Learning Hadoop 2

Design and implement data processing, lifecycle
management, and analytic workflows with the
cutting-edge toolbox of Hadoop 2

Garry Turkington

Gabriele Modena

[PACKT] open source*
PUBLISHING   community experience distilled

BIRMINGHAM - MUMBAI

Learning Hadoop 2

First published: February 2015

Production reference: 1060215

Published by Packt Publishing Ltd.
Livery Place
35 Livery Street
Birmingham B3 2PB, UK.

ISBN 978-1-78328-551-8

www.packtpub.com

Credits

About the Authors

Garry Turkington has over 15 years of industry experience, most of which has been focused on the design and implementation of large-scale distributed systems. In his current role as the CTO at Improve Digital, he is primarily responsible for the realization of systems that store, process, and extract value from the company's large data volumes. Before joining Improve Digital, he spent time at Amazon.co.uk, where he led several software development teams, building systems that process the Amazon catalog data for every item worldwide. Prior to this, he spent a decade in various government positions in both the UK and the USA.

He has BSc and PhD degrees in Computer Science from Queens University Belfast in Northern Ireland, and a Master's degree in Engineering in Systems Engineering from Stevens Institute of Technology in the USA. He is the author of *Hadoop Beginners Guide*, published by Packt Publishing in 2013, and is a committer on the Apache Samza project.

I would like to thank my wife Lea and mother Sarah for their support and patience through the writing of another book and my daughter Maya for frequently cheering me up and asking me hard questions. I would also like to thank Gabriele for being such an amazing co-author on this project.

Gabriele Modena is a data scientist at Improve Digital. In his current position, he uses Hadoop to manage, process, and analyze behavioral and machine-generated data. Gabriele enjoys using statistical and computational methods to look for patterns in large amounts of data. Prior to his current job in ad tech he held a number of positions in Academia and Industry where he did research in machine learning and artificial intelligence.

He holds a BSc degree in Computer Science from the University of Trento, Italy and a Research MSc degree in Artificial Intelligence: Learning Systems, from the University of Amsterdam in the Netherlands.

First and foremost, I want to thank Laura for her support, constant encouragement and endless patience putting up with far too many "can't do, I'm working on the Hadoop book". She is my rock and I dedicate this book to her.

A special thank you goes to Amit, Atdhe, Davide, Jakob, James and Valerie, whose invaluable feedback and commentary made this work possible.

Finally, I'd like to thank my co-author, Garry, for bringing me on board with this project; it has been a pleasure working together.

About the Reviewers

Atdhe Buja is a certified ethical hacker, DBA (MCITP, OCA11g), and developer with good management skills. He is a DBA at the Agency for Information Society / Ministry of Public Administration, where he also manages some projects of e-governance and has more than 10 years' experience working on SQL Server.

Atdhe is a regular columnist for UBT News. Currently, he holds an MSc degree in computer science and engineering and has a bachelor's degree in management and information. He specializes in and is certified in many technologies, such as SQL Server (all versions), Oracle 11*g*, CEH, Windows Server, MS Project, SCOM 2012 R2, BizTalk, and integration business processes.

He was the reviewer of the book, *Microsoft SQL Server 2012 with Hadoop*, published by Packt Publishing. His capabilities go beyond the aforementioned knowledge!

I thank Donika and my family for all the encouragement and support.

Amit Gurdasani is a software engineer at Amazon. He architects distributed systems to process product catalogue data. Prior to building high-throughput systems at Amazon, he was working on the entire software stack, both as a systems-level developer at Ericsson and IBM as well as an application developer at Manhattan Associates. He maintains a strong interest in bulk data processing, data streaming, and service-oriented software architectures.

Jakob Homan has been involved with big data and the Apache Hadoop ecosystem for more than 5 years. He is a Hadoop committer as well as a committer for the Apache Giraph, Spark, Kafka, and Tajo projects, and is a PMC member. He has worked in bringing all these systems to scale at Yahoo! and LinkedIn.

James Lampton is a seasoned practitioner of all things data (big or small) with 10 years of hands-on experience in building and using large-scale data storage and processing platforms. He is a believer in holistic approaches to solving problems using the right tool for the right job. His favorite tools include Python, Java, Hadoop, Pig, Storm, and SQL (which sometimes I like and sometimes I don't). He has recently completed his PhD from the University of Maryland with the release of Pig Squeal: a mechanism for running Pig scripts on Storm.

I would like to thank my spouse, Andrea, and my son, Henry, for giving me time to read work-related things at home. I would also like to thank Garry, Gabriele, and the folks at Packt Publishing for the opportunity to review this manuscript and for their patience and understanding, as my free time was consumed when writing my dissertation.

Davide Setti, after graduating in physics from the University of Trento, joined the SoNet research unit at the Fondazione Bruno Kessler in Trento, where he applied large-scale data analysis techniques to understand people's behaviors in social networks and large collaborative projects such as Wikipedia.

In 2010, Davide moved to Fondazione, where he led the development of data analytic tools to support research on civic media, citizen journalism, and digital media.

In 2013, Davide became the CTO of SpazioDati, where he leads the development of tools to perform semantic analysis of massive amounts of data in the business information sector.

When not solving hard problems, Davide enjoys taking care of his family vineyard and playing with his two children.

www.PacktPub.com

Support files, eBooks, discount offers, and more

For support files and downloads related to your book, please visit www.PacktPub.com.

Did you know that Packt offers eBook versions of every book published, with PDF and ePub files available? You can upgrade to the eBook version at www.PacktPub.com and as a print book customer, you are entitled to a discount on the eBook copy. Get in touch with us at service@packtpub.com for more details.

At www.PacktPub.com, you can also read a collection of free technical articles, sign up for a range of free newsletters and receive exclusive discounts and offers on Packt books and eBooks.

https://www2.packtpub.com/books/subscription/packtlib

Do you need instant solutions to your IT questions? PacktLib is Packt's online digital book library. Here, you can search, access, and read Packt's entire library of books.

Why subscribe?

- Fully searchable across every book published by Packt
- Copy and paste, print, and bookmark content
- On demand and accessible via a web browser

Free access for Packt account holders

If you have an account with Packt at www.PacktPub.com, you can use this to access PacktLib today and view 9 entirely free books. Simply use your login credentials for immediate access.

Table of Contents

Preface

This book will take you on a hands-on exploration of the wonderful world that is Hadoop 2 and its rapidly growing ecosystem. Building on the solid foundation from the earlier versions of the platform, Hadoop 2 allows multiple data processing frameworks to be executed on a single Hadoop cluster.

To give an understanding of this significant evolution, we will explore both how these new models work and also show their applications in processing large data volumes with batch, iterative, and near-real-time algorithms.

What this book covers

Chapter 1, *Introduction*, gives the background to Hadoop and the Big Data problems it looks to solve. We also highlight the areas in which Hadoop 1 had room for improvement.

Chapter 2, *Storage*, delves into the Hadoop Distributed File System, where most data processed by Hadoop is stored. We examine the particular characteristics of HDFS, show how to use it, and discuss how it has improved in Hadoop 2. We also introduce ZooKeeper, another storage system within Hadoop, upon which many of its high-availability features rely.

Chapter 3, *Processing – MapReduce and Beyond*, first discusses the traditional Hadoop processing model and how it is used. We then discuss how Hadoop 2 has generalized the platform to use multiple computational models, of which MapReduce is merely one.

Chapter 4, Real-time Computation with Samza, takes a deeper look at one of these alternative processing models enabled by Hadoop 2. In particular, we look at how to process real-time streaming data with Apache Samza.

Chapter 5, Iterative Computation with Spark, delves into a very different alternative processing model. In this chapter, we look at how Apache Spark provides the means to do iterative processing.

Chapter 6, Data Analysis with Pig, demonstrates how Apache Pig makes the traditional computational model of MapReduce easier to use by providing a language to describe data flows.

Chapter 7, Hadoop and SQL, looks at how the familiar SQL language has been implemented atop data stored in Hadoop. Through the use of Apache Hive and describing alternatives such as Cloudera Impala, we show how Big Data processing can be made possible using existing skills and tools.

Chapter 8, Data Lifecycle Management, takes a look at the bigger picture of just how to manage all that data that is to be processed in Hadoop. Using Apache Oozie, we show how to build up workflows to ingest, process, and manage data.

Chapter 9, Making Development Easier, focuses on a selection of tools aimed at helping a developer get results quickly. Through the use of Hadoop streaming, Apache Crunch and Kite, we show how the use of the right tool can speed up the development loop or provide new APIs with richer semantics and less boilerplate.

Chapter 10, Running a Hadoop Cluster, takes a look at the operational side of Hadoop. By focusing on the areas of interest to developers, such as cluster management, monitoring, and security, this chapter should help you to work better with your operations staff.

Chapter 11, Where to Go Next, takes you on a whirlwind tour through a number of other projects and tools that we feel are useful, but could not cover in detail in the book due to space constraints. We also give some pointers on where to find additional sources of information and how to engage with the various open source communities.

What you need for this book

Because most people don't have a large number of spare machines sitting around, we use the Cloudera QuickStart virtual machine for most of the examples in this book. This is a single machine image with all the components of a full Hadoop cluster pre-installed. It can be run on any host machine supporting either the VMware or the VirtualBox virtualization technology.

We also explore Amazon Web Services and how some of the Hadoop technologies can be run on the AWS Elastic MapReduce service. The AWS services can be managed through a web browser or a Linux command-line interface.

Who this book is for

This book is primarily aimed at application and system developers interested in learning how to solve practical problems using the Hadoop framework and related components. Although we show examples in a few programming languages, a strong foundation in Java is the main prerequisite.

Data engineers and architects might also find the material concerning data life cycle, file formats, and computational models useful.

Conventions

In this book, you will find a number of styles of text that distinguish between different kinds of information. Here are some examples of these styles, and an explanation of their meaning.

Code words in text, database table names, folder names, filenames, file extensions, pathnames, dummy URLs, user input, and Twitter handles are shown as follows: "If Avro dependencies are not present in the classpath, we need to add the Avro MapReduce.jar file to our environment before accessing individual fields."

A block of code is set as follows:

```
topic_edges_grouped = FOREACH topic_edges_grouped {
  GENERATE
    group.topic_id as topic,
    group.source_id as source,
    topic_edges.(destination_id,w) as edges;
}
```

Any command-line input or output is written as follows:

```
$ hdfs dfs -put target/elephant-bird-pig-4.5.jar hdfs:///jar/
$ hdfs dfs -put target/elephant-bird-hadoop-compat-4.5.jar hdfs:///jar/
$ hdfs dfs -put elephant-bird-core-4.5.jar hdfs:///jar/
```

New terms and **important words** are shown in bold. Words that you see on the screen, in menus or dialog boxes, appear in the text like this: "Once the form is filled in, we need to review and accept the terms of service and click on the **Create Application** button in the bottom-left corner of the page."

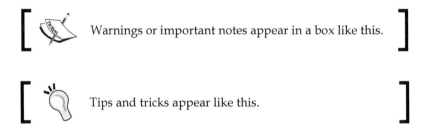

> Warnings or important notes appear in a box like this.

> Tips and tricks appear like this.

Reader feedback

Feedback from our readers is always welcome. Let us know what you think about this book—what you liked or disliked. Reader feedback is important for us as it helps us develop titles that you will really get the most out of.

To send us general feedback, simply e-mail feedback@packtpub.com, and mention the book's title in the subject of your message.

If there is a topic that you have expertise in and you are interested in either writing or contributing to a book, see our author guide at www.packtpub.com/authors.

Customer support

Now that you are the proud owner of a Packt book, we have a number of things to help you to get the most from your purchase.

Downloading the example code

The source code for this book can be found on GitHub at https://github.com/learninghadoop2/book-examples. The authors will be applying any errata to this code and keeping it up to date as the technologies evolve. In addition you can download the example code files from your account at http://www.packtpub.com for all the Packt Publishing books you have purchased. If you purchased this book elsewhere, you can visit http://www.packtpub.com/support and register to have the files e-mailed directly to you.

Errata

Although we have taken every care to ensure the accuracy of our content, mistakes do happen. If you find a mistake in one of our books—maybe a mistake in the text or the code—we would be grateful if you could report this to us. By doing so, you can save other readers from frustration and help us improve subsequent versions of this book. If you find any errata, please report them by visiting `http://www.packtpub.com/submit-errata`, selecting your book, clicking on the **Errata Submission Form** link, and entering the details of your errata. Once your errata are verified, your submission will be accepted and the errata will be uploaded to our website or added to any list of existing errata under the Errata section of that title.

To view the previously submitted errata, go to `https://www.packtpub.com/books/content/support` and enter the name of the book in the search field. The required information will appear under the **Errata** section.

Piracy

Piracy of copyright material on the Internet is an ongoing problem across all media. At Packt, we take the protection of our copyright and licenses very seriously. If you come across any illegal copies of our works, in any form, on the Internet, please provide us with the location address or website name immediately so that we can pursue a remedy.

Please contact us at `copyright@packtpub.com` with a link to the suspected pirated material.

We appreciate your help in protecting our authors, and our ability to bring you valuable content.

Questions

You can contact us at `questions@packtpub.com` if you are having a problem with any aspect of the book, and we will do our best to address it.

1
Introduction

This book will teach you how to build amazing systems using the latest release of Hadoop. Before you change the world though, we need to do some groundwork, which is where this chapter comes in.

In this introductory chapter, we will cover the following topics:

- A brief refresher on the background to Hadoop
- A walk-through of Hadoop's evolution
- The key elements in Hadoop 2
- The Hadoop distributions we'll use in this book
- The dataset we'll use for examples

A note on versioning

In Hadoop 1, the version history was somewhat convoluted with multiple forked branches in the 0.2x range, leading to odd situations, where a 1.x version could, in some situations, have fewer features than a 0.23 release. In the version 2 codebase, this is fortunately much more straightforward, but it's important to clarify exactly which version we will use in this book.

Hadoop 2.0 was released in alpha and beta versions, and along the way, several incompatible changes were introduced. There was, in particular, a major API stabilization effort between the beta and final release stages.

Hadoop 2.2.0 was the first **general availability** (**GA**) release of the Hadoop 2 codebase, and its interfaces are now declared stable and forward compatible. We will therefore use the 2.2 product and interfaces in this book. Though the principles will be usable on a 2.0 beta, in particular, there will be API incompatibilities in the beta. This is particularly important as MapReduce v2 was back-ported to Hadoop 1 by several distribution vendors, but these products were based on the beta and not the GA APIs. If you are using such a product, then you will encounter these incompatible changes. It is recommended that a release based upon Hadoop 2.2 or later is used for both the development and the production deployments of any Hadoop 2 workloads.

The background of Hadoop

We're assuming that most readers will have a little familiarity with Hadoop, or at the very least, with big data-processing systems. Consequently, we won't give a detailed background as to why Hadoop is successful or the types of problem it helps to solve in this book. However, particularly because of some aspects of Hadoop 2 and the other products we will use in later chapters, it is useful to give a sketch of how we see Hadoop fitting into the technology landscape and which are the particular problem areas where we believe it gives the most benefit.

In ancient times, before the term "big data" came into the picture (which equates to maybe a decade ago), there were few options to process datasets of sizes in terabytes and beyond. Some commercial databases could, with very specific and expensive hardware setups, be scaled to this level, but the expertise and capital expenditure required made it an option for only the largest organizations. Alternatively, one could build a custom system aimed at the specific problem at hand. This suffered from some of the same problems (expertise and cost) and added the risk inherent in any cutting-edge system. On the other hand, if a system was successfully constructed, it was likely a very good fit to the need.

Few small- to mid-size companies even worried about this space, not only because the solutions were out of their reach, but they generally also didn't have anything close to the data volumes that required such solutions. As the ability to generate very large datasets became more common, so did the need to process that data.

Even though large data became more democratized and was no longer the domain of the privileged few, major architectural changes were required if the data-processing systems could be made affordable to smaller companies. The first big change was to reduce the required upfront capital expenditure on the system; that means no high-end hardware or expensive software licenses. Previously, high-end hardware would have been utilized most commonly in a relatively small number of very large servers and storage systems, each of which had multiple approaches to avoid hardware failures. Though very impressive, such systems are hugely expensive, and moving to a larger number of lower-end servers would be the quickest way to dramatically reduce the hardware cost of a new system. Moving more toward commodity hardware instead of the traditional enterprise-grade equipment would also mean a reduction in capabilities in the area of resilience and fault tolerance. Those responsibilities would need to be taken up by the software layer. *Smarter software, dumber hardware.*

Google started the change that would eventually be known as Hadoop, when in 2003, and in 2004, they released two academic papers describing the **Google File System (GFS)** (http://research.google.com/archive/gfs.html) and MapReduce (http://research.google.com/archive/mapreduce.html). The two together provided a platform for very large-scale data processing in a highly efficient manner. Google had taken the build-it-yourself approach, but instead of constructing something aimed at one specific problem or dataset, they instead created a platform on which multiple processing applications could be implemented. In particular, they utilized large numbers of commodity servers and built GFS and MapReduce in a way that assumed hardware failures would be commonplace and were simply something that the software needed to deal with.

At the same time, Doug Cutting was working on the Nutch open source web crawler. He was working on elements within the system that resonated strongly once the Google GFS and MapReduce papers were published. Doug started work on open source implementations of these Google ideas, and Hadoop was soon born, firstly, as a subproject of Lucene, and then as its own top-level project within the Apache Software Foundation.

Yahoo! hired Doug Cutting in 2006 and quickly became one of the most prominent supporters of the Hadoop project. In addition to often publicizing some of the largest Hadoop deployments in the world, Yahoo! allowed Doug and other engineers to contribute to Hadoop while employed by the company, not to mention contributing back some of its own internally developed Hadoop improvements and extensions.

Components of Hadoop

The broad Hadoop umbrella project has many component subprojects, and we'll discuss several of them in this book. At its core, Hadoop provides two services: storage and computation. A typical Hadoop workflow consists of loading data into the **Hadoop Distributed File System (HDFS)** and processing using the **MapReduce** API or several tools that rely on MapReduce as an execution framework.

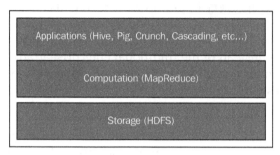

Hadoop 1: HDFS and MapReduce

Both layers are direct implementations of Google's own GFS and MapReduce technologies.

Common building blocks

Both HDFS and MapReduce exhibit several of the architectural principles described in the previous section. In particular, the common principles are as follows:

- Both are designed to run on clusters of commodity (that is, low to medium specification) servers

- Both scale their capacity by adding more servers (scale-out) as opposed to the previous models of using larger hardware (scale-up)

- Both have mechanisms to identify and work around failures

- Both provide most of their services transparently, allowing the user to concentrate on the problem at hand

- Both have an architecture where a software cluster sits on the physical servers and manages aspects such as application load balancing and fault tolerance, without relying on high-end hardware to deliver these capabilities

Storage

HDFS is a filesystem, though not a POSIX-compliant one. This basically means that it does not display the same characteristics as that of a regular filesystem. In particular, the characteristics are as follows:

- HDFS stores files in blocks that are typically at least 64 MB or (more commonly now) 128 MB in size, much larger than the 4-32 KB seen in most filesystems

- HDFS is optimized for throughput over latency; it is very efficient at streaming reads of large files but poor when seeking for many small ones

- HDFS is optimized for workloads that are generally write-once and read-many

- Instead of handling disk failures by having physical redundancies in disk arrays or similar strategies, HDFS uses replication. Each of the blocks comprising a file is stored on multiple nodes within the cluster, and a service called the NameNode constantly monitors to ensure that failures have not dropped any block below the desired replication factor. If this does happen, then it schedules the making of another copy within the cluster.

Computation

MapReduce is an API, an execution engine, and a processing paradigm; it provides a series of transformations from a source into a result dataset. In the simplest case, the input data is fed through a map function and the resultant temporary data is then fed through a reduce function.

MapReduce works best on semistructured or unstructured data. Instead of data conforming to rigid schemas, the requirement is instead that the data can be provided to the map function as a series of key-value pairs. The output of the map function is a set of other key-value pairs, and the reduce function performs aggregation to collect the final set of results.

Hadoop provides a standard specification (that is, interface) for the map and reduce phases, and the implementation of these are often referred to as mappers and reducers. A typical MapReduce application will comprise a number of mappers and reducers, and it's not unusual for several of these to be extremely simple. The developer focuses on expressing the transformation between the source and the resultant data, and the Hadoop framework manages all aspects of job execution and coordination.

Better together

It is possible to appreciate the individual merits of HDFS and MapReduce, but they are even more powerful when combined. They can be used individually, but when they are together, they bring out the best in each other, and this close interworking was a major factor in the success and acceptance of Hadoop 1.

When a MapReduce job is being planned, Hadoop needs to decide on which host to execute the code in order to process the dataset most efficiently. If the MapReduce cluster hosts are all pulling their data from a single storage host or array, then this largely doesn't matter as the storage system is a shared resource that will cause contention. If the storage system was more transparent and allowed MapReduce to manipulate its data more directly, then there would be an opportunity to perform the processing closer to the data, building on the principle of it being less expensive to move processing than data.

The most common deployment model for Hadoop sees the HDFS and MapReduce clusters deployed on the same set of servers. Each host that contains data and the HDFS component to manage the data also hosts a MapReduce component that can schedule and execute data processing. When a job is submitted to Hadoop, it can use the locality optimization to schedule data on the hosts where data resides as much as possible, thus minimizing network traffic and maximizing performance.

Hadoop 2 – what's the big deal?

If we look at the two main components of the core Hadoop distribution, storage and computation, we see that Hadoop 2 has a very different impact on each of them. Whereas the HDFS found in Hadoop 2 is mostly a much more feature-rich and resilient product than the HDFS in Hadoop 1, for MapReduce, the changes are much more profound and have, in fact, altered how Hadoop is perceived as a processing platform in general. Let's look at HDFS in Hadoop 2 first.

Storage in Hadoop 2

We'll discuss the HDFS architecture in more detail in *Chapter 2, Storage*, but for now, it's sufficient to think of a master-slave model. The slave nodes (called DataNodes) hold the actual filesystem data. In particular, each host running a DataNode will typically have one or more disks onto which files containing the data for each HDFS block are written. The DataNode itself has no understanding of the overall filesystem; its role is to store, serve, and ensure the integrity of the data for which it is responsible.

The master node (called the NameNode) is responsible for knowing which of the DataNodes holds which block and how these blocks are structured to form the filesystem. When a client looks at the filesystem and wishes to retrieve a file, it's via a request to the NameNode that the list of required blocks is retrieved.

This model works well and has been scaled to clusters with tens of thousands of nodes at companies such as Yahoo! So, though it is scalable, there is a resiliency risk; if the NameNode becomes unavailable, then the entire cluster is rendered effectively useless. No HDFS operations can be performed, and since the vast majority of installations use HDFS as the storage layer for services, such as MapReduce, they also become unavailable even if they are still running without problems.

More catastrophically, the NameNode stores the filesystem metadata to a persistent file on its local filesystem. If the NameNode host crashes in a way that this data is not recoverable, then all data on the cluster is effectively lost forever. The data will still exist on the various DataNodes, but the mapping of which blocks comprise which files is lost. This is why, in Hadoop 1, the best practice was to have the NameNode synchronously write its filesystem metadata to both local disks and at least one remote network volume (typically via NFS).

Several NameNode **high-availability (HA)** solutions have been made available by third-party suppliers, but the core Hadoop product did not offer such resilience in Version 1. Given this architectural single point of failure and the risk of data loss, it won't be a surprise to hear that **NameNode HA** is one of the major features of HDFS in Hadoop 2 and is something we'll discuss in detail in later chapters. The feature provides both a standby NameNode that can be automatically promoted to service all requests should the active NameNode fail, but also builds additional resilience for the critical filesystem metadata atop this mechanism.

HDFS in Hadoop 2 is still a non-POSIX filesystem; it still has a very large block size and it still trades latency for throughput. However, it does now have a few capabilities that can make it look a little more like a traditional filesystem. In particular, the core HDFS in Hadoop 2 now can be remotely mounted as an NFS volume. This is another feature that was previously offered as a proprietary capability by third-party suppliers but is now in the main Apache codebase.

Overall, the HDFS in Hadoop 2 is more resilient and can be more easily integrated into existing workflows and processes. It's a strong evolution of the product found in Hadoop 1.

Computation in Hadoop 2

The work on HDFS 2 was started before a direction for MapReduce crystallized. This was likely due to the fact that features such as NameNode HA were such an obvious path that the community knew the most critical areas to address. However, MapReduce didn't really have a similar list of areas of improvement, and that's why, when the MRv2 initiative started, it wasn't completely clear where it would lead.

Perhaps the most frequent criticism of MapReduce in Hadoop 1 was how its batch processing model was ill-suited to problem domains where faster response times were required. Hive, for example, which we'll discuss in *Chapter 7, Hadoop and SQL*, provides a SQL-like interface onto HDFS data, but, behind the scenes, the statements are converted into MapReduce jobs that are then executed like any other. A number of other products and tools took a similar approach, providing a specific user-facing interface that hid a MapReduce translation layer.

Though this approach has been very successful, and some amazing products have been built, the fact remains that in many cases, there is a mismatch as all of these interfaces, some of which expect a certain type of responsiveness, are behind the scenes, being executed on a batch-processing platform. When looking to enhance MapReduce, improvements could be made to make it a better fit to these use cases, but the fundamental mismatch would remain. This situation led to a significant change of focus of the MRv2 initiative; perhaps MapReduce itself didn't need change, but the real need was to enable different processing models on the Hadoop platform. Thus was born **Yet Another Resource Negotiator (YARN)**.

Looking at MapReduce in Hadoop 1, the product actually did two quite different things; it provided the processing framework to execute MapReduce computations, but it also managed the allocation of this computation across the cluster. Not only did it direct data to and between the specific map and reduce tasks, but it also determined where each task would run, and managed the full job life cycle, monitoring the health of each task and node, rescheduling if any failed, and so on.

This is not a trivial task, and the automated parallelization of workloads has always been one of the main benefits of Hadoop. If we look at MapReduce in Hadoop 1, we see that after the user defines the key criteria for the job, everything else is the responsibility of the system. Critically, from a scale perspective, the same MapReduce job can be applied to datasets of any volume hosted on clusters of any size. If the data is 1 GB in size and on a single host, then Hadoop will schedule the processing accordingly. If the data is instead 1 PB in size and hosted across 1,000 machines, then it does likewise. From the user's perspective, the actual scale of the data and cluster is transparent, and aside from affecting the time taken to process the job, it does not change the interface with which to interact with the system.

In Hadoop 2, this role of job scheduling and resource management is separated from that of executing the actual application, and is implemented by YARN.

YARN is responsible for managing the cluster resources, and so MapReduce exists as an application that runs atop the YARN framework. The MapReduce interface in Hadoop 2 is completely compatible with that in Hadoop 1, both semantically and practically. However, under the covers, MapReduce has become a hosted application on the YARN framework.

The significance of this split is that other applications can be written that provide processing models more focused on the actual problem domain and can offload all the resource management and scheduling responsibilities to YARN. The latest versions of many different execution engines have been ported onto YARN, either in a production-ready or experimental state, and it has shown that the approach can allow a single Hadoop cluster to run everything from batch-oriented MapReduce jobs through fast-response SQL queries to continuous data streaming and even to implement models such as graph processing and the **Message Passing Interface** (**MPI**) from the **High Performance Computing** (**HPC**) world. The following diagram shows the architecture of Hadoop 2:

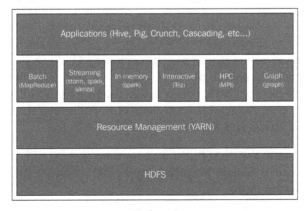

Hadoop 2

This is why much of the attention and excitement around Hadoop 2 has been focused on YARN and frameworks that sit on top of it, such as Apache Tez and Apache Spark. With YARN, the Hadoop cluster is no longer just a batch-processing engine; it is the single platform on which a vast array of processing techniques can be applied to the enormous data volumes stored in HDFS. Moreover, applications can build on these computation paradigms and execution models.

The analogy that is achieving some traction is to think of YARN as the processing kernel upon which other domain-specific applications can be built. We'll discuss YARN in more detail in this book, particularly in *Chapter 3, Processing – MapReduce and Beyond, Chapter 4, Real-time Computation with Samza*, and *Chapter 5, Iterative Computation with Spark*.

Distributions of Apache Hadoop

In the very early days of Hadoop, the burden of installing (often building from source) and managing each component and its dependencies fell on the user. As the system became more popular and the ecosystem of third-party tools and libraries started to grow, the complexity of installing and managing a Hadoop deployment increased dramatically to the point where providing a coherent offer of software packages, documentation, and training built around the core Apache Hadoop has become a business model. Enter the world of distributions for Apache Hadoop.

Hadoop distributions are conceptually similar to how Linux distributions provide a set of integrated software around a common core. They take the burden of bundling and packaging software themselves and provide the user with an easy way to install, manage, and deploy Apache Hadoop and a selected number of third-party libraries. In particular, the distribution releases deliver a series of product versions that are certified to be mutually compatible. Historically, putting together a Hadoop-based platform was often greatly complicated by the various version interdependencies.

Cloudera (`http://www.cloudera.com`), Hortonworks (`http://www.hortonworks.com`), and MapR (`http://www.mapr.com`) are amongst the first to have reached the market, each characterized by different approaches and selling points. Hortonworks positions itself as the open source player; Cloudera is also committed to open source but adds proprietary bits for configuring and managing Hadoop; MapR provides a hybrid open source/proprietary Hadoop distribution characterized by a proprietary NFS layer instead of HDFS and a focus on providing services.

Another strong player in the distributions ecosystem is Amazon, which offers a version of Hadoop called **Elastic MapReduce (EMR)** on top of the **Amazon Web Services (AWS)** infrastructure.

With the advent of Hadoop 2, the number of available distributions for Hadoop has increased dramatically, far in excess of the four we mentioned. A possibly incomplete list of software offerings that includes Apache Hadoop can be found at `http://wiki.apache.org/hadoop/Distributions%20and%20Commercial%20Support`.

A dual approach

In this book, we will discuss both the building and the management of local Hadoop clusters in addition to showing how to push the processing into the cloud via EMR.

The reason for this is twofold: firstly, though EMR makes Hadoop much more accessible, there are aspects of the technology that only become apparent when manually administering the cluster. Although it is also possible to use EMR in a more manual mode, we'll generally use a local cluster for such explorations. Secondly, though it isn't necessarily an either/or decision, many organizations use a mixture of in-house and cloud-hosted capacities, sometimes due to a concern of over reliance on a single external provider, but practically speaking, it's often convenient to do development and small-scale tests on local capacity and then deploy at production scale into the cloud.

In a few of the later chapters, where we discuss additional products that integrate with Hadoop, we'll mostly give examples of local clusters, as there is no difference between how the products work regardless of where they are deployed.

AWS – infrastructure on demand from Amazon

AWS is a set of cloud-computing services offered by Amazon. We will use several of these services in this book.

Simple Storage Service (S3)

Amazon's **Simple Storage Service (S3)**, found at `http://aws.amazon.com/s3/`, is a storage service that provides a simple key-value storage model. Using web, command-line, or programmatic interfaces to create objects, which can be anything from text files to images to MP3s, you can store and retrieve your data based on a hierarchical model. In this model, you create buckets that contain objects. Each bucket has a unique identifier, and within each bucket, every object is uniquely named. This simple strategy enables an extremely powerful service for which Amazon takes complete responsibility (for service scaling, in addition to reliability and availability of data).

Elastic MapReduce (EMR)

Amazon's Elastic MapReduce, found at http://aws.amazon.com/
elasticmapreduce/, is basically Hadoop in the cloud. Using any of the multiple
interfaces (web console, CLI, or API), a Hadoop workflow is defined with attributes
such as the number of Hadoop hosts required and the location of the source data.
The Hadoop code implementing the MapReduce jobs is provided, and the virtual
Go button is pressed.

In its most impressive mode, EMR can pull source data from S3, process it on a
Hadoop cluster it creates on Amazon's virtual host on-demand service EC2, push the
results back into S3, and terminate the Hadoop cluster and the EC2 virtual machines
hosting it. Naturally, each of these services has a cost (usually on per GB stored and
server-time usage basis), but the ability to access such powerful data-processing
capabilities with no need for dedicated hardware is a powerful one.

Getting started

We will now describe the two environments we will use throughout the book:
Cloudera's QuickStart virtual machine will be our reference system on which we
will show all examples, but we will additionally demonstrate some examples on
Amazon's EMR when there is some particularly valuable aspect to running the
example in the on-demand service.

Although the examples and code provided are aimed at being as general-purpose
and portable as possible, our reference setup, when talking about a local cluster,
will be Cloudera running atop CentOS Linux.

For the most part, we will show examples that make use of, or are executed from,
a terminal prompt. Although Hadoop's graphical interfaces have improved
significantly over the years (for example, the excellent HUE and Cloudera Manager),
when it comes to development, automation, and programmatic access to the system,
the command line is still the most powerful tool for the job.

All examples and source code presented in this book can be downloaded from
https://github.com/learninghadoop2/book-examples. In addition, we have
a home page for the book where we will publish updates and related material at
http://learninghadoop2.com.

Cloudera QuickStart VM

One of the advantages of Hadoop distributions is that they give access to easy-to-install, packaged software. Cloudera takes this one step further and provides a freely downloadable Virtual Machine instance of its latest distribution, known as the CDH QuickStart VM, deployed on top of CentOS Linux.

In the remaining parts of this book, we will use the CDH5.0.0 VM as the reference and baseline system to run examples and source code. Images of the VM are available for VMware (`http://www.vmware.com/nl/products/player/`), KVM (`http://www.linux-kvm.org/page/Main_Page`), and VirtualBox (`https://www.virtualbox.org/`) virtualization systems.

Amazon EMR

Before using **Elastic MapReduce**, we need to set up an AWS account and register it with the necessary services.

Creating an AWS account

Amazon has integrated its general accounts with AWS, which means that, if you already have an account for any of the Amazon retail websites, this is the only account you will need to use AWS services.

 Note that AWS services have a cost; you will need an active credit card associated with the account to which charges can be made.

If you require a new Amazon account, go to `http://aws.amazon.com`, select **Create a new AWS account**, and follow the prompts. Amazon has added a free tier for some services, so you might find that in the early days of testing and exploration, you are keeping many of your activities within the noncharged tier. The scope of the free tier has been expanding, so make sure you know what you will and won't be charged for.

Signing up for the necessary services

Once you have an Amazon account, you will need to register it for use with the required AWS services, that is, **Simple Storage Service (S3)**, **Elastic Compute Cloud (EC2)**, and **Elastic MapReduce**. There is no cost to simply sign up to any AWS service; the process just makes the service available to your account.

Go to the S3, EC2, and EMR pages linked from `http://aws.amazon.com`, click on the **Sign up** button on each page, and then follow the prompts.

Using Elastic MapReduce

Having created an account with AWS and registered all the required services, we can proceed to configure programmatic access to EMR.

Getting Hadoop up and running

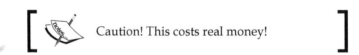 Caution! This costs real money!

Before going any further, it is critical to understand that use of AWS services will incur charges that will appear on the credit card associated with your Amazon account. Most of the charges are quite small and increase with the amount of infrastructure consumed; storing 10 GB of data in S3 costs 10 times more than 1 GB, and running 20 EC2 instances costs 20 times as much as a single one. There are tiered cost models, so the actual costs tend to have smaller marginal increases at higher levels. But you should read carefully through the pricing sections for each service before using any of them. Note also that currently data transfer out of AWS services, such as EC2 and S3, is chargeable, but data transfer between services is not. This means it is often most cost-effective to carefully design your use of AWS to keep data within AWS through as much of the data processing as possible. For information regarding AWS and EMR, consult `http://aws.amazon.com/elasticmapreduce/#pricing`.

How to use EMR

Amazon provides both web and command-line interfaces to EMR. Both interfaces are just a frontend to the very same system; a cluster created with the command-line interface can be inspected and managed with the web tools and vice-versa.

For the most part, we will be using the command-line tools to create and manage clusters programmatically and will fall back on the web interface cases where it makes sense to do so.

AWS credentials

Before using either programmatic or command-line tools, we need to look at how an account holder authenticates to AWS to make such requests.

Each AWS account has several identifiers, such as the following, that are used when accessing the various services:

- **Account ID**: each AWS account has a numeric ID.
- **Access key**: the associated access key is used to identify the account making the request.
- **Secret access key**: the partner to the access key is the secret access key. The access key is not a secret and could be exposed in service requests, but the secret access key is what you use to validate yourself as the account owner. Treat it like your credit card.
- **Key pairs**: these are the key pairs used to log in to EC2 hosts. It is possible to either generate public/private key pairs within EC2 or to import externally generated keys into the system.

User credentials and permissions are managed via a web service called **Identity and Access Management (IAM)**, which you need to sign up to in order to obtain access and secret keys.

If this sounds confusing, it's because it is, at least at first. When using a tool to access an AWS service, there's usually the single, upfront step of adding the right credentials to a configured file, and then everything just works. However, if you do decide to explore programmatic or command-line tools, it will be worth investing a little time to read the documentation for each service to understand how its security works. More information on creating an AWS account and obtaining access credentials can be found at http://docs.aws.amazon.com/iam.

The AWS command-line interface

Each AWS service historically had its own set of command-line tools. Recently though, Amazon has created a single, unified command-line tool that allows access to most services. The Amazon CLI can be found at http://aws.amazon.com/cli.

It can be installed from a tarball or via the pip or easy_install package managers.

On the CDH QuickStart VM, we can install awscli using the following command:

```
$ pip install awscli
```

In order to access the API, we need to configure the software to authenticate to AWS using our access and secret keys.

This is also a good moment to set up an EC2 key pair by following the instructions provided at `https://console.aws.amazon.com/ec2/home?region=us-east-1#c=EC2&s=KeyPairs`.

Although a key pair is not strictly necessary to run an EMR cluster, it will give us the capability to remotely log in to the master node and gain low-level access to the cluster.

The following command will guide you through a series of configuration steps and store the resulting configuration in the `.aws/credential` file:

```
$ aws configure
```

Once the CLI is configured, we can query AWS with `aws <service> <arguments>`. To create and query an S3 bucket use something like the following command. Note that S3 buckets need to be globally unique across all AWS accounts, so most common names, such as `s3://mybucket`, will not be available:

```
$ aws s3 mb s3://learninghadoop2
$ aws s3 ls
```

We can provision an EMR cluster with five `m1.xlarge` nodes using the following commands:

```
$ aws emr create-cluster --name "EMR cluster" \
--ami-version 3.2.0 \
--instance-type m1.xlarge  \
--instance-count 5 \
--log-uri s3://learninghadoop2/emr-logs
```

Where `--ami-version` is the ID of an Amazon Machine Image template (`http://docs.aws.amazon.com/AWSEC2/latest/UserGuide/AMIs.html`), and `--log-uri` instructs EMR to collect logs and store them in the `learninghadoop2` S3 bucket.

> If you did not specify a default region when setting up the AWS CLI, then you will also have to add one to most EMR commands in the AWS CLI using the --region argument; for example, `--region eu-west-1` is run to use the EU Ireland region. You can find details of all available AWS regions at `http://docs.aws.amazon.com/general/latest/gr/rande.html`.

We can submit workflows by adding steps to a running cluster using the following command:

```
$ aws emr add-steps --cluster-id <cluster> --steps <steps>
```

To terminate the cluster, use the following command line:

```
$ aws emr terminate-clusters --cluster-id <cluster>
```

In later chapters, we will show you how to add steps to execute MapReduce jobs and Pig scripts.

More information on using the AWS CLI can be found at `http://docs.aws.amazon.com/ElasticMapReduce/latest/DeveloperGuide/emr-manage.html`.

Running the examples

The source code of all examples is available at `https://github.com/learninghadoop2/book-examples`.

Gradle (`http://www.gradle.org/`) scripts and configurations are provided to compile most of the Java code. The `gradlew` script included with the example will bootstrap Gradle and use it to fetch dependencies and compile code.

JAR files can be created by invoking the `jar` task via a `gradlew` script, as follows:

```
./gradlew jar
```

Jobs are usually executed by submitting a JAR file using the `hadoop jar` command, as follows:

```
$ hadoop jar example.jar <MainClass> [-libjars $LIBJARS] arg1 arg2 ... argN
```

The optional `-libjars` parameter specifies runtime third-party dependencies to ship to remote nodes.

 Some of the frameworks we will work with, such as Apache Spark, come with their own build and package management tools. Additional information and resources will be provided for these particular cases.

The `copyJar` Gradle task can be used to download third-party dependencies into `build/libjars/<example>/lib`, as follows:

```
./gradlew copyJar
```

For convenience, we provide a `fatJar` Gradle task that bundles the example classes and their dependencies into a single JAR file. Although this approach is discouraged in favor of using `-libjar`, it might come in handy when dealing with dependency issues.

The following command will generate `build/libs/<example>-all.jar`:

```
$ ./gradlew fatJar
```

Data processing with Hadoop

In the remaining chapters of this book, we will introduce the core components of the Hadoop ecosystem as well as a number of third-party tools and libraries that will make writing robust, distributed code an accessible and hopefully enjoyable task. While reading this book, you will learn how to collect, process, store, and extract information from large amounts of structured and unstructured data.

We will use a dataset generated from Twitter's (`http://www.twitter.com`) real-time fire hose. This approach will allow us to experiment with relatively small datasets locally and, once ready, scale the examples up to production-level data sizes.

Why Twitter?

Thanks to its programmatic APIs, Twitter provides an easy way to generate datasets of arbitrary size and inject them into our local- or cloud-based Hadoop clusters. Other than the sheer size, the dataset that we will use has a number of properties that fit several interesting data modeling and processing use cases.

Twitter data possesses the following properties:

- **Unstructured**: each status update is a text message that can contain references to media content such as URLs and images
- **Structured**: tweets are timestamped, sequential records
- **Graph**: relationships such as replies and mentions can be modeled as a network of interactions
- **Geolocated**: the location where a tweet was posted or where a user resides
- **Real time**: all data generated on Twitter is available via a real-time fire hose

These properties will be reflected in the type of application that we can build with Hadoop. These include examples of sentiment analysis, social network, and trend analysis.

Building our first dataset

Twitter's terms of service prohibit redistribution of user-generated data in any form; for this reason, we cannot make available a common dataset. Instead, we will use a Python script to programmatically access the platform and create a dump of user tweets collected from a live stream.

One service, multiple APIs

Twitter users share more than 200 million tweets, also known as status updates, a day. The platform offers access to this corpus of data via four types of APIs, each of which represents a facet of Twitter and aims at satisfying specific use cases, such as linking and interacting with twitter content from third-party sources (Twitter for Products), programmatic access to specific users' or sites' content (REST), search capabilities across users' or sites' timelines (Search), and access to all content created on the Twitter network in real time (Streaming).

The Streaming API allows direct access to the Twitter stream, tracking keywords, retrieving geotagged tweets from a certain region, and much more. In this book, we will make use of this API as a data source to illustrate both the batch and real-time capabilities of Hadoop. We will not, however, interact with the API itself; rather, we will make use of third-party libraries to offload chores such as authentication and connection management.

Anatomy of a Tweet

Each tweet object returned by a call to the real-time APIs is represented as a serialized JSON string that contains a set of attributes and metadata in addition to a textual message. This additional content includes a numerical ID that uniquely identifies the tweet, the location where the tweet was shared, the user who shared it (user object), whether it was republished by other users (retweeted) and how many times (retweet count), the machine-detected language of its text, whether the tweet was posted in reply to someone and, if so, the user and tweet IDs it replied to, and so on.

The structure of a Tweet, and any other object exposed by the API, is constantly evolving. An up-to-date reference can be found at `https://dev.twitter.com/docs/platform-objects/tweets`.

Twitter credentials

Twitter makes use of the OAuth protocol to authenticate and authorize access from third-party software to its platform.

The application obtains through an external channel, for instance a web form, the following pair of credentials:

- Consumer key
- Consumer secret

The consumer secret is never directly transmitted to the third party as it is used to sign each request.

The user authorizes the application to access the service via a three-way process that, once completed, grants the application a token consisting of the following:

- Access token
- Access secret

Similarly, to the consumer, the access secret is never directly transmitted to the third party, and it is used to sign each request.

In order to use the Streaming API, we will first need to register an application and grant it programmatic access to the system. If you require a new Twitter account, proceed to the signup page at `https://twitter.com/signup`, and fill in the required information. Once this step is completed, we need to create a sample application that will access the API on our behalf and grant it the proper authorization rights. We will do so using the web form found at `https://dev.twitter.com/apps`.

When creating a new app, we are asked to give it a name, a description, and a URL. The following screenshot shows the settings of a sample application named `Learning Hadoop 2 Book Dataset`. For the purpose of this book, we do not need to specify a valid URL, so we used a placeholder instead.

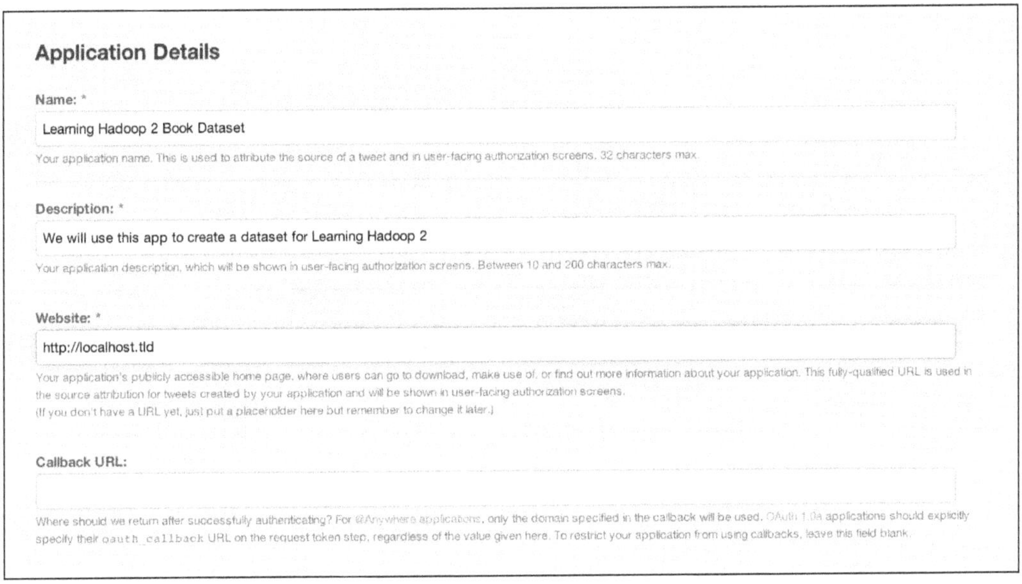

Once the form is filled in, we need to review and accept the terms of service and click on the **Create Application** button in the bottom-left corner of the page.

We are now presented with a page that summarizes our application details as seen in the following screenshot; the authentication and authorization credentials can be found under the OAuth Tool tab.

We are finally ready to generate our very first Twitter dataset.

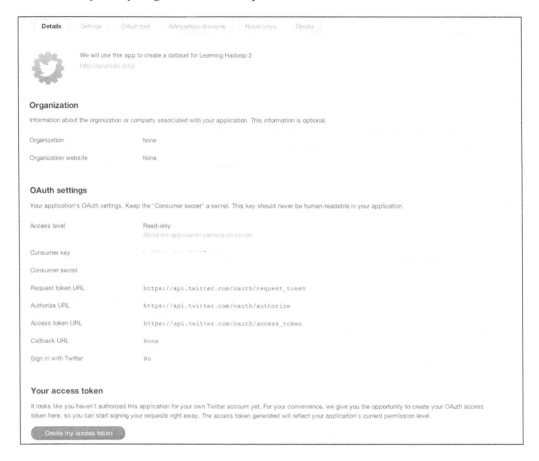

Programmatic access with Python

In this section, we will use Python and the `tweepy` library, found at
`https://github.com/tweepy/tweepy`, to collect Twitter's data. The `stream.py`
file found in the `ch1` directory of the book code archive instantiates a listener
to the real-time fire hose, grabs a data sample, and echoes each tweet's text to
standard output.

The `tweepy` library can be installed using either the `easy_install` or `pip` package
managers or by cloning the repository at `https://github.com/tweepy/tweepy`.

On the CDH QuickStart VM, we can install `tweepy` using the following
command line:

```
$ pip install tweepy
```

When invoked with the -j parameter, the script will output a JSON tweet to standard output; -t extracts and prints the text field. We specify how many tweets to print with-n <num tweets>. When –n is not specified, the script will run indefinitely. Execution can be terminated by pressing *Ctrl + C*.

The script expects OAuth credentials to be stored as shell environment variables; the following credentials will have to be set in the terminal session from where stream.py will be executed.

```
$ export TWITTER_CONSUMER_KEY="your_consumer_key"
$ export TWITTER_CONSUMER_SECRET="your_consumer_secret"
$ export TWITTER_ACCESS_KEY="your_access_key"
$ export TWITTER_ACCESS_SECRET="your_access_secret"
```

Once the required dependency has been installed and the OAuth data in the shell environment has been set, we can run the program as follows:

```
$ python stream.py -t -n 1000 > tweets.txt
```

We are relying on Linux's shell I/O to redirect the output with the > operator of stream.py to a file called tweets.txt. If everything was executed correctly, you should see a wall of text, where each line is a tweet.

Notice that in this example, we did not make use of Hadoop at all. In the next chapters, we will show how to import a dataset generated from the Streaming API into Hadoop and analyze its content on the local cluster and Amazon EMR.

For now, let's take a look at the source code of stream.py, which can be found at https://github.com/learninghadoop2/book-examples/blob/master/ch1/stream.py:

```
import tweepy
import os
import json
import argparse

consumer_key = os.environ['TWITTER_CONSUMER_KEY']
consumer_secret = os.environ['TWITTER_CONSUMER_SECRET']
access_key = os.environ['TWITTER_ACCESS_KEY']
access_secret = os.environ['TWITTER_ACCESS_SECRET']

class EchoStreamListener(tweepy.StreamListener):
```

```python
    def __init__(self, api, dump_json=False, numtweets=0):
        self.api = api
        self.dump_json = dump_json
        self.count = 0
        self.limit = int(numtweets)
        super(tweepy.StreamListener, self).__init__()

    def on_data(self, tweet):
        tweet_data = json.loads(tweet)
        if 'text' in tweet_data:
            if self.dump_json:
                print tweet.rstrip()
            else:
                print tweet_data['text'].encode("utf-8").rstrip()

            self.count = self.count+1
            return False if self.count == self.limit else True

    def on_error(self, status_code):
        return True

    def on_timeout(self):
        return True
...
if __name__ == '__main__':
    parser = get_parser()
    args = parser.parse_args()

    auth = tweepy.OAuthHandler(consumer_key, consumer_secret)
    auth.set_access_token(access_key, access_secret)
    api = tweepy.API(auth)
    sapi = tweepy.streaming.Stream(
        auth, EchoStreamListener(
            api=api,
            dump_json=args.json,
            numtweets=args.numtweets))
    sapi.sample()
```

First, we import three dependencies: `tweepy`, and the `os` and `json` modules, which come with the Python interpreter version 2.6 or greater.

We then define a class, `EchoStreamListener`, that inherits and extends `StreamListener` from `tweepy`. As the name suggests, `StreamListener` listens for events and tweets being published on the real-time stream and performs actions accordingly.

Whenever a new event is detected, it triggers a call to `on_data()`. In this method, we extract the `text` field from a tweet object and print it to standard output with UTF-8 encoding. Alternatively, if the script is invoked with `-j`, we print the whole JSON tweet. When the script is executed, we instantiate a `tweepy.OAuthHandler` object with the OAuth credentials that identify our Twitter account, and then we use this object to authenticate with the application access and secret key. We then use the `auth` object to create an instance of the `tweepy.API` class (`api`)

Upon successful authentication, we tell Python to listen for events on the real-time stream using `EchoStreamListener`.

An http GET request to the `statuses/sample` endpoint is performed by `sample()`. The request returns a random sample of all public statuses.

 Beware! By default, `sample()` will run indefinitely. Remember to explicitly terminate the method call by pressing *Ctrl + C*.

Summary

This chapter gave a whirlwind tour of where Hadoop came from, its evolution, and why the version 2 release is such a major milestone. We also described the emerging market in Hadoop distributions and how we will use a combination of local and cloud distributions in the book.

Finally, we described how to set up the needed software, accounts, and environments required in subsequent chapters and demonstrated how to pull data from the Twitter stream that we will use for examples.

With this background out of the way, we will now move on to a detailed examination of the storage layer within Hadoop.

2
Storage

After the overview of Hadoop in the previous chapter, we will now start looking at its various component parts in more detail. We will start at the conceptual bottom of the stack in this chapter: the means and mechanisms for storing data within Hadoop. In particular, we will discuss the following topics:

- Describe the architecture of the **Hadoop Distributed File System (HDFS)**
- Show what enhancements to HDFS have been made in Hadoop 2
- Explore how to access HDFS using command-line tools and the Java API
- Give a brief description of ZooKeeper — another (sort of) filesystem within Hadoop
- Survey considerations for storing data in Hadoop and the available file formats

In *Chapter 3, Processing – MapReduce and Beyond*, we will describe how Hadoop provides the framework to allow data to be processed.

The inner workings of HDFS

In *Chapter 1, Introduction*, we gave a very high-level overview of HDFS; we will now explore it in a little more detail. As mentioned in that chapter, HDFS can be viewed as a filesystem, though one with very specific performance characteristics and semantics. It's implemented with two main server processes: the **NameNode** and the **DataNodes**, configured in a master/slave setup. If you view the NameNode as holding all the filesystem metadata and the DataNodes as holding the actual filesystem data (blocks), then this is a good starting point. Every file placed onto HDFS will be split into multiple blocks that might reside on numerous DataNodes, and it's the NameNode that understands how these blocks can be combined to construct the files.

Cluster startup

Let's explore the various responsibilities of these nodes and the communication between them by assuming we have an HDFS cluster that was previously shut down and then examining the startup behavior.

NameNode startup

We'll firstly consider the startup of the NameNode (though there is no actual ordering requirement for this and we are doing it for narrative reasons alone). The NameNode actually stores two types of data about the filesystem:

- The structure of the filesystem, that is, directory names, filenames, locations, and attributes
- The blocks that comprise each file on the filesystem

This data is stored in files that the NameNode reads at startup. Note that the NameNode does not persistently store the mapping of the blocks that are stored on particular DataNodes; we'll see how that information is communicated shortly.

Because the NameNode relies on this in-memory representation of the filesystem, it tends to have quite different hardware requirements compared to the DataNodes. We'll explore hardware selection in more detail in *Chapter 10, Running a Hadoop Cluster*; for now, just remember that the NameNode tends to be quite memory hungry. This is particularly true on very large clusters with many (millions or more) files, particularly if these files have very long names. This scaling limitation on the NameNode has also led to an additional Hadoop 2 feature that we will not explore in much detail: NameNode federation, whereby multiple NameNodes (or NameNode HA pairs) work collaboratively to provide the overall metadata for the full filesystem.

The main file written by the NameNode is called `fsimage`; this is the single most important piece of data in the entire cluster, as without it, the knowledge of how to reconstruct all the data blocks into the usable filesystem is lost. This file is read into memory and all future modifications to the filesystem are applied to this in-memory representation of the filesystem. The NameNode does not write out new versions of `fsimage` as new changes are applied after it is run; instead, it writes another file called `edits`, which is a list of the changes that have been made since the last version of `fsimage` was written.

The NameNode startup process is to first read the `fsimage` file, then to read the `edits` file, and apply all the changes stored in the `edits` file to the in-memory copy of `fsimage`. It then writes to disk a new up-to-date version of the `fsimage` file and is ready to receive client requests.

DataNode startup

When the DataNodes start up, they first catalog the blocks for which they hold copies. Typically, these blocks will be written simply as files on the local DataNode filesystem. The DataNode will perform some block consistency checking and then report to the NameNode the list of blocks for which it has valid copies. This is how the NameNode constructs the final mapping it requires — by learning which blocks are stored on which DataNodes. Once the DataNode has registered itself with the NameNode, an ongoing series of heartbeat requests will be sent between the nodes to allow the NameNode to detect DataNodes that have shut down, become unreachable, or have newly entered the cluster.

Block replication

HDFS replicates each block onto multiple DataNodes; the default replication factor is 3, but this is configurable on a per-file level. HDFS can also be configured to be able to determine whether given DataNodes are in the same physical hardware rack or not. Given smart block placement and this knowledge of the cluster topology, HDFS will attempt to place the second replica on a different host but in the same equipment rack as the first and the third on a host outside the rack. In this way, the system can survive the failure of as much as a full rack of equipment and still have at least one live replica for each block. As we'll see in *Chapter 3, Processing – MapReduce and Beyond*, knowledge of block placement also allows Hadoop to schedule processing as near as possible to a replica of each block, which can greatly improve performance.

Remember that replication is a strategy for resilience but is not a backup mechanism; if you have data mastered in HDFS that is critical, then you need to consider backup or other approaches that give protection for errors, such as accidentally deleted files, against which replication will not defend.

When the NameNode starts up and is receiving the block reports from the DataNodes, it will remain in safe mode until a configurable threshold of blocks (the default is 99.9 percent) have been reported as live. While in safe mode, clients cannot make any modifications to the filesystem.

Command-line access to the HDFS filesystem

Within the Hadoop distribution, there is a command-line utility called `hdfs`, which is the primary way to interact with the filesystem from the command line. Run this without any arguments to see the various subcommands available. There are many, though; several are used to do things like starting or stopping various HDFS components. The general form of the `hdfs` command is:

```
hdfs <sub-command> <command> [arguments]
```

The two main subcommands we will use in this book are:

- `dfs`: This is used for general filesystem access and manipulation, including reading/writing and accessing files and directories

- `dfsadmin`: This is used for administration and maintenance of the filesystem. We will not cover this command in detail, though. Have a look at the `-report` command, which gives a listing of the state of the filesystem and all DataNodes:

  ```
  $ hdfs dfsadmin -report
  ```

 Note that the `dfs` and `dfsadmin` commands can also be used with the main Hadoop command-line utility, for example, `hadoop fs -ls /`. This was the approach in earlier versions of Hadoop but is now deprecated in favor of the `hdfs` command.

Exploring the HDFS filesystem

Run the following to get a list of the available commands provided by the `dfs` subcommand:

```
$ hdfs dfs
```

As will be seen from the output of the preceding command, many of these look similar to standard Unix filesystem commands and, not surprisingly, they work as would be expected. In our test VM, we have a user account called `cloudera`. Using this user, we can list the root of the filesystem as follows:

```
$ hdfs dfs -ls /
```

```
Found 7 items
```

```
drwxr-xr-x   - hbase hbase            0 2014-04-04 15:18 /hbase
drwxr-xr-x   - hdfs  supergroup       0 2014-10-21 13:16 /jar
drwxr-xr-x   - hdfs  supergroup       0 2014-10-15 15:26 /schema
drwxr-xr-x   - solr  solr             0 2014-04-04 15:16 /solr
drwxrwxrwt   - hdfs  supergroup       0 2014-11-12 11:29 /tmp
drwxr-xr-x   - hdfs  supergroup       0 2014-07-13 09:05 /user
drwxr-xr-x   - hdfs  supergroup       0 2014-04-04 15:15 /var
```

The output is very similar to the Unix `ls` command. The file attributes work the same as the `user/group/world` attributes on a Unix filesystem (including the `t` sticky bit as can be seen) plus details of the owner, group, and modification time of the directories. The column between the group name and the modified date is the size; this is 0 for directories but will have a value for files as we'll see in the code following the next information box:

> If relative paths are used, they are taken from the home directory of the user. If there is no home directory, we can create it using the following commands:
>
> ```
> $ sudo -u hdfs hdfs dfs –mkdir /user/cloudera
> $ sudo -u hdfs hdfs dfs –chown cloudera:cloudera /user/
> cloudera
> ```
>
> The `mkdir` and `chown` steps require superuser privileges
> (`sudo -u hdfs`).

```
$ hdfs dfs -mkdir testdir
$ hdfs dfs -ls
Found 1 items
drwxr-xr-x   - cloudera cloudera       0 2014-11-13 11:21 testdir
```

Then, we can create a file, copy it to HDFS, and read its contents directly from its location on HDFS, as follows:

```
$ echo "Hello world" > testfile.txt
$ hdfs dfs -put testfile.txt testdir
```

Note that there is an older command called `-copyFromLocal`, which works in the same way as `-put`; you might see it in older documentation online. Now, run the following command and check the output:

```
$ hdfs dfs -ls testdir
Found 1 items
-rw-r--r--   3 cloudera cloudera      12 2014-11-13 11:21 testdir/
testfile.txt
```

Note the new column between the file attributes and the owner; this is the replication factor of the file. Now, finally, run the following command:

```
$ hdfs dfs -tail testdir/testfile.txt
Hello world
```

Much of the rest of the `dfs` subcommands are pretty intuitive; play around. We'll explore snapshots and programmatic access to HDFS later in this chapter.

Protecting the filesystem metadata

Because the `fsimage` file is so critical to the filesystem, its loss is a catastrophic failure. In Hadoop 1, where the NameNode was a single point of failure, the best practice was to configure the NameNode to synchronously write the `fsimage` and edits files to both local storage plus at least one other location on a remote filesystem (often NFS). In the event of NameNode failure, a replacement NameNode could be started using this up-to-date copy of the filesystem metadata. The process would require non-trivial manual intervention, however, and would result in a period of complete cluster unavailability.

Secondary NameNode not to the rescue

The most unfortunately named component in all of Hadoop 1 was the Secondary NameNode, which, not unreasonably, many people expect to be some sort of backup or standby NameNode. It is not; instead, the Secondary NameNode was responsible only for periodically reading the latest version of the `fsimage` and edits file and creating a new up-to-date `fsimage` with the outstanding edits applied. On a busy cluster, this checkpoint could significantly speed up the restart of the NameNode by reducing the number of edits it had to apply before being able to service clients.

In Hadoop 2, the naming is more clear; there are Checkpoint nodes, which do the role previously performed by the Secondary NameNode, plus Backup NameNodes, which keep a local up-to-date copy of the filesystem metadata even though the process to promote a Backup node to be the primary NameNode is still a multistage manual process.

Hadoop 2 NameNode HA

In most production Hadoop 2 clusters, however, it makes more sense to use the full High Availability (HA) solution instead of relying on Checkpoint and Backup nodes. It is actually an error to try to combine NameNode HA with the Checkpoint and Backup node mechanisms.

The core idea is for a pair (currently no more than two are supported) of NameNodes configured in an active/passive cluster. One NameNode acts as the live master that services all client requests, and the second remains ready to take over should the primary fail. In particular, Hadoop 2 HDFS enables this HA through two mechanisms:

- Providing a means for both NameNodes to have consistent views of the filesystem
- Providing a means for clients to always connect to the master NameNode

Keeping the HA NameNodes in sync

There are actually two mechanisms by which the active and standby NameNodes keep their views of the filesystem consistent; use of an **NFS** share or **Quorum Journal Manager** (QJM).

In the NFS case, there is an obvious requirement on an external remote NFS file share—note that as use of NFS was best practice in Hadoop 1 for a second copy of filesystem metadata many clusters already have one. If high availability is a concern, though it should be borne in mind that making NFS highly available often requires high-end and expensive hardware. In Hadoop 2, HA uses NFS; however, the NFS location becomes the primary location for the filesystem metadata. As the active NameNode writes all filesystem changes to the NFS share, the standby node detects these changes and updates its copy of the filesystem metadata accordingly.

The QJM mechanism uses an external service (the Journal Managers) instead of a filesystem. The Journal Manager cluster is an odd number of services (3, 5, and 7 are the most common) running on that number of hosts. All changes to the filesystem are submitted to the QJM service, and a change is treated as committed only when a majority of the QJM nodes have committed the change. The standby NameNode receives change updates from the QJM service and uses this information to keep its copy of the filesystem metadata up to date.

The QJM mechanism does not require additional hardware as the Checkpoint nodes are lightweight and can be co-located with other services. There is also no single point of failure in the model. Consequently, the QJM HA is usually the preferred option.

In either case, both in NFS-based HA and QJM-based HA, the DataNodes send block status reports to both NameNodes to ensure that both have up-to-date information of the mapping of blocks to DataNodes. Remember that this block assignment information is not held in the `fsimage`/edits data.

Client configuration

The clients to the HDFS cluster remain mostly unaware of the fact that NameNode HA is being used. The configuration files need to include the details of both NameNodes, but the mechanisms for determining which is the active NameNode — and when to switch to the standby — are fully encapsulated in the client libraries. The fundamental concept though is that instead of referring to an explicit NameNode host as in Hadoop 1, HDFS in Hadoop 2 identifies a nameservice ID for the NameNode within which multiple individual NameNodes (each with its own NameNode ID) are defined for HA. Note that the concept of nameservice ID is also used by NameNode federation, which we briefly mentioned earlier.

How a failover works

Failover can be either manual or automatic. A manual failover requires an administrator to trigger the switch that promotes the standby to the currently active NameNode. Though automatic failover has the greatest impact on maintaining system availability, there might be conditions in which this is not always desirable. Triggering a manual failover requires running only a few commands and, therefore, even in this mode, the failover is significantly easier than in the case of Hadoop 1 or with Hadoop 2 Backup nodes, where the transition to a new NameNode requires substantial manual effort.

Regardless of whether the failover is triggered manually or automatically, it has two main phases: confirmation that the previous master is no longer serving requests and the promotion of the standby to be the master.

The greatest risk in a failover is to have a period in which both NameNodes are servicing requests. In such a situation, it is possible that conflicting changes might be made to the filesystem on the two NameNodes or that they might become out of sync. Even though this should not be possible if the QJM is being used (it only ever accepts connections from a single client), out-of-date information might be served to clients, who might then try to make incorrect decisions based on this stale metadata. This is, of course, particularly likely if the previous master NameNode is behaving incorrectly in some way, which is why the need for the failover is identified in the first place.

To ensure only one NameNode is active at any time, a fencing mechanism is used to validate that the existing NameNode master has been shut down. The simplest included mechanism will try to ssh into the NameNode host and actively kill the process though a custom script can also be executed, so the mechanism is flexible. The failover will not continue until the fencing is successful and the system has confirmed that the previous master NameNode is now dead and has released any required resources.

Once fencing succeeds, the standby NameNode becomes the master and will start writing to the NFS-mounted `fsimage` and edits logs if NFS is being used for HA or will become the single client to the QJM if that is the HA mechanism.

Before discussing automatic failover, we need a slight segue to introduce another Apache project that is used to enable this feature.

Apache ZooKeeper – a different type of filesystem

Within Hadoop, we will mostly talk about HDFS when discussing filesystems and data storage. But, inside almost all Hadoop 2 installations, there is another service that looks somewhat like a filesystem, but which provides significant capability crucial to the proper functioning of distributed systems. This service is Apache ZooKeeper (`http://zookeeper.apache.org`) and, as it is a key part of the implementation of HDFS HA, we will introduce it in this chapter. It is, however, also used by multiple other Hadoop components and related projects, so we will touch on it several more times throughout the book.

ZooKeeper started out as a subcomponent of HBase and was used to enable several operational capabilities of the service. When any complex distributed system is built, there are a series of activities that are almost always required and which are always difficult to get right. These activities include things such as handling shared locks, detecting component failure, and supporting leader election within a group of collaborating services. ZooKeeper was created as the coordination service that would provide a series of primitive operations upon which HBase could implement these types of operationally critical features. Note that ZooKeeper also takes inspiration from the Google Chubby system described at `http://research.google.com/archive/chubby-osdi06.pdf`.

ZooKeeper runs as a cluster of instances referred to as an ensemble. The ensemble provides a data structure, which is somewhat analogous to a filesystem. Each location in the structure is called a ZNode and can have children as if it were a directory but can also have content as if it were a file. Note that ZooKeeper is not a suitable place to store very large amounts of data, and by default, the maximum amount of data in a ZNode is 1 MB. At any point in time, one server in the ensemble is the master and makes all decisions about client requests. There are very well-defined rules around the responsibilities of the master, including that it has to ensure that a request is only committed when a majority of the ensemble have committed the change, and that once committed any conflicting change is rejected.

You should have ZooKeeper installed within your Cloudera Virtual Machine. If not, use Cloudera Manager to install it as a single node on the host. In production systems, ZooKeeper has very specific semantics around absolute majority voting, so some of the logic only makes sense in a larger ensemble (3, 5, or 7 nodes are the most common sizes).

There is a command-line client to ZooKeeper called `zookeeper-client` in the Cloudera VM; note that in the vanilla ZooKeeper distribution it is called `zkCli.sh`. If you run it with no arguments, it will connect to the ZooKeeper server running on the local machine. From here, you can type `help` to get a list of commands.

The most immediately interesting commands will be `create`, `ls`, and `get`. As the names suggest, these create a ZNode, list the ZNodes at a particular point in the filesystem, and get the data stored at a particular ZNode. Here are some examples of usage.

- Create a ZNode with no data:

  ```
  $ create /zk-test ''
  ```

- Create a child of the first ZNode and store some text in it:

  ```
  $ create /zk-test/child1 'sampledata'
  ```

- Retrieve the data associated with a particular ZNode:

  ```
  $ get /zk-test/child1
  ```

The client can also register a watcher on a given ZNode — this will raise an alert if the ZNode in question changes, either its data or children being modified.

This might not sound very useful, but ZNodes can additionally be created as both sequential and ephemeral nodes, and this is where the magic starts.

Implementing a distributed lock with sequential ZNodes

If a ZNode is created within the CLI with the `-s` option, it will be created as a sequential node. ZooKeeper will suffix the supplied name with a 10-digit integer guaranteed to be unique and greater than any other sequential children of the same ZNode. We can use this mechanism to create a distributed lock. ZooKeeper itself is not holding the actual lock; the client needs to understand what particular states in ZooKeeper mean in terms of their mapping to the application locks in question.

If we create a (non-sequential) ZNode at `/zk-lock`, then any client wishing to hold the lock will create a sequential child node. For example, the `create -s /zk-lock/ locknode` command might create the node, `/zk-lock/locknode-0000000001`, in the first case, with increasing integer suffixes for subsequent calls. When a client creates a ZNode under the lock, it will then check if its sequential node has the lowest integer suffix. If it does, then it is treated as having the lock. If not, then it will need to wait until the node holding the lock is deleted. The client will usually put a watch on the node with the next lowest suffix and then be alerted when that node is deleted, indicating that it now holds the lock.

Implementing group membership and leader election using ephemeral ZNodes

Any ZooKeeper client will send heartbeats to the server throughout the session, showing that it is alive. For the ZNodes we have discussed until now, we can say that they are persistent and will survive across sessions. We can, however, create a ZNode as ephemeral, meaning it will disappear once the client that created it either disconnects or is detected as being dead by the ZooKeeper server. Within the CLI an ephemeral ZNode is created by adding the `-e` flag to the create command.

Ephemeral ZNodes are a good mechanism to implement group membership discovery within a distributed system. For any system where nodes can fail, join, and leave without notice, knowing which nodes are alive at any point in time is often a difficult task. Within ZooKeeper, we can provide the basis for such discovery by having each node create an ephemeral ZNode at a certain location in the ZooKeeper filesystem. The ZNodes can hold data about the service nodes, such as host name, IP address, port number, and so on. To get a list of live nodes, we can simply list the child nodes of the parent group ZNode. Because of the nature of ephemeral nodes, we can have confidence that the list of live nodes retrieved at any time is up to date.

If we have each service node create ZNode children that are not just ephemeral but also sequential, then we can also build a mechanism for leader election for services that need to have a single master node at any one time. The mechanism is the same for locks; the client service node creates the sequential and ephemeral ZNode and then checks if it has the lowest sequence number. If so, then it is the master. If not, then it will register a watcher on the next lowest sequence node to be alerted when it might become the master.

Java API

The `org.apache.zookeeper.ZooKeeper` class is the main programmatic client to access a ZooKeeper ensemble. Refer to the javadocs for the full details, but the basic interface is relatively straightforward with obvious one-to-one correspondence to commands in the CLI. For example:

- `create`: is equivalent to CLI `create`
- `getChildren`: is equivalent to CLI `ls`
- `getData`: is equivalent to CLI `get`

Building blocks

As can be seen, ZooKeeper provides a small number of well-defined operations with very strong semantic guarantees that can be built into higher-level services, such as the locks, group membership, and leader election we discussed earlier. It's best to think of ZooKeeper as a toolkit of well-engineered and reliable functions critical to distributed systems that can be built upon without having to worry about the intricacies of their implementation. The provided ZooKeeper interface is quite low-level though, and there are a few higher-level interfaces emerging that provide more of the mapping of the low-level primitives into application-level logic. The Curator project (`http://curator.apache.org/`) is a good example of this.

ZooKeeper was used sparingly within Hadoop 1, but it's now quite ubiquitous. It's used by both MapReduce and HDFS for the high availability of their JobTracker and NameNode components. Hive and Impala, which we will explore later, use it to place locks on data tables that are being accessed by multiple concurrent jobs. Kafka, which we'll discuss in the context of Samza, uses ZooKeeper for node (broker in Kafka terminology), leader election, and state management.

Further reading

We have not described ZooKeeper in much detail and have completely omitted aspects such as its ability to apply quotas and access control lists to ZNodes within the filesystem and the mechanisms to build callbacks. Our purpose here was to give enough of the details so that you would have some idea of how it was being used within the Hadoop services we explore in this book. For more information, consult the project home page.

Automatic NameNode failover

Now that we have introduced ZooKeeper, we can show how it is used to enable **automatic NameNode** failover.

Automatic NameNode failover introduces two new components to the system, a **ZooKeeper quorum**, and the **ZooKeeper Failover Controller** (ZKFC), which runs on each NameNode host. The ZKFC creates an ephemeral ZNode in ZooKeeper and holds this ZNode for as long as it detects the local NameNode to be alive and functioning correctly. It determines this by continuously sending simple health-check requests to the NameNode, and if the NameNode fails to respond correctly over a short period of time the ZKFC will assume the NameNode has failed. If a NameNode machine crashes or otherwise fails, the ZKFC session in ZooKeeper will be closed and the ephemeral ZNode will also be automatically removed.

The ZKFC processes are also monitoring the ZNodes of the other NameNodes in the cluster. If the ZKFC on the standby NameNode host sees the existing master ZNode disappear, it will assume the master has failed and will attempt a failover. It does this by trying to acquire the lock for the NameNode (through the protocol described in the ZooKeeper section) and if successful will initiate a failover through the same fencing/promotion mechanism described earlier.

HDFS snapshots

We mentioned earlier that HDFS replication alone is not a suitable backup strategy. In the Hadoop 2 filesystem, snapshots have been added, which brings another level of data protection to HDFS.

Filesystem snapshots have been used for some time across a variety of technologies. The basic idea is that it becomes possible to view the exact state of the filesystem at particular points in time. This is achieved by taking a copy of the filesystem metadata at the point the snapshot is made and making this available to be viewed in the future.

As changes to the filesystem are made, any change that would affect the snapshot is treated specially. For example, if a file that exists in the snapshot is deleted then, even though it will be removed from the current state of the filesystem, its metadata will remain in the snapshot, and the blocks associated with its data will remain on the filesystem though not accessible through any view of the system other than the snapshot.

An example might illustrate this point. Say, you have a filesystem containing the following files:

```
/data1 (5 blocks)
/data2 (10 blocks)
```

You take a snapshot and then delete the file /data2. If you view the current state of the filesystem, then only /data1 will be visible. If you examine the snapshot, you will see both files. Behind the scenes, all 15 blocks still exist, but only those associated with the un-deleted file /data1 are part of the current filesystem. The blocks for the file /data2 will be released only when the snapshot is itself removed—snapshots are read-only views.

Snapshots in Hadoop 2 can be applied at either the full filesystem level or only on particular paths. A path needs to be set as snapshottable, and note that you cannot have a path snapshottable if any of its children or parent paths are themselves snapshottable.

Let's take a simple example based on the directory we created earlier to illustrate the use of snapshots. The commands we are going to illustrate need to be executed with superuser privileges, which can be obtained with sudo -u hdfs.

First, use the dfsadmin subcommand of the hdfs CLI utility to enable snapshots of a directory, as follows:

```
$ sudo -u hdfs hdfs dfsadmin -allowSnapshot \
/user/cloudera/testdir
Allowing snapshot on testdir succeeded
```

Now, we create the snapshot and examine it; snapshots are available through the .snapshot subdirectory of the snapshottable directory. Note that the .snapshot directory will not be visible in a normal listing of the directory. Here's how we create a snapshot and examine it:

```
$ sudo -u hdfs hdfs dfs -createSnapshot \
/user/cloudera/testdir sn1
Created snapshot /user/cloudera/testdir/.snapshot/sn1

$ sudo -u hdfs hdfs dfs -ls \
/user/cloudera/testdir/.snapshot/sn1

Found 1 items -rw-r--r--   1 cloudera cloudera        12 2014-11-13
11:21 /user/cloudera/testdir/.snapshot/sn1/testfile.txt
```

Now, we remove the test file from the main directory and verify that it is now empty:

```
$ sudo -u hdfs hdfs dfs -rm \
/user/cloudera/testdir/testfile.txt
14/11/13 13:13:51 INFO fs.TrashPolicyDefault: Namenode trash
configuration: Deletion interval = 1440 minutes, Emptier interval = 0
minutes. Moved: 'hdfs://localhost.localdomain:8020/user/cloudera/testdir/
testfile.txt' to trash at: hdfs://localhost.localdomain:8020/user/hdfs/.
Trash/Current
$ hdfs dfs -ls /user/cloudera/testdir
$
```

Note the mention of trash directories; by default, HDFS will copy any deleted files into a .Trash directory in the user's home directory, which helps to defend against slipping fingers. These files can be removed through hdfs dfs -expunge or will be automatically purged in 7 days by default.

Now, we examine the snapshot where the now-deleted file is still available:

```
$ hdfs dfs -ls testdir/.snapshot/sn1
Found 1 items drwxr-xr-x   - cloudera cloudera        0 2014-11-13
13:12 testdir/.snapshot/sn1
$ hdfs dfs -tail testdir/.snapshot/sn1/testfile.txt
Hello world
```

Then, we can delete the snapshot, freeing up any blocks held by it, as follows:

```
$ sudo -u hdfs hdfs dfs -deleteSnapshot \
/user/cloudera/testdir sn1
$ hdfs dfs -ls testdir/.snapshot
$
```

As can be seen, the files within a snapshot are fully available to be read and copied, providing access to the historical state of the filesystem at the point when the snapshot was made. Each directory can have up to 65,535 snapshots, and HDFS manages snapshots in such a way that they are quite efficient in terms of impact on normal filesystem operations. They are a great mechanism to use prior to any activity that might have adverse effects, such as trying a new version of an application that accesses the filesystem. If the new software corrupts files, the old state of the directory can be restored. If after a period of validation the software is accepted, then the snapshot can instead be deleted.

Hadoop filesystems

Until now, we referred to HDFS as *the* Hadoop filesystem. In reality, Hadoop has a rather abstract notion of filesystem. HDFS is only one of several implementations of the `org.apache.hadoop.fs.FileSystem` Java abstract class. A list of available filesystems can be found at `https://hadoop.apache.org/docs/r2.5.0/api/org/apache/hadoop/fs/FileSystem.html`. The following table summarizes some of these filesystems, along with the corresponding URI scheme and Java implementation class.

Filesystem	URI scheme	Java implementation
Local	`file`	`org.apache.hadoop.fs.LocalFileSystem`
HDFS	`hdfs`	`org.apache.hadoop.hdfs.DistributedFileSystem`
S3 (native)	`s3n`	`org.apache.hadoop.fs.s3native.NativeS3FileSystem`
S3 (block-based)	`s3`	`org.apache.hadoop.fs.s3.S3FileSystem`

There exist two implementations of the S3 filesystem. Native—`s3n`—is used to read and write regular files. Data stored using `s3n` can be accessed by any tool and conversely can be used to read data generated by other S3 tools. `s3n` cannot handle files larger than 5TB or rename operations.

Much like HDFS, the block-based S3 filesystem stores files in blocks and requires an S3 bucket to be dedicated to the filesystem. Files stored in an S3 filesystem can be larger than 5 TB, but they will not be interoperable with other S3 tools. Additionally block-based S3 supports rename operations.

Hadoop interfaces

Hadoop is written in Java, and not surprisingly, all interaction with the system happens via the Java API. The command-line interface we used through the `hdfs` command in previous examples is a Java application that uses the `FileSystem` class to carry out input/output operations on the available filesystems.

Java FileSystem API

The Java API, provided by the `org.apache.hadoop.fs` package, exposes Apache Hadoop filesystems.

`org.apache.hadoop.fs.FileSystem` is the abstract class each filesystem implements and provides a general interface to interact with data in Hadoop. All code that uses HDFS should be written with the capability of handling a `FileSystem` object.

Libhdfs

Libhdfs is a C library that, despite its name, can be used to access any Hadoop filesystem and not just HDFS. It is written using the Java Native Interface (JNI) and mimics the Java FileSystem class.

Thrift

Apache Thrift (`http://thrift.apache.org`) is a framework for building cross-language software through data serialization and remote method invocation mechanisms. The Hadoop Thrift API, available in `contrib`, exposes Hadoop filesystems as a Thrift service. This interface makes it easy for non-Java code to access data stored in a Hadoop filesystem.

Other than the aforementioned interfaces, there exist other interfaces that allow access to Hadoop filesystems via HTTP and FTP — these for HDFS only — as well as WebDAV.

Managing and serializing data

Having a filesystem is all well and good, but we also need mechanisms to represent data and store it on the filesystems. We will explore some of these mechanisms now.

The Writable interface

It is useful, to us as developers, if we can manipulate higher-level data types and have Hadoop look after the processes required to serialize them into bytes to write to a file system and reconstruct from a stream of bytes when it is read from the file system.

The `org.apache.hadoop.io package` contains the Writable interface, which provides this mechanism and is specified as follows:

```
public interface Writable
{
void write(DataOutput out) throws IOException ;
void readFields(DataInput in) throws IOException ;
}
```

The main purpose of this interface is to provide mechanisms for the serialization and deserialization of data as it is passed across the network or read and written from the disk.

When we explore processing frameworks on Hadoop in later chapters, we will often see instances where the requirement is for a data argument to be of the type Writable. If we use data structures that provide a suitable implementation of this interface, then the Hadoop machinery can automatically manage the serialization and deserialization of the data type without knowing anything about what it represents or how it is used.

Introducing the wrapper classes

Fortunately, you don't have to start from scratch and build Writable variants of all the data types you will use. Hadoop provides classes that wrap the Java primitive types and implement the Writable interface. They are provided in the `org.apache.hadoop.io` package.

These classes are conceptually similar to the primitive wrapper classes, such as Integer and Long, found in `java.lang`. They hold a single primitive value that can be set either at construction or via a setter method. They are as follows:

- `BooleanWritable`
- `ByteWritable`
- `DoubleWritable`
- `FloatWritable`
- `IntWritable`
- `LongWritable`
- `VIntWritable`: a variable length integer type
- `VLongWritable`: a variable length long type
- There is also Text, which wraps `java.lang.String`.

Array wrapper classes

Hadoop also provides some collection-based wrapper classes. These classes provide Writable wrappers for arrays of other Writable objects. For example, an instance could either hold an array of `IntWritable` or `DoubleWritable`, but not arrays of the raw int or float types. A specific subclass for the required Writable class will be required. They are as follows:

```
ArrayWritable
TwoDArrayWritable
```

The Comparable and WritableComparable interfaces

We were slightly inaccurate when we said that the wrapper classes implement `Writable`; they actually implement a composite interface called `WritableComparable` in the `org.apache.hadoop.io` package that combines `Writable` with the standard `java.lang.Comparable` interface:

```
public interface WritableComparable extends Writable, Comparable
{}
```

The need for `Comparable` will only become apparent when we explore MapReduce in the next chapter, but for now, just remember that the wrapper classes provide mechanisms for them to be both serialized and sorted by Hadoop or any of its frameworks.

Storing data

Until now, we introduced the architecture of HDFS and how to programmatically store and retrieve data using the command-line tools and the Java API. In the examples seen until now, we have implicitly assumed that our data was stored as a text file. In reality, some applications and datasets will require ad hoc data structures to hold the file's contents. Over the years, file formats have been created to address both the requirements of MapReduce processing—for instance, we want data to be splittable—and to satisfy the need to model both structured and unstructured data. Currently, a lot of focus has been dedicated to better capture the use cases of relational data storage and modeling. In the remainder of this chapter, we will introduce some of the popular file format choices available within the Hadoop ecosystem.

Serialization and Containers

When talking about file formats, we are assuming two types of scenarios, which are as follows:

- **Serialization:** we want to encode data structures generated and manipulated at processing time to a format we can store to a file, transmit, and at a later stage, retrieve and translate back for further manipulation

- **Containers:** once data is serialized to files, containers provide means to group multiple files together and add additional metadata

Compression

When working with data, file compression can often lead to significant savings both in terms of the space necessary to store files as well as on the data I/O across the network and from/to local disks.

In broad terms, when using a processing framework, compression can occur at three points in the processing pipeline:

- input files to be processed
- output files that result after processing is completed
- intermediate/temporary files produced internally within the pipeline

When we add compression at any of these stages, we have an opportunity to dramatically reduce the amount of data to be read or written to the disk or across the network. This is particularly useful with frameworks such as MapReduce that can, for example, produce volumes of temporary data that are larger than either the input or output datasets.

Apache Hadoop comes with a number of compression codecs: gzip, bzip2, LZO, snappy—each with its own tradeoffs. Picking a codec is an educated choice that should consider both the kind of data being processed as well as the nature of the processing framework itself.

Other than the general space/time tradeoff, where the largest space savings come at the expense of compression and decompression speed (and vice versa), we need to take into account that data stored in HDFS will be accessed by parallel, distributed software; some of this software will also add its own particular requirements on file formats. MapReduce, for example, is most efficient on files that can be split into valid subfiles.

This can complicate decisions, such as the choice of whether to compress and which codec to use if so, as most compression codecs (such as gzip) do not support splittable files, whereas a few (such as LZO) do.

General-purpose file formats

The first class of file formats are those general-purpose ones that can be applied to any application domain and make no assumptions on data structure or access patterns.

- **Text**: the simplest approach to storing data on HDFS is to use flat files. Text files can be used both to hold unstructured data—a web page or a tweet—as well as structured data—a CSV file that is a few million rows long. Text files are splittable, though one needs to consider how to handle boundaries between multiple elements (for example, lines) in the file.

- **SequenceFile**: a SequenceFile is a flat data structure consisting of binary key/value pairs, introduced to address specific requirements of MapReduce-based processing. It is still extensively used in MapReduce as an input/output format. As we will see in *Chapter 3, Processing – MapReduce and Beyond*, internally, the temporary outputs of maps are stored using SequenceFile.

SequenceFile provides `Writer`, `Reader`, and `Sorter` classes to write, read, and, sort data, respectively.

Depending on the compression mechanism in use, three variations of SequenceFile can be distinguished:

- Uncompressed key/value records.
- Record compressed key/value records. Only 'values' are compressed.
- Block compressed key/value records. Keys and values are collected in blocks of arbitrary size and compressed separately.

In each case, however, the SequenceFile remains splittable, which is one of its biggest strengths.

Column-oriented data formats

In the relational database world, column-oriented data stores organize and store tables based on the columns; generally speaking, the data for each column will be stored together. This is a significantly different approach compared to most relational DBMS that organize data per row. Column-oriented storage has significant performance advantages; for example, if a query needs to read only two columns from a very wide table containing hundreds of columns, then only the required column data files are accessed. A traditional row-oriented database would have to read all columns for each row for which data was required. This has the greatest impact on workloads where aggregate functions are computed over large numbers of similar items, such as with OLAP workloads typical of data warehouse systems.

In *Chapter 7, Hadoop and SQL*, we will see how Hadoop is becoming a SQL backend for the data warehouse world thanks to projects such as Apache Hive and Cloudera Impala. As part of the expansion into this domain, a number of file formats have been developed to account for both relational modeling and data warehousing needs.

RCFile, ORC, and Parquet are three state-of-the-art column-oriented file formats developed with these use cases in mind.

RCFile

Row Columnar File (RCFile) was originally developed by Facebook to be used as the backend storage for their Hive data warehouse system that was the first mainstream SQL-on-Hadoop system available as open source.

RCFile aims to provide the following:

- fast data loading
- fast query processing
- efficient storage utilization
- adaptability to dynamic workloads

More information on RCFile can be found at `http://www.cse.ohio-state.edu/ hpcs/WWW/HTML/publications/abs11-4.html`.

ORC

The Optimized Row Columnar file format (ORC) aims to combine the performance of the RCFile with the flexibility of Avro. It is primarily intended to work with Apache Hive and has been initially developed by Hortonworks to overcome the perceived limitations of other available file formats.

More details can be found at `http://docs.hortonworks.com/HDPDocuments/ HDP2/HDP-2.0.0.2/ds_Hive/orcfile.html`.

Parquet

Parquet, found at `http://parquet.incubator.apache.org`, was originally a joint effort of Cloudera, Twitter, and Criteo, and now has been donated to the Apache Software Foundation. The goals of Parquet are to provide a modern, performant, columnar file format to be used with Cloudera Impala. As with Impala, Parquet has been inspired by the Dremel paper (`http://research.google.com/pubs/ pub36632.html`). It allows complex, nested data structures and allows efficient encoding on a per-column level.

Avro

Apache Avro (`http://avro.apache.org`) is a schema-oriented binary data serialization format and file container. Avro will be our preferred binary data format throughout this book. It is both splittable and compressible, making it an efficient format for data processing with frameworks such as MapReduce.

Numerous other projects also have built-in specific Avro support and integration, however, so it is very widely applicable. When data is stored in an Avro file, its schema — defined as a JSON object — is stored with it. A file can be later processed by a third party with no a priori notion of how data is encoded. This makes data self-describing and facilitates use with dynamic and scripting languages. The schema-on-read model also helps Avro records to be efficient to store as there is no need for the individual fields to be tagged.

In later chapters, you will see how these properties can make data life cycle management easier and allow non-trivial operations such as schema migrations.

Using the Java API

We'll now demonstrate the use of the Java API to parse Avro schemas, read and write Avro files, and use Avro's code generation facilities. Note that the format is intrinsically language independent; there are APIs for most languages, and files created by Java will seamlessly be read from any other language.

Avro schemas are described as JSON documents and represented by the `org.apache.avro.Schema` class. To demonstrate the API for manipulating Avro documents, we'll look ahead to an Avro specification we use for a Hive table in *Chapter 7, Hadoop and SQL*. The following code can be found at `https://github.com/learninghadoop2/book-examples/blob/master/ch2/src/main/java/com/learninghadoop2/avro/AvroParse.java`.

In the following code, we will use the Avro Java API to create an Avro file containing a tweet record and then re-read the file, using the schema in the file to extract the details of the stored records:

```
public static void testGenericRecord() {
    try {
        Schema schema = new Schema.Parser()
.parse(new File("tweets_avro.avsc"));
        GenericRecord tweet = new GenericData
.Record(schema);

        tweet.put("text", "The generic tweet text");

        File file = new File("tweets.avro");
        DatumWriter<GenericRecord> datumWriter =
            new GenericDatumWriter<>(schema);
        DataFileWriter<GenericRecord> fileWriter =
            new DataFileWriter<>( datumWriter );
```

```
        fileWriter.create(schema, file);
        fileWriter.append(tweet);
        fileWriter.close();

        DatumReader<GenericRecord> datumReader =
            new GenericDatumReader<>(schema);
        DataFileReader<GenericRecord> fileReader =
            new DataFileReader(file, datumReader);
        GenericRecord genericTweet = null;

        while (fileReader.hasNext()) {
            genericTweet = (GenericRecord) fileReader
                .next(genericTweet);

            for (Schema.Field field :
                genericTweet.getSchema().getFields()) {
                Object val = genericTweet.get(field.name());

                if (val != null) {
                    System.out.println(val);
                }
            }

        }
    } catch (IOException ie) {
        System.out.println("Error parsing or writing file.");
    }
}
```

The tweets_avro.avsc schema, found at https://github.com/learninghadoop2/
book-examples/blob/master/ch2/tweets_avro.avsc, describes a tweet with
multiple fields. To create an Avro object of this type, we first parse the schema file.
We then use Avro's concept of a GenericRecord to build an Avro document that
complies with this schema. In this case, we only set a single attribute—the tweet
text itself.

To write this Avro file—containing a single object—we then use Avro's I/O
capabilities. To read the file, we do not need to start with the schema, as we can
extract this from the GenericRecord we read from the file. We then walk through
the schema structure and dynamically process the document based on the discovered
fields. This is particularly powerful, as it is the key enabler of clients remaining
independent of the Avro schema and how it evolves over time.

If we have the schema file in advance, however, we can use Avro code generation to create a customized class that makes manipulating Avro records much easier. To generate the code, we will use the compile class in the `avro-tools.jar`, passing it the name of the schema file and the desired output directory:

```
$ java -jar /opt/cloudera/parcels/CDH-5.0.0-1.cdh5.0.0.p0.47/lib/avro/
avro-tools.jar compile schema tweets_avro.avsc src/main/java
```

The class will be placed in a directory structure based on any namespace defined in the schema. Since we created this schema in the `com.learninghadoop2.avrotables` namespace, we see the following:

```
$ ls src/main/java/com/learninghadoop2/avrotables/tweets_avro.java
```

With this class, let's revisit the creation and the act of reading and writing Avro objects, as follows:

```java
public static void testGeneratedCode() {
    tweets_avro tweet = new tweets_avro();
    tweet.setText("The code generated tweet text");

    try {
        File file = new File("tweets.avro");
        DatumWriter<tweets_avro> datumWriter =
            new SpecificDatumWriter<>(tweets_avro.class);
        DataFileWriter<tweets_avro> fileWriter =
            new DataFileWriter<>(datumWriter);

        fileWriter.create(tweet.getSchema(), file);
        fileWriter.append(tweet);
        fileWriter.close();

        DatumReader<tweets_avro> datumReader =
            new SpecificDatumReader<>(tweets_avro.class);
        DataFileReader<tweets_avro> fileReader =
            new DataFileReader<>(file, datumReader);

        while (fileReader.hasNext()) {
            tweet = fileReader.next(tweet);
            System.out.println(tweet.getText());
        }
    } catch (IOException ie) {
        System.out.println("Error in parsing or writing
            files.");
    }
}
```

Because we used code generation, we now use the Avro `SpecificRecord` mechanism alongside the generated class that represents the object in our domain model. Consequently, we can directly instantiate the object and access its attributes through familiar get/set methods.

Writing the file is similar to the action performed before, except that we use specific classes and also retrieve the schema directly from the tweet object when needed. Reading is similarly eased through the ability to create instances of a specific class and use get/set methods.

Summary

This chapter has given a whistle-stop tour through storage on a Hadoop cluster. In particular, we covered:

- The high-level architecture of HDFS, the main filesystem used in Hadoop
- How HDFS works under the covers and, in particular, its approach to reliability
- How Hadoop 2 has added significantly to HDFS, particularly in the form of NameNode HA and filesystem snapshots
- What ZooKeeper is and how it is used by Hadoop to enable features such as NameNode automatic failover
- An overview of the command-line tools used to access HDFS
- The API for filesystems in Hadoop and how at a code level HDFS is just one implementation of a more flexible filesystem abstraction
- How data can be serialized onto a Hadoop filesystem and some of the support provided in the core classes
- The various file formats available in which data is most frequently stored in Hadoop and some of their particular use cases

In the next chapter, we will look in detail at how Hadoop provides processing frameworks that can be used to process the data stored within it.

3
Processing – MapReduce and Beyond

In Hadoop 1, the platform had two clear components: HDFS for data storage and MapReduce for data processing. The previous chapter described the evolution of HDFS in Hadoop 2 and in this chapter we'll discuss data processing.

The picture with processing in Hadoop 2 has changed more significantly than has storage, and Hadoop now supports multiple processing models as first-class citizens. In this chapter we'll explore both MapReduce and other computational models in Hadoop2. In particular, we'll cover:

- What MapReduce is and the Java API required to write applications for it
- How MapReduce is implemented in practice
- How Hadoop reads data into and out of its processing jobs
- YARN, the Hadoop2 component that allows processing beyond MapReduce on the platform
- An introduction to several computational models implemented on YARN

MapReduce

MapReduce is the primary processing model supported in Hadoop 1. It follows a divide and conquer model for processing data made popular by a 2006 paper by Google (http://research.google.com/archive/mapreduce.html) and has foundations both in functional programming and database research. The name itself refers to two distinct steps applied to all input data, a map function and a reduce function.

Every MapReduce application is a sequence of jobs that build atop this very simple model. Sometimes, the overall application may require multiple jobs, where the output of the `reduce` stage from one is the input to the `map` stage of another, and sometimes there might be multiple `map` or `reduce` functions, but the core concepts remain the same.

We will introduce the MapReduce model by looking at the nature of the `map` and `reduce` functions and then describe the Java API required to build implementations of the functions. After showing some examples, we will walk through a MapReduce execution to give more insight into how the actual MapReduce framework executes code at runtime.

Learning the MapReduce model can be a little counter-intuitive; it's often difficult to appreciate how very simple functions can, when combined, provide very rich processing on enormous datasets. But it does work, trust us!

As we explore the nature of the `map` and `reduce` functions, think of them as being applied to a stream of records being retrieved from the source dataset. We'll describe how that happens later; for now, think of the source data being sliced into smaller chunks, each of which gets fed to a dedicated instance of the map function. Each record has the map function applied, producing a set of intermediary data. Records are retrieved from this temporary dataset and all associated records are fed together through the `reduce` function. The final output of the `reduce` function for all the sets of records is the overall result for the complete job.

From a functional perspective, MapReduce transforms data structures from one list of (key, value) pairs into another. During the *Map* phase, data is loaded from HDFS, and a function is applied in parallel to every input (key, value) and a new list of (key, value) pairs is the output:

```
map(k1,v1) -> list(k2,v2)
```

The framework then collects all pairs with the same key from all lists and groups them together, creating one group for each key. A *Reduce* function is applied in parallel to each group, which in turn produces a list of values:

```
reduce(k2, list (v2)) → k3,list(v3)
```

The output is then written back to HDFS in the following manner:

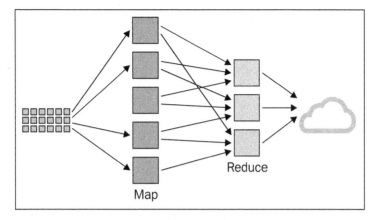

Map and Reduce phases

Java API to MapReduce

The Java API to MapReduce is exposed by the `org.apache.hadoop.mapreduce` package. Writing a MapReduce program, at its core, is a matter of subclassing Hadoop-provided `Mapper` and `Reducer` base classes, and overriding the `map()` and `reduce()` methods with our own implementation.

The Mapper class

For our own `Mapper` implementations, we will subclass the `Mapper` base class and override the `map()` method, as follows:

```
class Mapper<K1, V1, K2, V2>
{
        void map(K1 key, V1 value Mapper.Context context)
                throws IOException, InterruptedException

        ...
}
```

The class is defined in terms of the key/value input and output types, and then the `map` method takes an input key/value pair as its parameter. The other parameter is an instance of the `Context` class that provides various mechanisms to communicate with the Hadoop framework, one of which is to output the results of a `map` or `reduce` method.

Notice that the map method only refers to a single instance of K1 and V1 key/value pairs. This is a critical aspect of the MapReduce paradigm in which you write classes that process single records, and the framework is responsible for all the work required to turn an enormous dataset into a stream of key/value pairs. You will never have to write map or reduce classes that try to deal with the full dataset. Hadoop also provides mechanisms through its InputFormat and OutputFormat classes that provide implementations of common file formats and likewise remove the need for having to write file parsers for any but custom file types.

There are three additional methods that sometimes may be required to be overridden:.

```
protected void setup( Mapper.Context context)
    throws IOException, InterruptedException
```

This method is called once before any key/value pairs are presented to the map method. The default implementation does nothing:

```
protected void cleanup( Mapper.Context context)
    throws IOException, InterruptedException
```

This method is called once after all key/value pairs have been presented to the map method. The default implementation does nothing:

```
protected void run( Mapper.Context context)
    throws IOException, InterruptedException
```

This method controls the overall flow of task processing within a JVM. The default implementation calls the setup method once before repeatedly calling the map method for each key/value pair in the split and then finally calls the cleanup method.

The Reducer class

The Reducer base class works very similarly to the Mapper class and usually requires only subclasses to override a single reduce() method. Here is the cut-down class definition:

```
public class Reducer<K2, V2, K3, V3>
{
    void reduce(K2 key, Iterable<V2> values,
        Reducer.Context context)
          throws IOException, InterruptedException
    ...
}
```

Again, notice the class definition in terms of the broader data flow (the `reduce` method accepts K2/V2 as input and provides K3/V3 as output), while the actual `reduce` method takes only a single key and its associated list of values. The Context object is again the mechanism to output the result of the method.

This class also has the setup, run and cleanup methods with similar default implementations as with the `Mapper` class that can optionally be overridden:

```
protected void setup(Reducer.Context context)
throws IOException, InterruptedException
```

The `setup()` method is called once before any key/lists of values are presented to the `reduce` method. The default implementation does nothing:

```
protected void cleanup(Reducer.Context context)
throws IOException, InterruptedException
```

The `cleanup()` method is called once after all key/lists of values have been presented to the `reduce` method. The default implementation does nothing:

```
protected void run(Reducer.Context context)
throws IOException, InterruptedException
```

The `run()` method controls the overall flow of processing the task within the JVM. The default implementation calls the setup method before repeatedly and potentially concurrently calling the `reduce` method for as many key/value pairs provided to the `Reducer` class, and then finally calls the cleanup method.

The Driver class

The Driver class communicates with the Hadoop framework and specifies the configuration elements needed to run a MapReduce job. This involves aspects such as telling Hadoop which `Mapper` and `Reducer` classes to use, where to find the input data and in what format, and where to place the output data and how to format it.

The driver logic usually exists in the main method of the class written to encapsulate a MapReduce job. There is no default parent Driver class to subclass:

```
public class ExampleDriver extends Configured implements Tool
    {
    ...
    public static void run(String[] args) throws Exception
    {
        // Create a Configuration object that is used to set other
options
```

```
        Configuration conf = getConf();

        // Get command line arguments
        args = new GenericOptionsParser(conf, args)
        .getRemainingArgs();

        // Create the object representing the job
        Job job = new Job(conf, "ExampleJob");

        // Set the name of the main class in the job jarfile
        job.setJarByClass(ExampleDriver.class);
        // Set the mapper class
        job.setMapperClass(ExampleMapper.class);

        // Set the reducer class
        job.setReducerClass(ExampleReducer.class);

        // Set the types for the final output key and value
        job.setOutputKeyClass(Text.class);
        job.setOutputValueClass(IntWritable.class);

        // Set input and output file paths
        FileInputFormat.addInputPath(job, new Path(args[0]));
        FileOutputFormat.setOutputPath(job, new Path(args[1]));

        // Execute the job and wait for it to complete
        System.exit(job.waitForCompletion(true) ? 0 : 1);
    }

    public static void main(String[] args) throws Exception
    {
        int exitCode = ToolRunner.run(new ExampleDriver(), args);
        System.exit(exitCode);
    }
}
```

In the preceding lines of code, `org.apache.hadoop.util.Tool` is an interface for handling command-line options. The actual handling is delegated to `ToolRunner.run`, which runs `Tool` with the given `Configuration` used to get and set a job's configuration options. By subclassing `org.apache.hadoop.conf.Configured`, we can set the `Configuration` object directly from command-line options via `GenericOptionsParser`.

Given our previous talk of jobs, it's not surprising that much of the setup involves operations on a job object. This includes setting the job name and specifying which classes are to be used for the mapper and reducer implementations.

Certain input/output configurations are set and, finally, the arguments passed to the main method are used to specify the input and output locations for the job. This is a very common model that you will see often.

There are a number of default values for configuration options, and we are implicitly using some of them in the preceding class. Most notably, we don't say anything about the format of the input files or how the output files are to be written. These are defined through the InputFormat and OutputFormat classes mentioned earlier; we will explore them in detail later. The default input and output formats are text files that suit our examples. There are multiple ways of expressing the format within text files in addition to particularly optimized binary formats.

A common model for less complex MapReduce jobs is to have the Mapper and Reducer classes as inner classes within the driver. This allows everything to be kept in a single file, which simplifies the code distribution.

Combiner

Hadoop allows the use of a combiner class to perform some early sorting of the output from the map method before it's retrieved by the reducer.

Much of Hadoop's design is predicated on reducing the expensive parts of a job that usually equate to disk and network I/O. The output of the mapper is often large; it's not infrequent to see it many times the size of the original input. Hadoop does allow configuration options to help reduce the impact of the reducers transferring such large chunks of data across the network. The combiner takes a different approach where it's possible to perform early aggregation to require less data to be transferred in the first place.

The combiner does not have its own interface; a combiner must have the same signature as the reducer, and hence also subclasses the Reduce class from the org. apache.hadoop.mapreduce package. The effect of this is to basically perform a mini-reduce on the mapper for the output destined for each reducer.

Hadoop does not guarantee whether the combiner will be executed. Sometimes, it may not be executed at all, while at other times it may be used once, twice, or more times depending on the size and number of output files generated by the mapper for each reducer.

Partitioning

One of the implicit guarantees of the Reduce interface is that a single reducer will be given all the values associated with a given key. With multiple reduce tasks running across a cluster, each mapper output must be partitioned into the separate outputs destined for each reducer. These partitioned files are stored on the local node filesystem.

The number of reduce tasks across the cluster is not as dynamic as that of mappers, and indeed we can specify the value as part of our job submission. Hadoop therefore, knows how many reducers will be needed to complete the job, and from this, it knows into how many partitions the mapper output should be split.

The optional partition function

Within the `org.apache.hadoop.mapreduce` package is the `Partitioner` class, an abstract class with the following signature:

```
public abstract class Partitioner<Key, Value>
{
  public abstract int getPartition(Key key, Value value,
    int numPartitions);
}
```

By default, Hadoop will use a strategy that hashes the output key to perform the partitioning. This functionality is provided by the `HashPartitioner` class within the `org.apache.hadoop.mapreduce.lib.partition` package, but it's necessary in some cases to provide a custom subclass of `Partitioner` with application-specific partitioning logic. Notice that the `getPartition` function takes the key, value, and number of partitions as parameters, any of which can be used by the custom partitioning logic.

A custom partitioning strategy would be particularly necessary if, for example, the data provided a very uneven distribution when the standard hash function was applied. Uneven partitioning can result in some tasks having to perform significantly more work than others, leading to much longer overall job execution time.

Hadoop-provided mapper and reducer implementations

We don't always have to write our own Mapper and Reducer classes from scratch. Hadoop provides several common Mapper and Reducer implementations that can be used in our jobs. If we don't override any of the methods in the Mapper and Reducer classes, the default implementations are the identity Mapper and Reducer classes, which simply output the input unchanged.

The mappers are found at `org.apache.hadoop.mapreduce.lib.mapper` and include the following:

- `InverseMapper`: returns (value, key) as an output, that is, the input key is output as the value and the input value is output as the key
- `TokenCounterMapper`: counts the number of discrete tokens in each line of input
- `IdentityMapper`: implements the identity function, mapping inputs directly to outputs

The reducers are found at `org.apache.hadoop.mapreduce.lib.reduce` and currently include the following:

- `IntSumReducer`: outputs the sum of the list of integer values per key
- `LongSumReducer`: outputs the sum of the list of long values per key
- `IdentityReducer`: implements the identity function, mapping inputs directly to outputs

Sharing reference data

Occasionally, we might want to share data across tasks. For instance, if we need to perform a lookup operation on an ID-to-string translation table, we might want such a data source to be accessible by the mapper or reducer. A straightforward approach is to store the data we want to access on HDFS and use the FileSystem API to query it as part of the Map or Reduce steps.

Hadoop gives us an alternative mechanism to achieve the goal of sharing reference data across all tasks in the job, the Distributed Cache defined by the `org.apache.hadoop.mapreduce.filecache.DistributedCache` class. This can be used to efficiently make available common read-only files that are used by the `map` or `reduce` tasks to all nodes.

The files can be text data as in this case, but could also be additional JARs, binary data, or archives; anything is possible. The files to be distributed are placed on HDFS and added to the DistributedCache within the job driver. Hadoop copies the files onto the local filesystem of each node prior to job execution, meaning every task has local access to the files.

An alternative is to bundle needed files into the job JAR submitted to Hadoop. This does tie the data to the job JAR, making it more difficult to share across jobs and requires the JAR to be rebuilt if the data changes.

Writing MapReduce programs

In this chapter, we will be focusing on batch workloads; given a set of historical data, we will look at properties of that dataset. In *Chapter 4*, *Real-time Computation with Samza*, and *Chapter 5*, *Iterative Computation with Spark*, we will show how a similar type of analysis can be performed over a stream of text collected in real time.

Getting started

In the following examples, we will assume a dataset generated by collecting 1,000 tweets using the `stream.py` script, as shown in *Chapter 1*, *Introduction*:

```
$ python stream.py -t -n 1000 > tweets.txt
```

We can then copy the dataset into HDFS with:

```
$ hdfs dfs -put tweets.txt <destination>
```

> Note that until now we have been working only with the text of tweets. In the remainder of this book, we'll extend `stream.py` to output additional tweet metadata in JSON format. Keep this in mind before dumping terabytes of messages with `stream.py`.

Our first MapReduce program will be the canonical WordCount example. A variation of this program will be used to determine trending topics. We will then analyze text associated with topics to determine whether it expresses a "positive" or "negative" sentiment. Finally, we will make use of a MapReduce pattern—ChainMapper—to pull things together and present a data pipeline to clean and prepare the textual data we'll feed to the trending topic and sentiment analysis model.

Running the examples

The full source code of the examples described in this section can be found at `https://github.com/learninghadoop2/book-examples/tree/master/ch3`.

Before we run our job in Hadoop, we must compile our code and collect the required class files into a single JAR file that we will submit to the system. Using Gradle, you can build the needed JAR file with:

```
$ ./gradlew jar
```

Local cluster

Jobs are executed on Hadoop using the JAR option to the Hadoop command-line utility. To use this, we specify the name of the JAR file, the main class within it, and any arguments that will be passed to the main class, as shown in the following command:

```
$ hadoop jar <job jarfile> <main class> <argument 1> … <argument 2>
```

Elastic MapReduce

Recall from *Chapter 1*, *Introduction*, that Elastic MapReduce expects the job JAR file and its input data to be located in an S3 bucket and conversely will dump its output back into S3.

 Be careful: this will cost money! For this example, we will use the smallest possible cluster configuration available for EMR, a single-node cluster

First of all, we will copy the tweet dataset and the list of positive and negative words to S3 using the `aws` command-line utility:

```
$ aws s3 put tweets.txt s3://<bucket>/input
$ aws s3 put job.jar s3://<bucket>
```

We can execute a job using the EMR command-line tool as follows by uploading the JAR file to `s3://<bucket>` and adding CUSTOM_JAR steps with the aws CLI:

```
$ aws emr add-steps --cluster-id <cluster-id> --steps \
Type=CUSTOM_JAR,\
```

```
Name=CustomJAR,\
Jar=s3://<bucket>/job.jar,\
MainClass=<class name>,\
Args=arg1,arg2,...argN
```

Here, `cluster-id` is the ID of a running EMR cluster, `<class name>` is the fully qualified name of the main class, and `arg1`, `arg2`, ..., `argN` are the job arguments.

WordCount, the Hello World of MapReduce

WordCount counts word occurrences in a dataset. The source code of this example can be found at https://github.com/learninghadoop2/book-examples/blob/master/ch3/src/main/java/com/learninghadoop2/mapreduce/WordCount.java. Consider the following block of code for example:

```java
public class WordCount extends Configured implements Tool
{
    public static class WordCountMapper
            extends Mapper<Object, Text, Text, IntWritable>
    {
        private final static IntWritable one = new IntWritable(1);
        private Text word = new Text();
        public void map(Object key, Text value, Context context
        ) throws IOException, InterruptedException {
            String[] words = value.toString().split(" ") ;
            for (String str: words)
            {
                word.set(str);
                context.write(word, one);
            }
        }
    }
    public static class WordCountReducer
            extends Reducer<Text,IntWritable,Text,IntWritable> {
        public void reduce(Text key, Iterable<IntWritable> values,
                        Context context
        ) throws IOException, InterruptedException {
            int total = 0;
            for (IntWritable val : values) {
                total++ ;
            }
            context.write(key, new IntWritable(total));
```

```
            }
       }

       public int run(String[] args) throws Exception {
           Configuration conf = getConf();

           args = new GenericOptionsParser(conf, args)
           .getRemainingArgs();

           Job job = Job.getInstance(conf);

           job.setJarByClass(WordCount.class);
           job.setMapperClass(WordCountMapper.class);
           job.setReducerClass(WordCountReducer.class);
           job.setOutputKeyClass(Text.class);
           job.setOutputValueClass(IntWritable.class);

           FileInputFormat.addInputPath(job, new Path(args[0]));
           FileOutputFormat.setOutputPath(job, new Path(args[1]));

           return (job.waitForCompletion(true) ? 0 : 1);
       }

       public static void main(String[] args) throws Exception {
           int exitCode = ToolRunner.run(new WordCount(), args);
           System.exit(exitCode);
       }
   }
```

This is our first complete MapReduce job. Look at the structure, and you should recognize the elements we have previously discussed: the overall Job class with the driver configuration in its main method and the Mapper and Reducer implementations defined as static nested classes.

We'll do a more detailed walkthrough of the mechanics of MapReduce in the next section, but for now, let's look at the preceding code and think of how it realizes the key/value transformations we discussed earlier.

The input to the Mapper class is arguably the hardest to understand, as the key is not actually used. The job specifies TextInputFormat as the format of the input data and, by default, this delivers to the mapper data where the key is the byte offset in the file and the value is the text of that line. In reality, you may never actually see a mapper that uses that byte offset key, but it's provided.

The mapper is executed once for each line of text in the input source, and every time it takes the line and breaks it into words. It then uses the Context object to output (more commonly known as emitting) each new key/value of the form (word, 1). These are our K2/V2 values.

We said before that the input to the reducer is a key and a corresponding list of values, and there is some magic that happens between the map and reduce methods to collect the values for each key that facilitates this—called the shuffle stage, which we won't describe right now. Hadoop executes the reducer once for each key, and the preceding reducer implementation simply counts the numbers in the Iterable object and gives output for each word in the form of (word, count). These are our K3/V3 values.

Take a look at the signatures of our mapper and reducer classes: the WordCountMapper class accepts IntWritable and Text as input and provides Text and IntWritable as output. The WordCountReducer class has Text and IntWritable accepted as both input and output. This is again quite a common pattern, where the map method performs an inversion on the key and values, and instead emits a series of data pairs on which the reducer performs aggregation.

The driver is more meaningful here, as we have real values for the parameters. We use arguments passed to the class to specify the input and output locations.

Run the job with:

```
$ hadoop jar build/libs/mapreduce-example.jar com.learninghadoop2.mapreduce.WordCount \
  twitter.txt output
```

Examine the output with a command such as the following; the actual filename might be different, so just look inside the directory called output in your home directory on HDFS:

```
$ hdfs dfs -cat output/part-r-00000
```

Word co-occurrences

Words occurring together are likely to be phrases and common—frequently occurring—phrases are likely to be important. In Natural Language Processing, a list of co-occurring terms is called an N-Gram. N-Grams are the foundation of several statistical methods for text analytics. We will give an example of the special case of an N-Gram—and a metric often encountered in analytics applications—composed of two terms (a bigram).

A naïve implementation in MapReduce would be an extension of WordCount that emits a multi-field key composed of two tab-separated words.

```
public class BiGramCount extends Configured implements Tool
{
    public static class BiGramMapper
            extends Mapper<Object, Text, Text, IntWritable> {
        private final static IntWritable one = new IntWritable(1);
        private Text word = new Text();

        public void map(Object key, Text value, Context context
        ) throws IOException, InterruptedException {
            String[] words = value.toString().split(" ");

            Text bigram = new Text();
            String prev = null;

            for (String s : words) {
                if (prev != null) {
                    bigram.set(prev + "\t+\t" + s);
                    context.write(bigram, one);
                }

                prev = s;
            }
        }
    }

    @Override
    public int run(String[] args) throws Exception {
        Configuration conf = getConf();

        args = new GenericOptionsParser(conf, args).
getRemainingArgs();
        Job job = Job.getInstance(conf);
        job.setJarByClass(BiGramCount.class);
        job.setMapperClass(BiGramMapper.class);
        job.setReducerClass(IntSumReducer.class);
        job.setOutputKeyClass(Text.class);
        job.setOutputValueClass(IntWritable.class);
```

```
            FileInputFormat.addInputPath(job, new Path(args[0]));
            FileOutputFormat.setOutputPath(job, new Path(args[1]));
            return (job.waitForCompletion(true) ? 0 : 1);
        }

    public static void main(String[] args) throws Exception {
        int exitCode = ToolRunner.run(new BiGramCount(), args);
        System.exit(exitCode);
    }
}
```

In this job, we replace `WordCountReducer` with `org.apache.hadoop.mapreduce.lib.reduce.IntSumReducer`, which implements the same logic. The source code of this example can be found at `https://github.com/learninghadoop2/book-examples/blob/master/ch3/src/main/java/com/learninghadoop2/mapreduce/BiGramCount.java`.

Trending topics

The # symbol, called a hashtag, is used to mark keywords or topics in a tweet. It was created organically by Twitter users as a way to categorize messages. Twitter Search (found at `https://twitter.com/search-home`) popularized the use of hashtags as a method to connect and find content related to specific topics as well as the people talking about such topics. By counting the frequency with which a hashtag is mentioned over a given time period, we can determine which topics are trending in the social network.

```
public class HashTagCount extends Configured implements Tool
{
    public static class HashTagCountMapper
            extends Mapper<Object, Text, Text, IntWritable>
    {
        private final static IntWritable one = new IntWritable(1);
        private Text word = new Text();

        private String hashtagRegExp -
 "(?:\\s|\\A|^)[##]+([A-Za-z0-9-_]+)";
```

```
        public void map(Object key, Text value, Context context)
                throws IOException, InterruptedException {
            String[] words = value.toString().split(" ") ;

            for (String str: words)
            {
                if (str.matches(hashtagRegExp)) {
                    word.set(str);
                    context.write(word, one);
                }
            }
        }
    }

    public int run(String[] args) throws Exception {
        Configuration conf = getConf();

        args = new GenericOptionsParser(conf, args)
        .getRemainingArgs();

        Job job = Job.getInstance(conf);

        job.setJarByClass(HashTagCount.class);
        job.setMapperClass(HashTagCountMapper.class);
        job.setCombinerClass(IntSumReducer.class);
        job.setReducerClass(IntSumReducer.class);
        job.setOutputKeyClass(Text.class);
        job.setOutputValueClass(IntWritable.class);

        FileInputFormat.addInputPath(job, new Path(args[0]));
        FileOutputFormat.setOutputPath(job, new Path(args[1]));

        return (job.waitForCompletion(true) ? 0 : 1);
    }

    public static void main(String[] args) throws Exception {
        int exitCode = ToolRunner.run(new HashTagCount(), args);
        System.exit(exitCode);
    }
}
```

As in the WordCount example, we tokenize text in the Mapper. We use a regular expression— `hashtagRegExp`—to detect the presence of a hashtag in Twitter's text and emit the hashtag and the number 1 when a hashtag is found. In the Reducer step, we then count the total number of emitted hashtag occurrences using `IntSumReducer`.

The full source code of this example can be found at `https://github.com/learninghadoop2/book-examples/blob/master/ch3/src/main/java/com/learninghadoop2/mapreduce/HashTagCount.java`.

This compiled class will be in the JAR file we built with Gradle earlier, so now we execute HashTagCount with the following command:

```
$ hadoop jar build/libs/mapreduce-example.jar \
com.learninghadoop2.mapreduce.HashTagCount twitter.txt output
```

Let's examine the output as before:

```
$ hdfs dfs -cat output/part-r-00000
```

You should see output similar to the following:

```
#whey           1
#willpower      1
#win            2
#winterblues    1
#winterstorm    1
#wipolitics     1
#women          6
#woodgrain      1
```

Each line is composed of a hashtag and the number of times it appears in the tweets dataset. As you can see, the MapReduce job orders results by key. If we want to find the most mentioned topics, we need to order the result set. The naïve approach would be to perform a total order of the aggregated values and selecting the top 10.

If the output dataset is small, we can pipe it to standard output and sort it using the `sort` utility:

```
$ hdfs dfs -cat output/part-r-00000 | sort -k2 -n -r | head -n 10
```

Another solution would be to write another MapReduce job to traverse the whole result set and sort by value. When data becomes large, this type of global sorting can become quite expensive. In the following section, we will illustrate an efficient design pattern to sort aggregated data

The Top N pattern

In the Top N pattern, we keep data sorted in a local data structure. Each mapper calculates a list of the top N records in its split and sends its list to the reducer. A single reducer task finds the top N global records.

We will apply this design pattern to implement a `TopTenHashTag` job that finds the top ten topics in our dataset. The job takes as input the output data generated by `HashTagCount` and returns a list of the ten most frequently mentioned hashtags.

In `TopTenMapper` we use `TreeMap` to keep a sorted list — in ascending order — of hashtags. The key of this map is the number of occurrences; the value is a tab-separated string of hashtags and their frequency . In `map()`, for each value, we update the `topN` map. When topN has more than ten items, we remove the smallest:

```
public static class TopTenMapper extends Mapper<Object, Text,
  NullWritable, Text> {

    private TreeMap<Integer, Text> topN = new TreeMap<Integer, Text>();
    private final static IntWritable one = new IntWritable(1);
    private Text word = new Text();
    public void map(Object key, Text value, Context context) throws
      IOException, InterruptedException {

    String[] words = value.toString().split("\t") ;
    if (words.length < 2) {
      return;
    }
    topN.put(Integer.parseInt(words[1]), new Text(value));
    if (topN.size() > 10) {
      topN.remove(topN.firstKey());
    }
  }
}
```

```
    @Override
    protected void cleanup(Context context) throws IOException,
        InterruptedException {
            for (Text t : topN.values()) {
                context.write(NullWritable.get(), t);
            }
        }
    }
}
```

We don't emit any key/value in the map function. We implement a `cleanup()` method that, once the mapper has consumed all its input, emits the (hashtag, count) values in `topN`. We use a `NullWritable` key because we want all values to be associated with the same key so that we can perform a global order over all mappers' top n lists. This implies that our job will execute only one reducer.

The reducer implements logic similar to what we have in `map()`. We instantiate `TreeMap` and use it to keep an ordered list of the top 10 values:

```
public static class TopTenReducer extends
        Reducer<NullWritable, Text, NullWritable, Text> {

    private TreeMap<Integer, Text> topN = new TreeMap<Integer,
        Text>();

    @Override
    public void reduce(NullWritable key, Iterable<Text> values,
        Context context) throws IOException, InterruptedException {
            for (Text value : values) {
                String[] words = value.toString().split("\t") ;

                topN.put(Integer.parseInt(words[1]),
                    new Text(value));

                if (topN.size() > 10) {
                    topN.remove(topN.firstKey());
                }
            }
```

```
            for (Text word : topN.descendingMap().values()) {
                context.write(NullWritable.get(), word);
            }
        }
    }
```

Finally, we traverse `topN` in descending order to generate the list of trending topics.

 Note that in this implementation, we override hashtags that have a frequency value already present in `TreeMap` when calling `topN`. `put()`. Depending on the use case, it's advised to use a different data structure—such as the ones offered by the Guava library (`https://code.google.com/p/guava-libraries/`)—or adjust the updating strategy.

In the driver, we enforce a single reducer by setting `job.setNumReduceTasks(1)`:

```
$ hadoop jar build/libs/mapreduce-example.jar \
com.learninghadoop2.mapreduce.TopTenHashTag \
output/part-r-00000 \
top-ten
```

We can inspect the top ten to list trending topics:

```
$ hdfs dfs -cat top-ten/part-r-00000
#Stalker48        150
#gameinsight      55
#12M      52
#KCA      46
#LORDJASONJEROME          29
#Valencia         19
#LesAnges6        16
#VoteLuan         15
#hadoop2      12
#Gameinsight      11
```

The source code of this example can be found at `https://github.com/learninghadoop2/book-examples/blob/master/ch3/src/main/java/com/learninghadoop2/mapreduce/TopTenHashTag.java`.

Sentiment of hashtags

The process of identifying subjective information in a data source is commonly referred to as sentiment analysis. In the previous example, we show how to detect trending topics in a social network; we'll now analyze the text shared around those topics to determine whether they express a mostly positive or negative sentiment.

A list of positive and negative words for the English language—a so-called opinion lexicon—can be found at `http://www.cs.uic.edu/~liub/FBS/opinion-lexicon-English.rar`.

These resources—and many more—have been collected by Prof. Bing Liu's group at the University of Illinois at Chicago and have been used, among others, in *Bing Liu, Minqing Hu and Junsheng Cheng. "Opinion Observer: Analyzing and Comparing Opinions on the Web." Proceedings of the 14th International World Wide Web conference (WWW-2005), May 10-14, 2005, Chiba, Japan.*

In this example, we'll present a bag-of-words method that, although simplistic in nature, can be used as a baseline to mine opinion in text. For each tweet and each hashtag, we will count the number of times a positive or a negative word appears and normalize this count by the text length.

The bag-of-words model is an approach used in Natural Language Processing and Information Retrieval to represent textual documents. In this model, text is represented as the set or bag—with multiplicity—of its words, disregarding grammar and morphological properties and even word order.

Uncompress the archive and place the word lists into HDFS with the following command line:

```
$ hdfs dfs -put positive-words.txt <destination>
$ hdfs dfs -put negative-words.txt <destination>
```

In the Mapper class, we define two objects that will hold the word lists: `positiveWords` and `negativeWords` as `Set<String>`:

```
    private Set<String> positiveWords = null;
    private Set<String> negativeWords = null;
```

We override the default `setup()` method of the Mapper so that a list of positive and negative words—specified by two configuration properties: `job.positivewords.path` and `job.negativewords.path`—is read from HDFS using the filesystem API we discussed in the previous chapter. We could have also used DistributedCache to share this data across the cluster. The helper method, `parseWordsList`, reads a list of word lists, strips out comments, and loads words into `HashSet<String>`:

```
private HashSet<String> parseWordsList(FileSystem fs, Path
wordsListPath)
{
    HashSet<String> words = new HashSet<String>();
    try {

        if (fs.exists(wordsListPath)) {
            FSDataInputStream fi = fs.open(wordsListPath);

            BufferedReader br =
new BufferedReader(new InputStreamReader(fi));
            String line = null;
            while ((line = br.readLine()) != null) {
                if (line.length() > 0 && !line.startsWith(BEGIN_
COMMENT)) {
                    words.add(line);
                }
            }

            fi.close();
        }
    }
    catch (IOException e) {
        e.printStackTrace();
    }

    return words;
}
```

In the Mapper step, we emit for each hashtag in the tweet the overall sentiment of the tweet (simply the positive word count minus the negative word count) and the length of the tweet.

We'll use these in the reducer to calculate an overall sentiment ratio weighted by the length of the tweets to estimate the sentiment expressed by a tweet on a hashtag, as follows:

```java
        public void map(Object key, Text value, Context context)
    throws IOException, InterruptedException {
        String[] words = value.toString().split(" ") ;
        Integer positiveCount = new Integer(0);
        Integer negativeCount = new Integer(0);

        Integer wordsCount = new Integer(0);

        for (String str: words)
        {
            if (str.matches(HASHTAG_PATTERN)) {
                hashtags.add(str);
            }

            if (positiveWords.contains(str)) {
                positiveCount += 1;
            } else if (negativeWords.contains(str)) {
                negativeCount += 1;
            }

            wordsCount += 1;
        }

        Integer sentimentDifference = 0;
        if (wordsCount > 0) {
          sentimentDifference = positiveCount - negativeCount;
        }

        String stats ;
        for (String hashtag : hashtags) {
            word.set(hashtag);
            stats = String.format("%d %d", sentimentDifference,
              wordsCount);
            context.write(word, new Text(stats));
        }
    }
}
```

In the Reducer step, we add together the sentiment scores given to each instance of the hashtag and divide by the total size of all the tweets in which it occurred:

```
public static class HashTagSentimentReducer
        extends Reducer<Text,Text,Text,DoubleWritable> {
    public void reduce(Text key, Iterable<Text> values,
                        Context context
    ) throws IOException, InterruptedException {
        double totalDifference = 0;
        double totalWords = 0;
        for (Text val : values) {
            String[] parts = val.toString().split(" ") ;
            totalDifference += Double.parseDouble(parts[0]) ;
            totalWords += Double.parseDouble(parts[1]) ;
        }
        context.write(key,
  new DoubleWritable(totalDifference/totalWords));
    }
}
```

The full source code of this example can be found at `https://github.com/learninghadoop2/book-examples/blob/master/ch3/src/main/java/com/learninghadoop2/mapreduce/HashTagSentiment.java`.

After running the preceding code, execute `HashTagSentiment` with the following command:

```
$ hadoop jar build/libs/mapreduce-example.jar com.learninghadoop2.
mapreduce.HashTagSentiment twitter.txt output-sentiment <positive words>
<negative words>
```

You can examine the output with the following command:

```
$ hdfs dfs -cat output-sentiment/part-r-00000
```

You should see an output similar to the following:

```
#1068    0.011861271213042056

#10YearsOfLove   0.012285135487494233

#11      0.011941109121333999

#12      0.011938693593171155

#12F     0.012339242266249566

#12M     0.011864286953783268

#12MCalleEnPazYaTeVasNicolas
```

In the preceding output, each line is composed of a hashtag and the sentiment polarity associated with it. This number is a heuristic that tells us whether a hashtag is associated mostly with positive (polarity > 0) or negative (polarity < 0) sentiment and the magnitude of such a sentiment — the higher or lower the number, the stronger the sentiment.

Text cleanup using chain mapper

In the examples presented until now, we ignored a key step of essentially every application built around text processing, which is the normalization and cleanup of the input data. Three common components of this normalization step are:

- Changing the letter case to either lower or upper
- Removal of stopwords
- Stemming

In this section, we will show how the ChainMapper class — found at org.apache. hadoop.mapreduce.lib.chain.ChainMapper — allows us to sequentially combine a series of Mappers to put together as the first step of a data cleanup pipeline. Mappers are added to the configured job using the following:

```
ChainMapper.addMapper(
JobConf job,
Class<? extends Mapper<K1,V1,K2,V2>> klass,
Class<? extends K1> inputKeyClass,
Class<? extends V1> inputValueClass,
Class<? extends K2> outputKeyClass,
Class<? extends V2> outputValueClass, JobConf mapperConf)
```

The static method, addMapper, requires the following arguments to be passed:

- job: JobConf to add the Mapper class
- class: Mapper class to add
- inputKeyClass: mapper input key class
- inputValueClass: mapper input value class
- outputKeyClass: mapper output key class
- outputValueClass: mapper output value class
- mapperConf: a JobConf with the configuration for the Mapper class

In this example, we will take care of the first item listed above: before computing the sentiment of each tweet, we will convert to lowercase each word present in its text. This will allow us to more accurately ascertain the sentiment of hashtags by ignoring differences in capitalization across tweets.

First of all, we define a new Mapper — LowerCaseMapper — whose map() function calls Java String's toLowerCase() method on its input value and emits the lower cased text:

```
public class LowerCaseMapper extends Mapper<LongWritable, Text,
IntWritable, Text> {
    private Text lowercased = new Text();
    public void map(LongWritable key, Text value, Context context)
throws IOException, InterruptedException {
        lowercased.set(value.toString().toLowerCase());
        context.write(new IntWritable(1), lowercased);
    }
}
```

In the HashTagSentimentChain driver, we configure the Job object so that both Mappers will be chained together and executed:

```
public class HashTagSentimentChain
extends Configured implements Tool
{

    public int run(String[] args) throws Exception {
        Configuration conf = getConf();
        args = new GenericOptionsParser(conf,args).
            getRemainingArgs();

        // location (on hdfs) of the positive words list
        conf.set("job.positivewords.path", args[2]);
        conf.set("job.negativewords.path", args[3]);

        Job job = Job.getInstance(conf);
        job.setJarByClass(HashTagSentimentChain.class);

        Configuration lowerCaseMapperConf = new
            Configuration(false);
        ChainMapper.addMapper(job,
                LowerCaseMapper.class,
                LongWritable.class, Text.class,
                IntWritable.class, Text.class,
```

```
                          lowerCaseMapperConf);

        Configuration hashTagSentimentConf = new
            Configuration(false);
        ChainMapper.addMapper(job,
            HashTagSentiment.HashTagSentimentMapper.class,
            IntWritable.class,
            Text.class, Text.class,
            Text.class,
            hashTagSentimentConf);
        job.setReducerClass(HashTagSentiment.
            HashTagSentimentReducer.class);


        job.setInputFormatClass(TextInputFormat.class);
        FileInputFormat.addInputPath(job, new Path(args[0]));

        job.setOutputFormatClass(TextOutputFormat.class);
        FileOutputFormat.setOutputPath(job, new Path(args[1]));

        return (job.waitForCompletion(true) ? 0 : 1);
    }

    public static void main (String[] args) throws Exception {
        int exitCode = ToolRunner.run(
new HashTagSentimentChain(), args);
        System.exit(exitCode);
    }
}
```

The `LowerCaseMapper` and `HashTagSentimentMapper` classes are invoked in a pipeline, where the output of the first becomes the input of the second. The output of the last Mapper will be written to the task's output. An immediate benefit of this design is a reduction of disk I/O operations. Mappers do not need to be aware that they are chained. It's therefore possible to reuse specialized Mappers that can be combined within a single task. Note that this pattern assumes that all Mappers — and the Reduce — use matching output and input (key, value) pairs. No casting or conversion is done by ChainMapper itself.

Finally, notice that the `addMapper` call for the last mapper in the chain specifies the output key/value classes applicable to the whole mapper pipeline when used as a composite.

The full source code of this example can be found at `https://github.com/learninghadoop2/book-examples/blob/master/ch3/src/main/java/com/learninghadoop2/mapreduce/HashTagSentimentChain.java`.

Execute `HashTagSentimentChain` with the command:

```
$ hadoop jar build/libs/mapreduce-example.jar com.learninghadoop2.
mapreduce.HashTagSentimentChain twitter.txt output <positive words>
<negative words>
```

You should see an output similar to the previous example. Notice that this time, the hashtag in each line is lowercased.

Walking through a run of a MapReduce job

To explore the relationship between mapper and reducer in more detail, and to expose some of Hadoop's inner workings, we'll now go through how a MapReduce job is executed. This applies to both MapReduce in Hadoop 1 and Hadoop 2 even though the latter is implemented very differently using YARN, which we'll discuss later in this chapter. Additional information on the services described in this section, as well as suggestions for troubleshooting MapReduce applications, can be found in *Chapter 10, Running a Hadoop Cluster.*

Startup

The driver is the only piece of code that runs on our local machine, and the call to `Job.waitForCompletion()` starts the communication with the JobTracker, which is the master node in the MapReduce system. The JobTracker is responsible for all aspects of job scheduling and execution, so it becomes our primary interface when performing any task related to job management.

To share resources on the cluster the JobTracker can use one of several scheduling approaches to handle incoming jobs. The general model is to have a number of queues to which jobs can be submitted along with policies to assign resources across the queues. The most commonly used implementations for these policies are Capacity and Fair Scheduler.

The JobTracker communicates with the NameNode on our behalf and manages all interactions relating to the data stored on HDFS.

Splitting the input

The first of these interactions happens when the JobTracker looks at the input data and determines how to assign it to map tasks. Recall that HDFS files are usually split into blocks of at least 64 MB and the JobTracker will assign each block to one map task. Our WordCount example, of course, used a trivial amount of data that was well within a single block. Picture a much larger input file measured in terabytes, and the split model makes more sense. Each segment of the file — or split, in MapReduce terminology — is processed uniquely by one map task. Once it has computed the splits, the JobTracker places them and the JAR file containing the Mapper and Reducer classes into a job-specific directory on HDFS, whose path will be passed to each task as it starts.

Task assignment

The TaskTracker service is responsible for allocating resources, executing and tracking the status of map and reduce tasks running on a node. Once the JobTracker has determined how many map tasks will be needed, it looks at the number of hosts in the cluster, how many TaskTrackers are working, and how many map tasks each can concurrently execute (a user-definable configuration variable). The JobTracker also looks to see where the various input data blocks are located across the cluster and attempts to define an execution plan that maximizes the cases when the TaskTracker processes a split/block located on the same physical host, or, failing that, it processes at least one in the same hardware rack. This data locality optimization is a huge reason behind Hadoop's ability to efficiently process such large datasets. Recall also that, by default, each block is replicated across three different hosts, so the likelihood of producing a task/host plan that sees most blocks processed locally is higher than it might seem at first.

Task startup

Each TaskTracker then starts up a separate Java virtual machine to execute the tasks. This does add a startup time penalty, but it isolates the TaskTracker from problems caused by misbehaving `map` or `reduce` tasks, and it can be configured to be shared between subsequently executed tasks.

If the cluster has enough capacity to execute all the map tasks at once, they will all be started and given a reference to the split they are to process and the job JAR file. If there are more tasks than the cluster capacity, the JobTracker will keep a queue of pending tasks and assign them to nodes as they complete their initially assigned map tasks.

We are now ready to see the executed data of map tasks. If all this sounds like a lot of work, it is; it explains why, when running any MapReduce job, there is always a non-trivial amount of time taken as the system gets started and performs all these steps.

Ongoing JobTracker monitoring

The JobTracker doesn't just stop work now and wait for the TaskTrackers to execute all the mappers and reducers. It's constantly exchanging heartbeat and status messages with the TaskTrackers, looking for evidence of progress or problems. It also collects metrics from the tasks throughout the job execution, some provided by Hadoop and others specified by the developer of the `map` and `reduce` tasks, although we don't use any in this example.

Mapper input

The driver class specifies the format and structure of the input file using `TextInputFormat`, and from this, Hadoop knows to treat this as text with the byte offset as the key and line contents as the value. Assume that our dataset contains the following text:

```
This is a test
Yes it is
```

The two invocations of the mapper will therefore be given the following output:

```
1 This is a test
2 Yes it is
```

Mapper execution

The key/value pairs received by the mapper are the offset in the file of the line and the line contents, respectively, because of how the job is configured. Our implementation of the map method in `WordCountMapper` discards the key, as we do not care where each line occurred in the file, and splits the provided value into words using the split method on the standard Java String class. Note that better tokenization could be provided by use of regular expressions or the `StringTokenizer` class, but for our purposes this simple approach will suffice. For each individual word, the mapper then emits a key comprised of the actual word itself, and a value of 1.

Mapper output and reducer input

The output of the mapper is a series of pairs of the form (word, 1); in our example, these will be:

```
(This,1), (is, 1), (a, 1), (test, 1), (Yes, 1), (it, 1), (is, 1)
```

These output pairs from the mapper are not passed directly to the reducer. Between mapping and reducing is the shuffle stage, where much of the magic of MapReduce occurs.

Reducer input

The reducer TaskTracker receives updates from the JobTracker that tell it which nodes in the cluster hold map output partitions that need to be processed by its local reduce task. It then retrieves these from the various nodes and merges them into a single file that will be fed to the reduce task.

Reducer execution

Our WordCountReducer class is very simple; for each word, it simply counts the number of elements in the array and emits the final (word, count) output for each word. For our invocation of WordCount on our sample input, all but one word has only one value in the list of values; *is* has two.

Reducer output

The final set of reducer output for our example is therefore:

```
(This, 1), (is, 2), (a, 1), (test, 1), (Yes, 1), (it, 1)
```

This data will be output to partition files within the output directory specified in the driver that will be formatted using the specified OutputFormat implementation. Each reduce task writes to a single file with the filename part-r-nnnnn, where nnnnn starts at 00000 and is incremented.

Shutdown

Once all tasks have completed successfully, the JobTracker outputs the final state of the job to the client, along with the final aggregates of some of the more important counters that it has been aggregating along the way. The full job and task history is available in the log directory on each node or, more accessibly, via the JobTracker web UI; point your browser to port 50030 on the JobTracker node.

Input/Output

We have talked about files being broken into splits as part of the job startup and the data in a split being sent to the mapper implementation. However, this overlooks two aspects: how the data is stored in the file and how the individual keys and values are passed to the mapper structure.

InputFormat and RecordReader

Hadoop has the concept of InputFormat for the first of these responsibilities. The InputFormat abstract class in the `org.apache.hadoop.mapreduce` package provides two methods as shown in the following code:

```
public abstract class InputFormat<K, V>
{
    public abstract List<InputSplit> getSplits( JobContext context);
    RecordReader<K, V> createRecordReader(InputSplit split,
        TaskAttemptContext context) ;
}
```

These methods display the two responsibilities of the InputFormat class:

- To provide details on how to divide an input file into the splits required for map processing
- To create a RecordReader that will generate the series of key/value pairs from a split

The RecordReader class is also an abstract class within the `org.apache.hadoop.mapreduce` package:

```
public abstract class RecordReader<Key, Value> implements Closeable
{
  public abstract void initialize(InputSplit split,
    TaskAttemptContext  context);
  public abstract boolean nextKeyValue()
    throws IOException, InterruptedException;
  public abstract Key getCurrentKey()
    throws IOException, InterruptedException;
  public abstract Value getCurrentValue()
    throws IOException, InterruptedException;
  public abstract float getProgress()
    throws IOException, InterruptedException;
  public abstract close() throws IOException;
}
```

A `RecordReader` instance is created for each split and calls `getNextKeyValue` to return a Boolean indicating whether another key/value pair is available, and, if so, the `getKey` and `getValue` methods are used to access the key and value respectively.

The combination of the `InputFormat` and `RecordReader` classes therefore are all that is required to bridge between any kind of input data and the key/value pairs required by MapReduce.

Hadoop-provided InputFormat

There are some Hadoop-provided InputFormat implementations within the `org.apache.hadoop.mapreduce.lib.input` package:

- `FileInputFormat`: is an abstract base class that can be the parent of any file-based input.
- `SequenceFileInputFormat`: is an efficient binary file format that will be discussed in an upcoming section.
- `TextInputFormat`: is used for plain text files.
- `KeyValueTextInputFormat`: is used for plain text files. Each line is divided into key and value parts by a separator byte.

Note that input formats are not restricted to reading from files; FileInputFormat is itself a subclass of InputFormat. It's possible to have Hadoop use data that is not based on files as the input to MapReduce jobs; common sources are relational databases or column-oriented databases, such as Amazon DynamoDB or HBase.

Hadoop-provided RecordReader

Hadoop provides a few common `RecordReader` implementations, which are also present within the `org.apache.hadoop.mapreduce.lib.input` package:

- `LineRecordReader`: implementation is the default `RecordReader` class for text files that presents the byte offset in the file as the key and the line contents as the value
- `SequenceFileRecordReader`: implementation reads the key/value from the binary `SequenceFile` container

OutputFormat and RecordWriter

There is a similar pattern for writing the output of a job coordinated by subclasses of OutputFormat and RecordWriter from the org.apache.hadoop.mapreduce package. We won't explore these in any detail here, but the general approach is similar, although OutputFormat does have a more involved API, as it has methods for tasks such as validation of the output specification.

It's this step that causes a job to fail if a specified output directory already exists. If you wanted different behavior, it would require a subclass of OutputFormat that overrides this method.

Hadoop-provided OutputFormat

The following output formats are provided in the org.apache.hadoop.mapreduce. output package:

- FileOutputFormat: is the base class for all file-based OutputFormats
- NullOutputFormat: is a dummy implementation that discards the output and writes nothing to the file
- SequenceFileOutputFormat: writes to the binary SequenceFile format
- TextOutputFormat: writes a plain text file

Note that these classes define their required RecordWriter implementations as static nested classes, so there are no separately provided RecordWriter implementations.

Sequence files

The SequenceFile class within the org.apache.hadoop.io package provides an efficient binary file format that is often useful as an output from a MapReduce job. This is especially true if the output from the job is processed as the input of another job. Sequence files have several advantages, as follows:

- As binary files, they are intrinsically more compact than text files
- They additionally support optional compression, which can also be applied at different levels, that is, they compress each record or an entire split
- They can be split and processed in parallel

This last characteristic is important as most binary formats – particularly those that are compressed or encrypted – cannot be split and must be read as a single linear stream of data. Using such files as input to a MapReduce job means that a single mapper will be used to process the entire file, causing a potentially large performance hit. In such a situation, it's preferable to use a splittable format, such as SequenceFile, or, if you cannot avoid receiving the file in another format, do a preprocessing step that converts it into a splittable format. This will be a tradeoff, as the conversion will take time, but in many cases – especially with complex map tasks – this will be outweighed by the time saved through increased parallelism.

YARN

YARN started out as part of the MapReduce v2 (MRv2) initiative but is now an independent sub-project within Hadoop (that is, it's at the same level as MapReduce). It grew out of a realization that MapReduce in Hadoop 1 conflated two related but distinct responsibilities: resource management and application execution.

Although it has enabled previously unimagined processing on enormous datasets, the MapReduce model at a conceptual level has an impact on performance and scalability. Implicit in the MapReduce model is that any application can only be composed of a series of largely linear MapReduce jobs, each of which follows a model of one or more maps followed by one or more reduces. This model is a great fit for some applications, but not all. In particular, it's a poor fit for workloads requiring very low-latency response times; the MapReduce startup times and sometimes lengthy job chains often greatly exceed the tolerance for a user-facing process. The model has also been found to be very inefficient for jobs that would more naturally be represented as a directed acyclic graph (DAG) of tasks where the nodes on the graph are processing steps, and the edges are data flows. If analyzed and executed as a DAG then the application may be performed in one step with high parallelism across the processing steps, but when viewed through the MapReduce lens, the result is usually an inefficient series of interdependent MapReduce jobs.

Numerous projects have built different types of processing atop MapReduce and although many are wildly successful (Apache Hive and Pig are two standout examples), the close coupling of MapReduce as a processing paradigm with the job scheduling mechanism in Hadoop1 made it very difficult for any new project to tailor either of these areas to its specific needs.

The result is **Yet Another Resource Negotiator** (**YARN**), which provides a highly capable job scheduling mechanism within Hadoop and the well-defined interfaces for different processing models to be implemented within it.

YARN architecture

To understand how YARN works, it's important to stop thinking about MapReduce and how it processes data. YARN itself says nothing about the nature of the applications that run atop it, rather it's focused on providing the machinery for the scheduling and execution of these jobs. As we'll see, YARN is just as capable of hosting long-running stream processing or low-latency, user-facing workloads as it is capable of hosting batch-processing workloads, such as MapReduce.

The components of YARN

YARN is comprised of two main components, the **ResourceManager** (**RM**), which manages resources across the cluster, and the **NodeManager** (**NM**), which runs on each host and manages the resources on the individual machine. The ResourceManager and NodeManagers deal with the scheduling and management of containers, an abstract notion of the memory, CPU, and I/O that will be dedicated to run a particular piece of application code. Using MapReduce as an example, when running atop YARN, the JobTracker and each TaskTracker all run in their own dedicated containers. Note though, that in YARN, each MapReduce job has its own dedicated JobTracker; there is no single instance that manages all jobs, as in Hadoop 1.

YARN itself is responsible only for the scheduling of tasks across the cluster; all notions of application-level progress, monitoring, and fault tolerance are handled in the application code. This is a very explicit design decision; by making YARN as independent as possible, it has a very clear set of responsibilities and does not artificially constrain the types of application that can be implemented on YARN.

As the arbiter of all cluster resources, YARN has the ability to efficiently manage the cluster as a whole and not focus on application-level resource requirements. It has a pluggable scheduling policy with the provided implementations similar to the existing Hadoop Capacity and Fair Scheduler. YARN also treats all application code as inherently untrusted and all application management and control tasks are performed in user space.

Anatomy of a YARN application

A submitted YARN application has two components: the **ApplicationMaster** (**AM**), which coordinates the overall application flow, and the specification of the code that will run on the worker nodes. For MapReduce atop YARN, the JobTracker implements the ApplicationMaster functionality and TaskTrackers are the application custom code deployed on the worker nodes.

As mentioned in the previous section, the responsibilities of application management, progress monitoring and fault tolerance are pushed to the application level in YARN. It's the ApplicationMaster that performs these tasks; YARN itself says nothing about the mechanisms for communication between the ApplicationMaster and the code running in the worker containers, for example.

This genericity allows YARN applications to not be tied to Java classes. The ApplicationManager can instead request a NodeManager to execute shell scripts, native applications, or any other type of processing that is made available on each node.

Life cycle of a YARN application

As with MapReduce jobs in Hadoop 1, YARN applications are submitted to the cluster by a client. When a YARN application is started, the client first calls the ResourceManager (more specifically the ApplicationManager portion of the ResourceManager) and requests the initial container within which to execute the ApplicationMaster. In most cases the ApplicationMaster will run from a hosted container in the cluster, just as will the rest of the application code. The ApplicationManager communicates with the other main component of the ResourceManager, the scheduler itself, which has the ultimate responsibility of managing all resources across the cluster.

The ApplicationMaster starts up in the provided container, registers itself with the ResourceManager, and begins the process of negotiating its required resources. The ApplicationMaster communicates with the ResourceManager and requests the containers it requires. The specification of the containers requested can also include additional information, such as desired placement within the cluster and concrete resource requirements, such as a particular amount of memory or CPU.

The ResourceManager provides the ApplicationMaster with the details of the containers it has been allocated, and the ApplicationMaster then communicates with the NodeManagers to start the application-specific task for each container. This is done by providing the NodeManager with the specification of the application to be executed, which as mentioned may be a JAR file, a script, a path to a local executable, or anything else that the NodeManager can invoke. Each NodeManager instantiates the container for the application code and starts the application based on the provided specification.

Fault tolerance and monitoring

From this point onward, the behavior is largely application specific. YARN will not manage application progress but does perform a number of ongoing tasks. The AMLivelinessMonitor within the ResourceManager receives heartbeats from all ApplicationMasters, and if it determines that an ApplicationMaster has failed or stopped working, it will de-register the failed ApplicationMaster and release all its allocated containers. The ResourceManager will then reschedule the application a configurable number of times.

Alongside this process the NMLivelinessMonitor within the ResourceManager receives heartbeats from the NodeManagers and keeps track of the health of each NodeManager in the cluster. Similar to the monitoring of ApplicationMaster health, a NodeManager will be marked as dead after receiving no heartbeats for a default time of 10 minutes, after which all allocated containers are marked as dead, and the node is excluded from future resource allocation.

At the same time, the NodeManager will actively monitor resource utilization of each allocated container and, for those resources not constrained by hard limits, will kill containers that exceed their resource allocation.

At a higher level, the YARN scheduler will always be looking to maximize the cluster utilization within the constraints of the sharing policy being employed. As with Hadoop 1, this will allow low-priority applications to use more cluster resources if contention is low, but the scheduler will then preempt these additional containers (that is, request them to be terminated) if higher-priority applications are submitted.

The rest of the responsibility for application-level fault tolerance and progress monitoring must be implemented within the application code. For MapReduce on YARN, for example, all the management of task scheduling and retries is provided at the application level and is not in any way delivered by YARN.

Thinking in layers

These last statements may suggest that writing applications to run on YARN is a lot of work, and this is true. The YARN API is quite low-level and likely intimidating for most developers who just want to run some processing tasks on their data. If all we had was YARN and every new Hadoop application had to have its own ApplicationMaster implemented, then YARN would not look quite as interesting as it does.

What makes the picture better is that, in general, the requirement isn't to implement each and every application on YARN, but instead use it for a smaller number of processing frameworks that provide much friendlier interfaces to be implemented. The first of these was MapReduce; with it hosted on YARN, the developer writes to the usual `map` and `reduce` interfaces and is largely unaware of the YARN mechanics.

But on the same cluster, another developer may be running a job that uses a different framework with significantly different processing characteristics, and YARN will manage both at the same time.

We'll give some more detail on several YARN processing models currently available, but they run the gamut from batch processing through low-latency queries to stream and graph processing and beyond.

As the YARN experience grows, however, there are a number of initiatives to make the development of these processing frameworks easier. On the one hand there are higher-level interfaces, such as Cloudera Kitten (`https://github.com/cloudera/kitten`) or Apache Twill (`http://twill.incubator.apache.org/`), that give friendlier abstractions above the YARN APIs. Perhaps a more significant development model, though, is the emergence of frameworks that provide richer tools to more easily construct applications with a common general class of performance characteristics.

Execution models

We have mentioned different YARN applications having distinct processing characteristics, but an emerging pattern has seen their execution models in general being a source of differentiation. By this, we refer to how the YARN application life cycle is managed, and we identify three main types: per-job application, per-session, and always-on.

Batch processing, such as MapReduce on YARN, sees the life cycle of the MapReduce framework tied to that of the submitted application. If we submit a MapReduce job, then the JobTracker and TaskTrackers that execute it are created specifically for the job and are terminated when the job completes. This works well for batch, but if we wish to provide a more interactive model then the startup overhead of establishing the YARN application and all its resource allocations will severely impact the user experience if every command issued suffers this penalty. A more interactive, or session-based, life cycle will see the YARN application start and then be available to service a number of submitted requests/commands. The YARN application terminates only when the session is exited.

Finally, we have the concept of long-running applications that process continuous data streams independent of any interactive input. For these it makes most sense for the YARN application to start and continuously process data that is retrieved through some external mechanism. The application will only exit when explicitly shut down or if an abnormal situation occurs.

YARN in the real world – Computation beyond MapReduce

The previous discussions have been a little abstract, so in this section, we will explore a few existing YARN applications to see just how they use the framework and how they provide a breadth of processing capability. Of particular interest is how the YARN frameworks take very different approaches to resource management, I/O pipelining, and fault tolerance.

The problem with MapReduce

Until now, we have looked at MapReduce in terms of API. MapReduce in Hadoop is more than that; up until Hadoop 2, it was the default execution engine for a number of tools, among which were Hive and Pig, which we will discuss in more detail later in this book. We have seen how MapReduce applications are, in fact, chains of jobs. This very aspect is one the biggest pain points and constraining factors of the frameworks. MapReduce checkpoints data to HDFS for intra-process communication:

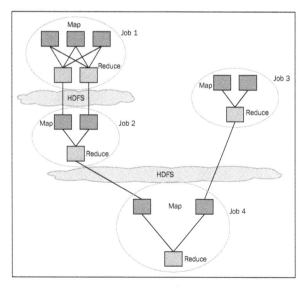

A chain of MapReduce jobs

At the end of each `reduce` phase, output is written to disk so that it can then be loaded by the mappers of the next job and used as its input. This I/O overhead introduces latency, especially when we have applications that require multiple passes on a dataset (hence multiple writes). Unfortunately, this type of iterative computation is at the core of many analytics applications.

Apache Tez and Apache Spark are two frameworks that address this problem by generalizing the MapReduce paradigm. We will briefly discuss them in the remainder of this section, next to Apache Samza, a framework that takes an entirely different approach to real-time processing.

Tez

Tez (`http://tez.apache.org`) is a low-level API and execution engine focused on providing low-latency processing, and is being used as the basis of the latest evolution of Hive, Pig and several other frameworks that implement standard join, filter, merge and group operations. Tez is an implementation and evolution of a programming model presented by Microsoft in the 2009 Dryad paper (`http://research.microsoft.com/en-us/projects/dryad/`). Tez is a generalization of MapReduce as dataflow that strives to achieve fast, interactive computing by pipelining I/O operations over a queue for intra-process communication. This avoids the expensive writes to disks that affect MapReduce. The API provides primitives expressing dependencies between jobs as a DAG. The full DAG is then submitted to a planner that can optimize the execution flow. The same application depicted in the preceding diagram would be executed in Tez as a single job, with I/O pipelined from reducers to reducers without HDFS writes and subsequent reads by mappers. An example can be seen in the following diagram:.

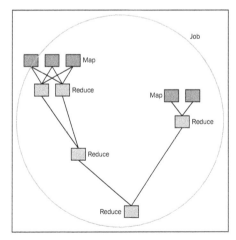

A Tez DAG is a generalization of MapReduce

The canonical WordCount example can be found at `https://github.com/apache/incubator-tez/blob/master/tez-mapreduce-examples/src/main/java/org/apache/tez/mapreduce/examples/WordCount.java`.

```
DAG dag = new DAG("WordCount");
dag.addVertex(tokenizerVertex)
.addVertex(summerVertex)
.addEdge(new Edge(tokenizerVertex, summerVertex,
edgeConf.createDefaultEdgeProperty()));
```

Even though the graph topology `dag` can be expressed with a few lines of code, the boilerplate required to execute the job is considerable. This code handles many of the low-level scheduling and execution responsibilities, including fault tolerance. When Tez detects a failed task, it walks back up the processing graph to find the point from which to re-execute the failed tasks.

Hive-on-tez

Hive 0.13 is the first high-profile project to use Tez as its execution engine. We'll discuss Hive in a lot more detail in *Chapter 7*, *Hadoop and SQL*, but for now we will just touch on how it's implemented on YARN.

Hive (`http://hive.apache.org`) is an engine for querying data stored on HDFS through standard SQL syntax. It has been enormously successful, as this type of capability greatly reduces the barriers to start analytic exploration of data in Hadoop.

In Hadoop 1, Hive had no choice, but to implement its SQL statements as a series of MapReduce jobs. When SQL is submitted to Hive, it generates the required MapReduce jobs behind the scenes and executes these on the cluster. This approach has two main drawbacks: there is a non-trivial startup penalty each time, and the constrained MapReduce model means that seemingly simple SQL statements are often translated into a lengthy series of multiple dependent MapReduce jobs. This is an example of the type of processing more naturally conceptualized as a DAG of tasks, as described earlier in this chapter.

Although some benefits are achieved when Hive executes within MapReduce, within YARN, the major benefits come in Hive 0.13 when the project is fully re-implemented using Tez. By exploiting the Tez APIs, which are focused on providing low-latency processing, Hive gains even more performance while making its codebase simpler.

Since Tez treats its workloads as the DAGs which provide a much better fit to translated SQL queries, Hive on Tez can perform any SQL statement as a single job with maximized parallelism.

Tez helps Hive support interactive queries by providing an always-running service instead of requiring the application to be instantiated from scratch for each SQL submission. This is important because, even though queries that process huge data volumes will simply take some time, the goal is for Hive to become less of a batch tool and instead move to be as much of an interactive tool as possible.

Apache Spark

Spark (`http://spark.apache.org`) is a processing framework that excels at iterative and near real-time processing. Created at UC Berkeley, it has been donated as an Apache project. Spark provides an abstraction that allows data in Hadoop to be viewed as a distributed data structure upon which a series of operations can be performed. The framework is based on the same concepts Tez draws inspiration from (Dryad), but excels with jobs that allow data to be held and processed in memory, and it can very efficiently schedule processing on the in-memory dataset across the cluster. Spark automatically controls replication of data across the cluster, ensuring that each element of the distributed dataset is held in memory on at least two machines, and provides replication-based fault tolerance somewhat akin to HDFS.

Spark started as a standalone system, but was ported to also run on YARN as of its 0.8 release. Spark is particularly interesting because, although its classic processing model is batch-oriented, with the Spark shell it provides an interactive frontend and with the Spark Streaming sub-project also offers near real-time processing of data streams. Spark is different things to different people; it's both a high-level API and an execution engine. At the time of writing, ports of Hive and Pig to Spark are in progress.

Apache Samza

Samza (`http://samza.apache.org`) is a stream-processing framework developed at LinkedIn and donated to the Apache Software Foundation. Samza processes conceptually infinite streams of data, which are seen by the application as a series of messages.

Samza currently integrates most tightly with Apache Kafka (`http://kafka.apache.org`) although it does have a pluggable architecture. Kafka itself is a messaging system that excels at large data volumes and provides a topic-based abstraction similar to most other messaging platforms, such as RabbitMQ. Publishers send messages to topics and interested clients consume messages from the topics as they arrive. Kafka has multiple aspects that set it apart from other messaging platforms, but for this discussion, the most interesting one is that Kafka stores messages for a period of time, which allows messages in topics to be replayed. Topics are partitioned across multiple hosts and partitions can be replicated across hosts to protect from node failure.

Samza builds its processing flow on its concept of streams, which when using Kafka map directly to Kafka partitions. A typical Samza job may listen to one topic for incoming messages, perform some transformations, and then write the output to a different topic. Multiple Samza jobs can then be composed to provide more complex processing structures.

As a YARN application, the Samza ApplicationMaster monitors the health of all running Samza tasks. If a task fails, then a replacement task is instantiated in a new container. Samza achieves fault tolerance by having each task write its progress to a new stream (again modeled as a Kafka topic), so any replacement task just needs to read the latest task state from this checkpoint topic and then replay the main message topic from the last processed position. Samza additionally offers support for local task state, which can be very useful for join and aggregation type workloads. This local state is again built atop the stream abstraction and hence is intrinsically resilient to host failure.

YARN-independent frameworks

An interesting point to note is that two of the preceding projects (Samza and Spark) run atop YARN but are not specific to YARN. Spark started out as a standalone service and has implementations for other schedulers, such as Apache Mesos or to run on Amazon EC2. Though Samza runs only on YARN today, its architecture explicitly is not YARN-specific, and there are discussions about providing realizations on other platforms.

If the YARN model of pushing as much as possible into the application has its downsides through implementation complexity, then this decoupling is one of its major benefits. An application written to use YARN need not be tied to it; by definition, all the functionality for the actual application logic and management is encapsulated within the application code and is independent of YARN or another framework. This is, of course, not saying that designing a scheduler-independent application is a trivial task, but it's now a tractable task; this was absolutely not the case pre-YARN.

YARN today and beyond

Though YARN has been used in production (at Yahoo! in particular) for some time, the final GA version was not released until late 2012. The interfaces to YARN were also somewhat fluid until quite late in the development cycle. Consequently, the fully forward compatible YARN as of Hadoop 2.2 is still relatively new.

YARN is fully functional today, and the future direction will see extensions to its current capabilities. Perhaps most notable among these will be the ability to specify and control container resources on more dimensions. Currently, only location, memory and CPU specifications are possible, and this will be expanded into areas such as storage and network I/O.

In addition, the ApplicationMaster currently has little control over the management of how containers are co-located or not. Finer-grained control here will allow the ApplicationMaster to specify policies around when containers may or may not be scheduled on the same node. In addition, the current resource allocation model is quite static, and it will be useful to allow an application to dynamically change the resources allocated to a running container.

Summary

This chapter explored how to process those large volumes of data that we discussed so much in the previous chapter. In particular we covered:

- How MapReduce was the only processing model available in Hadoop 1 and its conceptual model

- The Java API to MapReduce, and how to use this to build some examples, from a word count to sentiment analysis of Twitter hashtags

- The details of how MapReduce is implemented in practice, and we walked through the execution of a MapReduce job

- How Hadoop stores data and the classes involved to represent input and output formats and record readers and writers

- The limitations of MapReduce that led to the development of YARN, opening the door to multiple computational models on the Hadoop platform

- The YARN architecture and how applications are built atop it

In the next two chapters, we will move away from strictly batch processing and delve into the world of near real-time and iterative processing, using two of the YARN-hosted frameworks we introduced in this chapter, namely Samza and Spark.

4
Real-time Computation with Samza

The previous chapter discussed YARN, and frequently mentioned the breadth of computational models and processing frameworks outside of traditional batch-based MapReduce that it enables on the Hadoop platform. In this chapter and the next, we will explore two such projects in some depth, namely Apache Samza and Apache Spark. We chose these frameworks as they demonstrate the usage of stream and iterative processing and also provide interesting mechanisms to combine processing paradigms. In this chapter we will explore Samza and cover the following topics:

- What Samza is and how it integrates with YARN and other projects such as Apache Kafka
- How Samza provides a simple callback-based interface for stream processing
- How Samza composes multiple stream processing jobs into more complex workflows
- How Samza supports persistent local state within tasks and how this greatly enriches what it can enable

Stream processing with Samza

To explore a pure stream-processing platform, we will use Samza, which is available at `https://samza.apache.org`. The code shown here was tested with the current 0.8 release and we'll keep the GitHub repository updated as the project continues to evolve.

Samza was built at LinkedIn and donated to the Apache Software Foundation in September 2013. Over the years, LinkedIn has built a model that conceptualizes much of their data as streams, and from this they saw the need for a framework that can provide a developer-friendly mechanism to process these ubiquitous data streams.

The team at LinkedIn realized that when it came to data processing, much of the attention went to the extreme ends of the spectrum, for example, RPC workloads are usually implemented as synchronous systems with very low latency requirements or batch systems where the periodicity of jobs is often measured in hours. The ground in between has been relatively poorly supported and this is the area that Samza is targeted at; most of its jobs expect response times ranging from milliseconds to minutes. They also assume that data arrives in a theoretically infinite stream of continuous messages.

How Samza works

There are numerous stream-processing systems such as Storm (`http://storm.apache.org`), in the open source world, and many other (mostly commercial) tools such as **complex event processing** (**CEP**) systems that also target processing on continuous message streams. These systems have many similarities but also some major differences.

For Samza, perhaps the most significant difference is its assumptions about message delivery. Many systems work very hard to reduce the latency of each message, sometimes with an assumption that the goal is to get the message into and out of the system as fast as possible. Samza assumes almost the opposite; its streams are persistent and resilient and any message written to a stream can be re-read for a period of time after its first arrival. As we will see, this gives significant capability around fault tolerance. Samza also builds on this model to allow each of its tasks to hold resilient local state.

Samza is mostly implemented in Scala even though its public APIs are written in Java. We'll show Java examples in this chapter, but any JVM language can be used to implement Samza applications. We'll discuss Scala when we explore Spark in the next chapter.

Samza high-level architecture

Samza views the world as having three main layers or components: the streaming, execution, and processing layers.

Samza architecture

The streaming layer provides access to the data streams, both for consumption and publication. The execution layer provides the means by which Samza applications can be run, have resources such as CPU and memory allocated, and have their life cycles managed. The processing layer is the actual Samza framework itself, and its interfaces allow per-message functionality.

Samza provides pluggable interfaces to support the first two layers though the current main implementations use Kafka for streaming and YARN for execution. We'll discuss these further in the following sections.

Samza's best friend – Apache Kafka

Samza itself does not implement the actual message stream. Instead, it provides an interface for a message system with which it then integrates. The default stream implementation is built upon **Apache Kafka** (http://kafka.apache.org), a messaging system also built at LinkedIn but now a successful and widely adopted open source project.

Kafka can be viewed as a message broker akin to something like RabbitMQ or ActiveMQ, but as mentioned earlier, it writes all messages to disk and scales out across multiple hosts as a core part of its design. Kafka uses the concept of a publish/subscribe model through named topics to which producers write messages and from which consumers read messages. These work much like topics in any other messaging system.

Because Kafka writes all messages to disk, it might not have the same ultra-low latency message throughput as other messaging systems, which focus on getting the message processed as fast as possible and don't aim to store the message long term. Kafka can, however, scale exceptionally well and its ability to replay a message stream can be extremely useful. For example, if a consuming client fails, then it can re-read messages from a known good point in time, or if a downstream algorithm changes, then traffic can be replayed to utilize the new functionality.

When scaling across hosts, Kafka partitions topics and supports partition replication for fault tolerance. Each Kafka message has a key associated with the message and this is used to decide to which partition a given message is sent. This allows semantically useful partitioning, for example, if the key is a user ID in the system, then all messages for a given user will be sent to the same partition. Kafka guarantees ordered delivery within each partition so that any client reading a partition can know that they are receiving all messages for each key in that partition in the order in which they are written by the producer.

Samza periodically writes out checkpoints of the position upto which it has read in all the streams it is consuming. These checkpoint messages are themselves written to a Kafka topic. Thus, when a Samza job starts up, each task can reread its checkpoint stream to know from which position in the stream to start processing messages. This means that in effect Kafka also acts as a buffer; if a Samza job crashes or is taken down for upgrade, no messages will be lost. Instead, the job will just restart from the last checkpointed position when it restarts. This buffer functionality is also important, as it makes it easier for multiple Samza jobs to run as part of a complex workflow. When Kafka topics are the points of coordination between the jobs, one job might consume a topic being written to by another; in such cases, Kafka can help smooth out issues caused due to any given job running slower than others. Traditionally, the back pressure caused by a slow running job can be a real issue in a system comprised of multiple job stages, but Kafka as the resilient buffer allows each job to read and write at its own rate. Note that this is analogous to how multiple coordinating MapReduce jobs will use HDFS for similar purposes.

Kafka provides at-least once message delivery semantics, that is to say that any message written to Kafka will be guaranteed to be available to a client of the particular partition. Messages might be processed between checkpoints however; it is possible for duplicate messages to be received by the client. There are application-specific mechanisms to mitigate this, and both Kafka and Samza have exactly-once semantics on their roadmaps, but for now it is something you should take into consideration when designing jobs.

We won't explain Kafka further beyond what we need to demonstrate Samza. If you are interested, check out its website and wiki; there is a lot of good information, including some excellent papers and presentations.

YARN integration

As mentioned earlier, just as Samza utilizes Kafka for its streaming layer implementation, it uses YARN for the execution layer. Just like any YARN application described in *Chapter 3, Processing – MapReduce and Beyond*, Samza provides an implementation of both an `ApplicationMaster`, which controls the life cycle of the overall job, plus implementations of Samza-specific functionality (called tasks) that are executed in each container. Just as Kafka partitions its topics, tasks are the mechanism by which Samza partitions its processing. Each Kafka partition will be read by a single Samza task. If a Samza job consumes multiple streams, then a given task will be the only consumer within the job for every stream partition assigned to it.

The Samza framework is told by each job configuration about the Kafka streams that are of interest to the job, and Samza continuously polls these streams to determine if any new messages have arrived. When a new message is available, the Samza task invokes a user-defined callback to process the message, a model that shouldn't look too alien to MapReduce developers. This method is defined in an interface called `StreamTask` and has the following signature:

```
public void process(IncomingMessageEnvelope envelope,
  MessageCollector collector,
  TaskCoordinator coordinator)
```

This is the core of each Samza task and defines the functionality to be applied to received messages. The received message that is to be processed is wrapped in the `IncomingMessageEnvelope`; output messages can be written to the `MessageCollector`, and task management (such as Shutdown) can be performed via the `TaskCoordinator`.

As mentioned, Samza creates one task instance for each partition in the underlying Kafka topic. Each YARN container will manage one or more of these tasks. The overall model then is of the Samza Application Master coordinating multiple containers, each of which is responsible for one or more `StreamTask` instances.

An independent model

Though we will talk exclusively of Kafka and YARN as the providers of Samza's streaming and execution layers in this chapter, it is important to remember that the core Samza system uses well-defined interfaces for both the stream and execution systems. There are implementations of multiple stream sources (we'll see one in the next section) and alongside the YARN support, Samza ships with a `LocalJobRunner` class. This alternative method of running tasks can execute `StreamTask` instances in-process on the JVM instead of requiring a full YARN cluster, which can sometimes be a useful testing and debugging tool. There is also a discussion of Samza implementations on top of other cluster manager or virtualization frameworks.

Hello Samza!

Since not everyone already has ZooKeeper, Kafka, and YARN clusters ready to be used, the Samza team has created a wonderful way to get started with the product. Instead of just having a Hello world! program, there is a repository called Hello Samza, which is available by cloning the repository at `git://git.apache.org/ samza-hello-samza.git.`

This will download and install dedicated instances of ZooKeeper, Kafka, and YARN (the 3 major prerequisites for Samza), creating a full stack upon which you can submit Samza jobs.

There are also a number of example Samza jobs that process data from Wikipedia edit notifications. Take a look at the page at `http://samza.apache.org/startup/ hello-samza/0.8/` and follow the instructions given there. (At the time of writing, Samza is still a relatively young project and we'd rather not include direct information about the examples, which might be subject to change).

For the remainder of the Samza examples in this chapter, we'll assume you are either using the Hello Samza package to provide the necessary components (ZooKeeper/Kafka/YARN) or you have integrated with other instances of each.

This example has three different Samza jobs that build upon each other. The first reads the Wikipedia edits, the second parses these records, and the third produces statistics based on the processed records. We'll build our own multistream workflow shortly.

One interesting point is the WikipediaFeed example here; it uses Wikipedia as its message source instead of Kafka. Specifically, it provides another implementation of the Samza `SystemConsumer` interface to allow Samza to read messages from an external system. As mentioned earlier, Samza is not tied to Kafka and, as this example shows, building a new stream implementation does not have to be against a generic infrastructure component; it can be quite job-specific, as the work required is not huge.

 Note that the default configuration for both ZooKeeper and Kafka will write system data to directories under /tmp, which will be what you have set if you use Hello Samza. Be careful if you are using a Linux distribution that purges the contents of this directory on a reboot. If you plan to carry out any significant testing, then it's best to reconfigure these components to use less ephemeral locations. Change the relevant config files for each service; they are located in the service directory under the hello-samza/deploy directory.

Building a tweet parsing job

Let's build our own simple job implementation to show the full code required. We'll use parsing of the Twitter stream as the examples in this chapter and will later set up a pipe from our client consuming messages from the Twitter API into a Kafka topic. So, we need a Samza task that will read the stream of JSON messages, extract the actual tweet text, and write these to a topic of tweets.

Here is the main code from `TwitterParseStreamTask.java`, available at `https://github.com/learninghadoop2/book-examples/blob/master/ch4/src/main/java/com/learninghadoop2/samza/tasks/TwitterParseStreamTask.java`:

```java
package com.learninghadoop2.samza.tasks;
public class TwitterParseStreamTask implements StreamTask {
    @Override
    public void process(IncomingMessageEnvelope envelope,
        MessageCollector collector, TaskCoordinator coordinator) {
        String msg = ((String) envelope.getMessage());

        try {
            JSONParser parser  = new JSONParser();
            Object     obj     = parser.parse(msg);
            JSONObject jsonObj = (JSONObject) obj;
            String     text    = (String) jsonObj.get("text");

            collector.send(new OutgoingMessageEnvelope(new
                SystemStream("kafka", "tweets-parsed"), text));
        } catch (ParseException pe) {}
    }
}
```

The code is largely self-explanatory, but there are a few points of interest. We use JSON Simple (`http://code.google.com/p/json-simple/`) for our relatively straightforward JSON parsing requirements; we'll also use it later in this book.

The `IncomingMessageEnvelope` and its corresponding `OutputMessageEnvelope` are the main structures concerned with the actual message data. Along with the message payload, the envelope will also have data concerning the system, topic name, and (optionally) partition number in addition to other metadata. For our purposes, we just extract the message body from the incoming message and send the tweet text we extract from it via a new `OutgoingMessageEnvelope` to a topic called `tweets-parsed` within a system called `kafka`. Note the lower case name—we'll explain this in a moment.

The type of message in the IncomingMessageEnvelope is java.lang.Object. Samza does not currently enforce a data model and hence does not have strongly-typed message bodies. Therefore, when extracting the message contents, an explicit cast is usually required. Since each task needs to know the expected message format of the streams it processes, this is not the oddity that it may appear to be.

The configuration file

There was nothing in the previous code that said where the messages came from; the framework just presents them to the StreamTask implementation, but obviously Samza needs to know from where to fetch messages. There is a configuration file for each job that defines this and more. The following can be found as twitter-parse. properties at https://github.com/learninghadoop2/book-examples/blob/master/ch4/src/main/resources/twitter-parser.properties:

```
# Job
job.factory.class=org.apache.samza.job.yarn.YarnJobFactory
job.name=twitter-parser

# YARN
yarn.package.path=file:///home/gturkington/samza/build/distributions/
learninghadoop2-0.1.tar.gz

# Task
task.class=com.learninghadoop2.samza.tasks.TwitterParseStreamTask
task.inputs=kafka.tweets
task.checkpoint.factory=org.apache.samza.checkpoint.kafka.
KafkaCheckpointManagerFactory
task.checkpoint.system=kafka

# Normally, this would be 3, but we have only one broker.
task.checkpoint.replication.factor=1

# Serializers
serializers.registry.string.class=org.apache.samza.serializers.
StringSerdeFactory

# Systems
systems.kafka.samza.factory=org.apache.samza.system.kafka.
KafkaSystemFactory
```

```
systems.kafka.streams.tweets.samza.msg.serde=string
systems.kafka.streams.tweets-parsed.samza.msg.serde=string
systems.kafka.consumer.zookeeper.connect=localhost:2181/
systems.kafka.consumer.auto.offset.reset=largest
systems.kafka.producer.metadata.broker.list=localhost:9092
systems.kafka.producer.producer.type=sync
systems.kafka.producer.batch.num.messages=1
```

This may look like a lot, but for now we'll just consider the high-level structure and some key settings. The job section sets YARN as the execution framework (as opposed to the local job runner class) and gives the job a name. If we were to run multiple copies of this same job, we would also give each copy a unique ID. The task section specifies the implementation class of our task and also the name of the streams for which it should receive messages. Serializers tell Samza how to read and write messages to and from the stream and the system section defines systems by name and associates implementation classes with them.

In our case, we define only one system called `kafka` and we refer to this system when sending our message in the preceding task. Note that this name is arbitrary and we could call it whatever we want. Obviously, for clarity it makes sense to call the Kafka system by the same name but this is only a convention. In particular, sometimes you will need to give different names when dealing with multiple systems that are similar to each other, or sometimes even when treating the same system differently in different parts of a configuration file.

In this section, we will also specify the SerDe to be associated with the streams used by the task. Recall that Kafka messages have a body and an optional key that is used to determine to which partition the message is sent. Samza needs to know how to treat the contents of the keys and messages for these streams. Samza has support to treat these as raw bytes or specific types such as string, integer, and JSON, as mentioned earlier.

The rest of the configuration will be mostly unchanged from job to job, as it includes things such as the location of the ZooKeeper ensemble and Kafka clusters, and specifies how streams are to be checkpointed. Samza allows a wide variety of customizations and the full configuration options are detailed at `http://samza. apache.org/learn/documentation/0.8/jobs/configuration-table.html`.

Getting Twitter data into Kafka

Before we run the job, we do need to get some tweets into Kafka. Let's create a new Kafka topic called *tweets* to which we'll write the tweets.

To perform this and other Kafka-related operations, we'll use command-line tools located within the `bin` directory of the Kafka distribution. If you are running a job from within the stack created as part of the Hello Samza application; this will be `deploy/kafka/bin`.

`kafka-topics.sh` is a general-purpose tool that can be used to create, update, and describe topics. Most of its usages require arguments to specify the location of the local ZooKeeper cluster, where Kafka brokers store their details, and the name of the topic to be operated upon. To create a new topic, run the following command:

```
$ kafka-topics.sh  --zookeeper localhost:2181 --create -topic tweets
--partitions 1 --replication-factor 1
```

This creates a topic called *tweets* and explicitly sets its number of partitions and replication factor to 1. This is suitable if you are running Kafka within a local test VM, but clearly production deployments will have more partitions to scale out the load across multiple brokers and a replication factor of at least 2 to provide fault tolerance.

Use the list option of the `kafka-topics.sh` tool to simply show the topics in the system, or use `describe` to get more detailed information on specific topics:

```
$ kafka-topics.sh  --zookeeper localhost:2181 --describe --topic tweets
Topic:tweets      PartitionCount:1      ReplicationFactor:1      Configs:
    Topic: tweets  Partition: 0    Leader: 0    Replicas: 0    Isr: 0
```

The multiple 0s are possibly confusing as these are labels and not counts. Each broker in the system has an ID that usually starts from 0, as do the partitions within each topic. The preceding output is telling us that the topic called `tweets` has a single partition with ID 0, the broker acting as the leader for that partition is broker 0, and the set of **in-sync replicas (ISR)** for this partition is again only broker 0. This last value is particularly important when dealing with replication.

We'll use our Python utility from previous chapters to pull JSON tweets from the Twitter feed, and then use a Kafka CLI message producer to write the messages to a Kafka topic. This isn't a terribly efficient way of doing things, but it is suitable for illustration purposes. Assuming our Python script is in our home directory, run the following command from within the Kafka `bin` directory:

```
$ python ~/stream.py -j | ./kafka-console-producer.sh  --broker-list
localhost:9092 --topic tweets
```

This will run indefinitely so be careful not to leave it running overnight on a test VM with small disk space, not that the authors have ever done such a thing.

Running a Samza job

To run a Samza job, we need our code to be packaged along with the Samza components required to execute it into a `.tar.gz` archive that will be read by the YARN NodeManager. This is the file referred to by the `yarn.file.package` property in the Samza task configuration file.

When using the single node Hello Samza we can just use an absolute path on the filesystem, as seen in the previous configuration example. For jobs on larger YARN grids, the easiest way is to put the package onto HDFS and refer to it by an `hdfs://` URI or on a web server (Samza provides a mechanism to allow YARN to read the file via HTTP).

Because Samza has multiple subcomponents and each subcomponent has its own dependencies, the full YARN package can end up containing a lot of JAR files (over 100!). In addition, you need to include your custom code for the Samza task as well as some scripts from within the Samza distribution. It's not something to be done by hand. In the sample code for this chapter, found at `https://github.com/learninghadoop2/book-examples/tree/master/ch4`, we have set up a sample structure to hold the code and config files and provided some automation via Gradle to build the necessary task archive and start the tasks.

When in the root of the Samza example code directory for this book, perform the following command to build a single file archive containing all the classes of this chapter compiled together and bundled with all the other required files:

```
$ ./gradlew targz
```

This Gradle task will not only create the necessary `.tar.gz` archive in the `build/distributions` directory, but will also store an expanded version of the archive under `build/samza-package`. This will be useful, as we will use Samza scripts stored in the `bin` directory of the archive to actually submit the task to YARN.

So now, let's run our job. We need to have file paths for two things: the Samza `run-job.sh` script to submit a job to YARN and the configuration file for our job. Since our created job package has all the compiled tasks bundled together, it is by using a different configuration file that specifies a specific task implementation class in the `task.class` property that we tell Samza which task to run. To actually run the task, we can run the following command from within the exploded project archive under `build/samza-archives`:

```
$ bin/run-job.sh  --config-factory=org.apache.samza.config.factories.
PropertiesConfigFactory --config-path=] config/twitter-parser.properties
```

For convenience, we added a Gradle task to run this job:

```
$ ./gradlew runTwitterParser
```

To see the output of the job, we'll use the Kafka CLI client to consume messages:

```
$ ./kafka-console-consumer.sh -zookeeper localhost:2181 -topic tweets-
parsed
```

You should see a continuous stream of tweets appearing on the client.

> Note that we did not explicitly create the topic called tweets-parsed.
> Kafka can allow topics to be created dynamically when either a
> producer or consumer tries to use the topic. In many situations,
> though the default partitioning and replication values may not be
> suitable, and explicit topic creation will be required to ensure these
> critical topic attributes are correctly defined.

Samza and HDFS

You may have noticed that we just mentioned HDFS for the first time in our discussion of Samza. Though Samza integrates tightly with YARN, it has no direct integration with HDFS. At a logical level, Samza's stream-implementing systems (such as Kafka) are providing the storage layer that is usually provided by HDFS for traditional Hadoop workloads. In the terminology of Samza's architecture, as described earlier, YARN is the execution layer in both models, whereas Samza uses a streaming layer for its source and destination data, frameworks such as MapReduce use HDFS. This is a good example of how YARN enables alternative computational models that not only process data very differently than batch-oriented MapReduce, but that can also use entirely different storage systems for their source data.

Windowing functions

It's frequently useful to generate some data based on the messages received on a stream over a certain time window. An example of this may be to record the top *n* attribute values measured every minute. Samza supports this through the `WindowableTask` interface, which has the following single method to be implemented:

```
public void window(MessageCollector collector, TaskCoordinator
coordinator);
```

This should look similar to the `process` method in the `StreamTask` interface. However, because the method is called on a time schedule, its invocation is not associated with a received message. The `MessageCollector` and `TaskCoordinator` parameters are still there, however, as most windowable tasks will produce output messages and may also wish to perform some task management actions.

Let's take our previous task and add a window function that will output the number of tweets received in each windowed time period. This is the main class implementation of `TwitterStatisticsStreamTask.java` found at https://github.com/learninghadoop2/book-examples/blob/master/ch4/src/main/java/com/learninghadoop2/samza/tasks/TwitterStatisticsStreamTask.java:

```
public class TwitterStatisticsStreamTask implements StreamTask,
WindowableTask {
    private int tweets = 0;

    @Override
    public void process(IncomingMessageEnvelope envelope,
MessageCollector collector, TaskCoordinator coordinator) {
        tweets++;
    }

    @Override
    public void window(MessageCollector collector, TaskCoordinator
      coordinator) {
        collector.send(new OutgoingMessageEnvelope(new
          SystemStream("kafka", "tweet-stats"), "" + tweets));

        // Reset counts after windowing.
        tweets = 0;
    }
}
```

The `TwitterStatisticsStreamTask` class has a private member variable called `tweets` that is initialized to `0` and is incremented in every call to the `process` method. We therefore know that this variable will be incremented for each message passed to the task from the underlying stream implementation. Each Samza container has a single thread running in a loop that executes the process and window methods on all the tasks within the container. This means that we do not need to guard instance variables against concurrent modifications; only one method on each task within a container will be executing simultaneously.

In our `window` method, we send a message to a new topic we call `tweet-stats` and then reset the `tweets` variable. This is pretty straightforward and the only missing piece is how Samza will know when to call the `window` method. We specify this in the configuration file:

```
task.window.ms=5000
```

This tells Samza to call the `window` method on each task instance every 5 seconds. To run the `window` task, there is a Gradle task:

```
$ ./gradlew runTwitterStatistics
```

If we use `kafka-console-consumer.sh` to listen on the `tweet-stats` stream now, we will see the following output:

```
Number of tweets: 5012
Number of tweets: 5398
```

 Note that the term *window* in this context refers to Samza conceptually slicing the stream of messages into time ranges and providing a mechanism to perform processing at each range boundary. Samza does not directly provide an implementation of the other use of the term with regards to sliding windows, where a series of values is held and processed over time. However, the windowable task interface does provide the plumbing to implement such sliding windows.

Multijob workflows

As we saw with the Hello Samza examples, some of the real power of Samza comes from composition of multiple jobs and we'll use a text cleanup job to start demonstrating this capability.

In the following section, we'll perform tweet sentiment analysis by comparing tweets with a set of English positive and negative words. Simply applying this to the raw Twitter feed will have very patchy results, however, given how richly multilingual the Twitter stream is. We also need to consider things such as text cleanup, capitalization, frequent contractions, and so on. As anyone who has worked with any non-trivial dataset knows, the act of making the data fit for processing is usually where a large amount of effort (often the majority!) goes.

So before we try and detect tweet sentiments, let's do some simple text cleanup; in particular, we'll select only English language tweets and we will force their text to be lower case before sending them to a new output stream.

Language detection is a difficult problem and for this we'll use a feature of the Apache Tika library (http://tika.apache.org). Tika provides a wide array of functionality to extract text from various sources and then to extract further information from that text. If using our Gradle scripts, the Tika dependency is already specified and will automatically be included in the generated job package. If building through another mechanism, you will need to download the Tika JAR file from the home page and add it to your YARN job package. The following code can be found as TextCleanupStreamTask.java at https://github.com/learninghadoop2/book-examples/blob/master/ch4/src/main/java/com/learninghadoop2/samza/tasks/TextCleanupStreamTask.java:

```java
public class TextCleanupStreamTask implements StreamTask {
    @Override
    public void process(IncomingMessageEnvelope envelope,
MessageCollector collector, TaskCoordinator coordinator) {
        String rawtext = ((String) envelope.getMessage());

        if ("en".equals(detectLanguage(rawtext))) {
            collector.send(new OutgoingMessageEnvelope(new
SystemStream("kafka", "english-tweets"),
                    rawtext.toLowerCase()));
        }
    }

    private String detectLanguage(String text) {
        LanguageIdentifier li = new LanguageIdentifier(text);

        return li.getLanguage();
    }
}
```

This task is quite straightforward thanks to the heavy lifting performed by Tika. We create a utility method that wraps the creation and use of a Tika, `LanguageDetector`, and then we call this method on the message body of each incoming message in the `process` method. We only write to the output stream if the result of applying this utility method is `"en"`, that is, the two-letter code for English.

The configuration file for this task is similar to that of our previous task, with the specific values for the task name and implementing class. It is in the repository as `textcleanup.properties` at `https://github.com/learninghadoop2/book-examples/blob/master/ch4/src/main/resources/textcleanup.properties`. We also need to specify the input stream:

```
task.inputs=kafka.tweets-parsed
```

This is important because we need this task to parse the tweet text that was extracted in the earlier task and avoid duplicating the JSON parsing logic that is best encapsulated in one place. We can run this task with the following command:

```
$ ./gradlew runTextCleanup
```

Now, we can run all three tasks together; `TwitterParseStreamTask` and `TwitterStatisticsStreamTask` will consume the raw tweet stream, while `TextCleanupStreamTask` will consume the output from `TwitterParseStreamTask`.

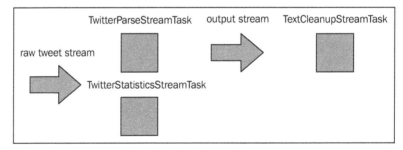

Data processing on streams

Tweet sentiment analysis

We'll now implement a task to perform tweet sentiment analysis similar to what we did using MapReduce in the previous chapter. This will also show us a useful mechanism offered by Samza: bootstrap streams.

Bootstrap streams

Generally speaking, most stream-processing jobs (in Samza or another framework) will start processing messages that arrive after they start up and generally ignore historical messages. Because of its concept of replayable streams, Samza doesn't have this limitation.

In our sentiment analysis job, we had two sets of reference terms: positive and negative words. Though we've not shown it so far, Samza can consume messages from multiple streams and the underlying machinery will poll all named streams and provide their messages, one at a time, to the `process` method. We can therefore create streams for the positive and negative words and push the datasets onto those streams. At first glance, we could plan to rewind these two streams to the earliest point and read tweets as they arrive. The problem is that Samza won't guarantee ordering of messages from multiple streams, and even though there is a mechanism to give streams higher priority, we can't assume that all negative and positive words will be processed before the first tweet arrives.

For such types of scenarios, Samza has the concept of bootstrap streams. If a task has any bootstrap streams defined, then it will read these streams from the earliest offset until they are fully processed (technically, it will read the streams till they get caught up, so that any new words sent to either stream will be treated without priority and will arrive interleaved between tweets).

We'll now create a new job called `TweetSentimentStreamTask` that reads two bootstrap streams, collects their contents into HashMaps, gathers running counts for sentiment trends, and uses a `window` function to output this data at intervals. This code can be found at `https://github.com/learninghadoop2/book-examples/blob/master/ch4/src/main/java/com/learninghadoop2/samza/tasks/TwitterSentimentStreamTask.java`:

```java
public class TwitterSentimentStreamTask implements StreamTask,
    WindowableTask {
    private Set<String>        positiveWords = new
        HashSet<String>();
    private Set<String>        negativeWords = new
        HashSet<String>();
    private int                tweets        = 0;
    private int                positiveTweets = 0;
    private int                negativeTweets = 0;
    private int                maxPositive    = 0;
    private int                maxNegative    = 0;
```

```
    @Override
    public void process(IncomingMessageEnvelope envelope,
        MessageCollector collector, TaskCoordinator coordinator) {
        if ("positive-words".equals(envelope.
getSystemStreamPartition().
            getStream())) {
            positiveWords.add(((String) envelope.getMessage()));
        } else if ("negative-words".equals(envelope.
getSystemStreamPartition().getStream())) {
            negativeWords.add(((String) envelope.getMessage()));
        } else if ("english-tweets".equals(envelope.
getSystemStreamPartition().getStream())) {
            tweets++;

            int    positive = 0;
            int    negative = 0;
            String words    = ((String) envelope.getMessage());

            for (String word : words.split(" ")) {
                if (positiveWords.contains(word)) {
                    positive++;
                } else if (negativeWords.contains(word)) {
                    negative++;
                }
            }

            if (positive > negative) {
                positiveTweets++;
            }

            if (negative > positive) {
                negativeTweets++;
            }

            if (positive > maxPositive) {
                maxPositive = positive;
            }

            if (negative > maxNegative) {
                maxNegative = negative;
            }
        }
    }
```

```
@Override
public void window(MessageCollector collector, TaskCoordinator
    coordinator) {
    String msg = String.format("Tweets: %d Positive: %d Negative:
        %d MaxPositive: %d MinPositive: %d", tweets, positiveTweets,
            negativeTweets, maxPositive, maxNegative);


    collector.send(new OutgoingMessageEnvelope(new
        SystemStream("kafka", "tweet-sentiment-stats"), msg));

    // Reset counts after windowing.
    tweets        = 0;
    positiveTweets = 0;
    negativeTweets = 0;
    maxPositive    = 0;
    maxNegative    = 0;
}

}
```

In this task, we add a number of private member variables that we will use to keep a running count of the number of overall tweets, how many were positive and negative, and the maximum positive and negative counts seen in a single tweet.

This task consumes from three Kafka topics. Even though we will configure two to be used as bootstrap streams, they are all still exactly the same type of Kafka topic from which messages are received; the only difference with bootstrap streams is that we tell Samza to use Kafka's rewinding capabilities to fully re-read each message in the stream. For the other stream of tweets, we just start reading new messages as they arrive.

As hinted earlier, if a task subscribes to multiple streams, the same `process` method will receive messages from each stream. That is why we use `envelope.getSystemStreamPartition().getStream()` to extract the stream name for each given message and then act accordingly. If the message is from either of the bootstrapped streams, we add its contents to the appropriate hashmap. We break a tweet message into its constituent words, test each word for positive or negative sentiment, and then update counts accordingly. As you can see, this task doesn't output the received tweets to another topic.

Since we don't perform any direct processing, there is no point in doing so; any other task that wishes to consume messages can just subscribe directly to the incoming tweets stream. However, a possible modification could be to write positive and negative sentiment tweets to dedicated streams for each.

The `window` method outputs a series of counts and then resets the variables (as it did before). Note that Samza does have support to directly expose metrics through JMX, which could possibly be a better fit for such simple windowing examples. However, we won't have space to cover that aspect of the project in this book.

To run this job, we need to modify the configuration file by setting the job and task names as usual, but we also need to specify multiple input streams now:

```
task.inputs=kafka.english-tweets,kafka.positive-words,kafka.negative-words
```

Then, we need to specify that two of our streams are bootstrap streams that should be read from the earliest offset. Specifically, we set three properties for the streams. We say they are to be bootstrapped, that is, fully read before other streams, and this is achieved by specifying that the offset on each stream needs to be reset to the oldest (first) position:

```
systems.kafka.streams.positive-words.samza.bootstrap=true
systems.kafka.streams.positive-words.samza.reset.offset=true
systems.kafka.streams.positive-words.samza.offset.default=oldest

systems.kafka.streams.negative-words.samza.bootstrap=true
systems.kafka.streams.negative-words.samza.reset.offset=true
systems.kafka.streams.negative-words.samza.offset.default=oldest
```

We can run this job with the following command:

```
$ ./gradlew runTwitterSentiment
```

After starting the job, look at the output of the messages on the `tweet-sentiment-stats` topic.

The sentiment detection job will bootstrap the positive and negative word streams before reading any of our newly detected lower-case English tweets.

With the sentiment detection job, we can now visualize our four collaborating jobs as shown in the following diagram:

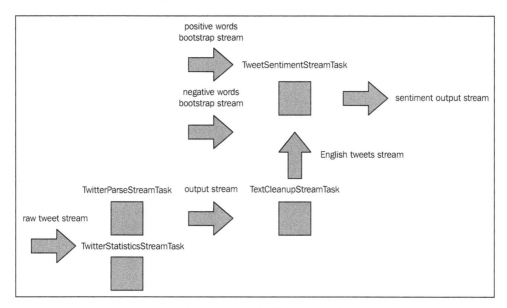

Bootstrap streams and collaborating tasks

To correctly run the jobs, it may seem necessary to start the JSON parser job followed by the cleanup job before finally starting the sentiment job, but this is not the case. Any unread messages remain buffered in Kafka, so it doesn't matter in which order the jobs of a multi-job workflow are started. Of course, the sentiment job will output counts of 0 tweets until it starts receiving data, but nothing will break if a stream job starts before those it depends on.

Stateful tasks

The final aspect of Samza that we will explore is how it allows the tasks processing stream partitions to have persistent local state. In the previous example, we used private variables to keep a track of running totals, but sometimes it is useful for a task to have richer local state. An example could be the act of performing a logical join on two streams, where it is useful to build up a state model from one stream and compare this with the other.

Note that Samza can utilize its concept of partitioned streams to greatly optimize the act of joining streams. If each stream to be joined uses the same partition key (for example, a user ID), then each task consuming these streams will receive all messages associated with each ID across all the streams.

Samza has another abstraction similar to its notion of the framework to manage its jobs and that which implements its tasks. It defines an abstract key-value store that can have multiple concrete implementations. Samza uses existing open source projects for the on-disk implementations and used LevelDB as of v0.7 and added RocksDB as of v0.8. There is also an in-memory store that does not persist the key-value data but that may be useful in testing or potentially very specific production workloads.

Each task can write to this key-value store and Samza manages its persistence to the local implementation. To support persistent states, the store is also modeled as a stream and all writes to the store are also pushed into a stream. If a task fails, then on restart, it can recover the state of its local key-value store by replaying the messages in the backing topic. An obvious concern here will be the number of messages that need to be replayed; however, when using Kafka, for example, it compacts messages with the same key so that only the latest update remains in the topic.

We'll modify our previous tweet sentiment example to add a lifetime count of the maximum positive and negative sentiment seen in any tweet. The following code can be found as `TwitterStatefulSentimentStateTask.java` at https://github. com/learninghadoop2/book-examples/blob/master/ch4/src/main/java/com/ learninghadoop2/samza/tasks/TwitterStatefulSentimentStreamTask.java. Note that the process method is the same as `TwitterSentimentStateTask.java`, so we have omitted it here for space reasons:

```java
public class TwitterStatefulSentimentStreamTask implements StreamTask,
WindowableTask, InitableTask {
    private Set<String> positiveWords  = new HashSet<String>();
    private Set<String> negativeWords  = new HashSet<String>();
    private int tweets = 0;
    private int positiveTweets = 0;
    private int negativeTweets = 0;
    private int maxPositive = 0;
    private int maxNegative = 0;
    private KeyValueStore<String, Integer> store;
```

```
    @SuppressWarnings("unchecked")
    @Override
    public void init(Config config, TaskContext context) {
        this.store = (KeyValueStore<String, Integer>) context.
getStore("tweet-store");
    }


    @Override
    public void process(IncomingMessageEnvelope envelope,
MessageCollector collector, TaskCoordinator coordinator) {
...
    }


    @Override
    public void window(MessageCollector collector, TaskCoordinator
coordinator) {
        Integer lifetimeMaxPositive = store.
get("lifetimeMaxPositive");
        Integer lifetimeMaxNegative = store.
get("lifetimeMaxNegative");

        if ((lifetimeMaxPositive == null) || (maxPositive >
lifetimeMaxPositive)) {
            lifetimeMaxPositive = maxPositive;
            store.put("lifetimeMaxPositive", lifetimeMaxPositive);
        }

        if ((lifetimeMaxNegative == null) || (maxNegative >
lifetimeMaxNegative)) {
            lifetimeMaxNegative = maxNegative;
            store.put("lifetimeMaxNegative", lifetimeMaxNegative);
        }

        String msg =
            String.format(
                "Tweets: %d Positive: %d Negative: %d MaxPositive: %d
MaxNegative: %d LifetimeMaxPositive: %d LifetimeMaxNegative: %d",
                tweets, positiveTweets, negativeTweets, maxPositive,
maxNegative, lifetimeMaxPositive,
                lifetimeMaxNegative);

        collector.send(new OutgoingMessageEnvelope(new
SystemStream("kafka", "tweet-stateful-sentiment-stats"), msg));
```

```
            // Reset counts after windowing.
            tweets          = 0;
            positiveTweets  = 0;
            negativeTweets  = 0;
            maxPositive     = 0;
            maxNegative     = 0;
        }
    }
```

This class implements a new interface called `InitableTask`. This has a single method called `init` and is used when a task needs to configure aspects of its configuration before it begins execution. We use the `init()` method here to create an instance of the `KeyValueStore` class and store it in a private member variable.

`KeyValueStore`, as the name suggests, provides a familiar `put/get` type interface. In this case, we specify that the keys are of the type String and the values are Integers. In our `window` method, we retrieve any previously stored values for the maximum positive and negative sentiment and if the count in the current window is higher, update the store accordingly. Then, we just output the results of the `window` method as before.

As you can see, the user does not need to deal with the details of either the local or remote persistence of the `KeyValueStore` instance; this is all handled by Samza. The efficiency of the mechanism also makes it tractable for tasks to hold sizeable amount of local state, which can be particularly valuable in cases such as long-running aggregations or stream joins.

The configuration file for the job can be found at `https://github.com/learninghadoop2/book-examples/blob/master/ch4/src/main/resources/twitter-stateful-sentiment.properties`. It needs to have a few entries added, which are as follows:

```
    stores.tweet-store.factory=org.apache.samza.storage.
    kv.KeyValueStorageEngineFactory
    stores.tweet-store.changelog=kafka.twitter-stats-state
    stores.tweet-store.key.serde=string
    stores.tweet-store.msg.serde=integer
```

The first line specifies the implementation class for the store, the second line specifies the Kafka topic to be used for persistent state, and the last two lines specify the type of the store key and value.

To run this job, use the following command:

```
$ ./gradlew runTwitterStatefulSentiment
```

For convenience, the following command will start up four jobs: the JSON parser, the text cleanup, the statistics job and the stateful sentiment jobs:

```
$ ./gradlew runTasks
```

Samza is a pure stream-processing system that provides pluggable implementations of its storage and execution layers. The most commonly used plugins are YARN and Kafka, and these demonstrate how Samza can integrate tightly with Hadoop YARN while using a completely different storage layer. Samza is still a relatively new project and the current features are only a subset of what is envisaged. It is recommended to consult its webpage to get the latest information on its current status.

Summary

This chapter focused much more on what can be done on Hadoop 2, and in particular YARN, than the details of Hadoop internals. This is almost certainly a good thing, as it demonstrates that Hadoop is realizing its goal of becoming a much more flexible and generic data processing platform that is no longer tied to batch processing. In particular, we highlighted how Samza shows that the processing frameworks that can be implemented on YARN can innovate and enable functionality vastly different from that available in Hadoop 1.

In particular, we saw how Samza goes to the opposite end of the latency spectrum from batch processing and enables per-message processing of individual messages as they arrive.

We also saw how Samza provides a callback mechanism that MapReduce developers will be familiar with, but uses it for a very different processing model. We also discussed the ways in which Samza utilizes YARN as its main execution framework and how it implements the model described in *Chapter 3, Processing – MapReduce and Beyond*.

In the next chapter, we will switch gears and explore Apache Spark. Though it has a very different data model than Samza, we'll see that it does also have an extension that supports processing of real time data streams, including the option of Kafka integration. However, both projects are so different that they are complimentary more than in competition.

5
Iterative Computation with Spark

In the previous chapter, we saw how Samza can enable near real-time stream data processing within Hadoop. This is quite a step away from the traditional batch processing model of MapReduce, but still keeps with the model of providing a well-defined interface against which business logic tasks can be implemented. In this chapter we will explore Apache Spark, which can be viewed both as a framework on which applications can be built as well as a processing framework in its own right. Not only are applications being built on Spark, but entire components within the Hadoop ecosystem are also being reimplemented to use Spark as their underlying processing framework. In particular, we will cover the following topics:

- What Spark is and how its core system can run on YARN
- The data model provided by Spark that enables hugely scalable and highly efficient data processing
- The breadth of additional Spark components and related projects

It's important to note upfront that although Spark has its own mechanism to process streaming data, this is but one part of what Spark has to offer. It's best to think of it as a much broader initiative.

Apache Spark

Apache Spark (`https://spark.apache.org/`) is a data processing framework based on a generalization of MapReduce. It was originally developed by the AMPLab at UC Berkeley (`https://amplab.cs.berkeley.edu/`). Like Tez, Spark acts as an execution engine that models data transformations as DAGs and strives to eliminate the I/O overhead of MapReduce in order to perform iterative computation at scale. While Tez's main goal was to provide a faster execution engine for MapReduce on Hadoop, Spark has been designed both as a standalone framework and an API for application development. The system is designed to perform general-purpose in-memory data processing, stream workflows, as well as interactive and iterative computation.

Spark is implemented in Scala, which is a statically typed programming language for the Java VM and exposes native programming interfaces for Java and Python in addition to Scala itself. Note that though Java code can call the Scala interface directly, there are some aspects of the type system that make such code pretty unwieldy, and hence we use the native Java API.

Scala ships with an interactive shell similar to that of Ruby and Python; this allows users to run Spark interactively from the interpreter to query any dataset.

The Scala interpreter operates by compiling a class for each line typed by the user, loading it into the JVM, and invoking a function on it. This class includes a singleton object that contains the variables or functions on that line and runs the line's code in an initialize method. In addition to its rich programming interfaces, Spark is becoming established as an execution engine, with popular tools of the Hadoop ecosystem (such as Pig and Hive) being ported to the framework.

Cluster computing with working sets

Spark's architecture is centered around the concept of **Resilient Distributed Datasets (RDDs)**, which is a read-only collection of Scala objects partitioned across a set of machines that can persist in memory. This abstraction was proposed in a 2012 research paper, *Resilient Distributed Datasets: A Fault-Tolerant Abstraction for In-Memory Cluster Computing*, which can be found at `https://www.cs.berkeley.edu/~matei/papers/2012/nsdi_spark.pdf`.

A Spark application consists of a driver program that executes parallel operations on a cluster of workers and long-lived processes that can store data partitions in memory by dispatching functions that run as parallel tasks, as shown in the following diagram:

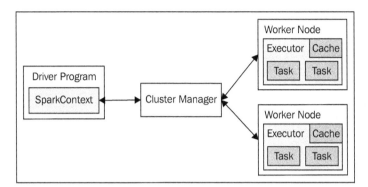

Spark cluster architecture

Processes are coordinated via a SparkContext instance. SparkContext connects to a resource manager (such as YARN), requests executors on worker nodes, and sends tasks to be executed. Executors are responsible for running tasks and managing memory locally.

Spark allows you to share variables between tasks, or between tasks and the driver, using an abstraction known as shared variables. Spark supports two types of shared variables: broadcast variables, which can be used to cache a value in memory on all nodes, and accumulators, which are additive variables such as counters and sums.

Resilient Distributed Datasets (RDDs)

An RDD is stored in memory, shared across machines and is used in MapReduce-like parallel operations. Fault tolerance is achieved through the notion of *lineage*: if a partition of an RDD is lost, the RDD has enough information about how it was derived from other RDDs to be able to rebuild just that partition. An RDD can be built in four ways:

- By reading data from a file stored in HDFS
- By dividing – parallelizing – a Scala collection into a number of partitions that are sent to workers
- By transforming an existing RDD using parallel operators
- By changing the persistence of an existing RDD

Spark shines when RDDs can fit in memory and can be cached across operations. The API exposes methods to persist RDDs and allows for several persistence strategies and storage levels, allowing for spill to disk as well as space-efficient binary serialization.

Actions

Operations are invoked by passing functions to Spark. The system deals with variables and side effects according to the functional programming paradigm. Closures can refer to variables in the scope where they are created. Examples of actions are `count` (returns the number of elements in the dataset), and `save` (outputs the dataset to storage). Other parallel operations on RDDs include the following:

- `map`: applies a function to each element of the dataset
- `filter`: selects elements from a dataset based on user-provided criteria
- `reduce`: combines dataset elements using an associative function
- `collect`: sends all elements of the dataset to the driver program
- `foreach`: passes each element through a user-provided function
- `groupByKey`: groups items together by a provided key
- `sortByKey`: sorts items by key

Deployment

Spark can run both in local mode, similar to a Hadoop single-node setup, or atop a resource manager. Currently supported resource managers include:

- Spark Standalone Cluster Mode
- YARN
- Apache Mesos

Spark on YARN

An ad-hoc-consolidated JAR needs to be built in order to deploy Spark on YARN. Spark launches an instance of the standalone deployed cluster within the ResourceManager. Cloudera and MapR both ship with Spark on YARN as part of their software distribution. At the time of writing, Spark is available for Hortonworks's HDP as a technology preview (`http://hortonworks.com/hadoop/spark/`).

Spark on EC2

Spark comes with a deployment script, `spark-ec2`, located in the `ec2` directory. This script automatically sets up Spark and HDFS on a cluster of EC2 instances. In order to launch a Spark cluster on the Amazon cloud, go to the `ec2` directory and run the following command:

```
./spark-ec2 -k <keypair> -i <key-file> -s <num-slaves> launch <cluster-name>
```

Here, `<keypair>` is the name of your EC2 key pair, `<key-file>` is the private key file for the key pair, `<num-slaves>` is the number of slave nodes to be launched, and `<cluster-name>` is the name to be given to your cluster. See *Chapter 1, Introduction*, for more details regarding the setup of key pairs, and verify that the cluster scheduler is up and sees all the slaves by going to its web UI, the address of which will be printed once the script completes.

You can specify a path in S3 as the input through a URI of the form `s3n://<bucket>/path`. You will also need to set your Amazon security credentials, either by setting the environment variables `AWS_ACCESS_KEY_ID` and `AWS_SECRET_ACCESS_KEY` before your program is executed, or through `SparkContext.hadoopConfiguration`.

Getting started with Spark

Spark binaries and source code are available on the project website at `http://spark.apache.org/`. The examples in the following section have been tested using Spark 1.1.0 built from source on the Cloudera CDH 5.0 QuickStart VM.

Download and uncompress the `gzip` archive with the following commands:

```
$ wget http://d3kbcqa49mib13.cloudfront.net/spark-1.1.0.tgz
$ tar xvzf spark-1.1.0.tgz
$ cd spark-1.1.0
```

Spark is built on Scala 2.10 and uses `sbt` (`https://github.com/sbt/sbt`) to build the source core and related examples:

```
$ ./sbt/sbt -Dhadoop.version=2.2.0  -Pyarn  assembly
```

With the `-Dhadoop.version=2.2.0` and `-Pyarn` options, we instruct `sbt` to build against Hadoop versions 2.2.0 or higher and enable YARN support.

Start Spark in standalone mode with the following command:

```
$ ./sbin/start-all.sh
```

This command will launch a local master instance at `spark://localhost:7077` as well as a worker node.

A web interface to the master node can be accessed at `http://localhost:8080/` and can be seen in the following screenshot:

Master node web interface

Spark can run interactively through `spark-shell`, which is a modified version of the Scala shell. As a first example, we will implement a word count of the Twitter dataset we used in *Chapter 3, Processing - MapReduce and Beyond*, using the Scala API.

Start an interactive `spark-shell` session by running the following command:

```
$ ./bin/spark-shell
```

The shell instantiates a `SparkContext` object, `sc`, that is responsible for handling driver connections to workers. We will describe its semantics later in this chapter.

To make things a bit easier, let's create a sample textual dataset that contains one status update per line:

```
$ stream.py -t -n 1000 > sample.txt
```

Then, copy it to HDFS:

```
$ hdfs dfs -put sample.txt /tmp
```

Within `spark-shell`, we first create an RDD - `file` - from the sample data:

```
val file = sc.textFile("/tmp/sample.txt")
```

Then, we apply a series of transformations to count the word occurrences in the file. Note that the output of the transformation chain - `counts` - is still an RDD:

```
val counts = file.flatMap(line => line.split(" "))
.map(word => (word, 1))
.reduceByKey((m, n) => m + n)
```

This chain of transformations corresponds to the map and reduce phases that we are familiar with. In the map phase, we load each line of the dataset (`flatMap`), tokenize each tweet into a sequence of words, count the occurrence of each word (`map`), and emit (`key`, `value`) pairs. In the reduce phase, we group by key (`word`) and sum values (`m`, `n`) together to obtain word counts.

Finally, we print the first ten elements, `counts.take(10)`, to the console:

```
counts.take(10).foreach(println)
```

Writing and running standalone applications

Spark allows standalone applications to be written using three APIs: Scala, Java, and Python.

Scala API

The first thing a Spark driver must do is to create a `SparkContext` object, which tells Spark how to access a cluster. After importing classes and implicit conversions into a program, as in the following:

```
import org.apache.spark.SparkContext
import org.apache.spark.SparkContext._
```

The `SparkContext` object can be created with the following constructor:

```
new SparkContext(master, appName, [sparkHome])
```

It can also be created through `SparkContext(conf)`, which takes a `SparkConf` object.

The master parameter is a string that specifies a cluster URI to connect to (such as `spark://localhost:7077`) or a `local` string to run in local mode. The `appName` term is the application name that will be shown in the cluster web UI.

It is not possible to override the default `SparkContext` class, nor is it possible to create a new one within a running Spark shell. It is however possible to specify which master the context connects to using the `MASTER` environment variable. For example, to run `spark-shell` on four cores, use the following:

```
$ MASTER=local[4] ./bin/spark-shell
```

Java API

The `org.apache.spark.api.java` package exposes all the Spark features available in the Scala version to Java. The Java API has a `JavaSparkContext` class that returns instances of `org.apache.spark.api.java.JavaRDD` and works with Java collections instead of Scala ones.

There are a few key differences between the Java and Scala APIs:

- Java 7 does not support anonymous or first-class functions; therefore, functions must be implemented by extending the `org.apache.spark.api.java.function.Function`, `Function2`, and other classes. As of Spark version 1.0 the API has been refactored to support Java 8 lambda expressions. With Java 8, Function classes can be replaced with inline expressions that act as a shorthand for anonymous functions.

- The RDD methods return Java collections

- Key-value pairs, which are simply written as (`key`, `value`) in Scala, are represented by the `scala.Tuple2` class.

- To maintain type safety, some RDD and function methods, such as those that handle key pairs and doubles, are implemented as specialized classes.

WordCount in Java

An example of WordCount in Java is included with the Spark source code distribution at `examples/src/main/java/org/apache/spark/examples/JavaWordCount.java`.

First of all, we create a context using the `JavaSparkContext` class:

```
    JavaSparkContext sc = new JavaSparkContext(master, "JavaWordCount",
        System.getenv("SPARK_HOME"), JavaSparkContext.
jarOfClass(JavaWordCount.class));

    JavaRDD<String> data = sc.textFile(infile, 1);
    JavaRDD<String> words = data.flatMap(new FlatMapFunction<String,
String>() {
        @Override
```

```
   public Iterable<String> call(String s) {
     return Arrays.asList(s.split(" "));
   }
 });

   JavaPairRDD<String, Integer> ones = words.map(new
 PairFunction<String, String, Integer>() {
     @Override
     public Tuple2<String, Integer> call(String s) {
       return new Tuple2<String, Integer>(s, 1);
     }
 });

   JavaPairRDD<String, Integer> counts = ones.reduceByKey(new
 Function2<Integer, Integer, Integer>() {
     @Override
     public Integer call(Integer i1, Integer i2) {
       return i1 + i2;
     }
 });
```

We then build an RDD from the HDFS location `infile`. In the first step of the transformation chain, we tokenize each tweet in the dataset and return a list of words. We use an instance of `JavaPairRDD<String, Integer>` to count occurrences of each word. Finally, we reduce the RDD to a new `JavaPairRDD<String, Integer>` instance that contains a list of tuples, each representing a word and the number of times it was found in the dataset.

Python API

PySpark requires Python version 2.6 or higher. RDDs support the same methods as their Scala counterparts but take Python functions and return Python collection types. Lambda syntax (`https://docs.python.org/2/reference/expressions.html`) is used to pass functions to RDDs.

The word count in `pyspark` is relatively similar to its Scala counterpart:

```
tweets = sc.textFile("/tmp/sample.txt")
counts = tweets.flatMap(lambda tweet: tweet.split(' ')) \
               .map(lambda word: (word, 1)) \
               .reduceByKey(lambda m,n:m+n)
```

The `lambda` construct creates anonymous functions at runtime. `lambda tweet:` `tweet.split(' ')` creates a function that takes a string `tweet` as the input and outputs a list of strings split by whitespace. Spark's `flatMap` applies this function to each line of the `tweets` dataset. In the `map` phase, for each `word` token, `lambda word:` `(word, 1)` returns `(word, 1)` tuples that indicate the occurrence of a word in the dataset. In `reduceByKey`, we group these tuples by key - word - and sum the values together to obtain the word count with `lambda m,n:m+n`.

The Spark ecosystem

Apache Spark powers a number of tools, both as a library and as an execution engine.

Spark Streaming

Spark Streaming (found at `http://spark.apache.org/docs/latest/streaming-programming-guide.html`) is an extension of the Scala API that allows data ingestion from streams such as Kafka, Flume, Twitter, ZeroMQ, and TCP sockets.

Spark Streaming receives live input data streams and divides the data into batches (arbitrarily sized time windows), which are then processed by the Spark core engine to generate the final stream of results in batches. This high-level abstraction is called DStream (`org.apache.spark.streaming.dstream.DStreams`) and is implemented as a sequence of RDDs. DStream allows for two kinds of operations: *transformations* and *output operations*. Transformations work on one or more DStreams to create new DStreams. As part of a chain of transformations, data can be persisted either to a storage layer (HDFS) or an output channel. Spark Streaming allows for transformations over a sliding window of data. A window-based operation needs to specify two parameters: the window length, the duration of the window and the slide interval, the interval at which the window-based operation is performed.

GraphX

GraphX (found at `https://spark.apache.org/docs/latest/graphx-programming-guide.html`) is an API for graph computation that exposes a set of operators and algorithms for graph-oriented computation as well as an optimized variant of Pregel.

MLlib

MLlib (found at `http://spark.apache.org/docs/latest/mllib-guide.html`) provides common **Machine Learning** (**ML**) functionality, including tests and data generators. MLlib currently supports four types of algorithms: binary classification, regression, clustering, and collaborative filtering.

Spark SQL

Spark SQL is derived from Shark, which is an implementation of the Hive data warehousing system that uses Spark as an execution engine. We will discuss Hive in *Chapter 7, Hadoop and SQL*. With Spark SQL, it is possible to mix SQL-like queries with Scala or Python code. The result sets returned by a query are themselves RDDs, and as such, they can be manipulated by Spark core methods or MLlib and GraphX.

Processing data with Apache Spark

In this section, we will implement the examples from *Chapter 3, Processing – MapReduce and Beyond*, using the Scala API. We will consider both the batch and real-time processing scenarios. We will show you how Spark Streaming can be used to compute statistics on the live Twitter stream.

Building and running the examples

Scala source code for the examples can be found at `https://github.com/learninghadoop2/book-examples/tree/master/ch5`. We will be using `sbt` to build, manage, and execute code.

The `build.sbt` file controls the codebase metadata and software dependencies; these include the version of the Scala interpreter that Spark links to, a link to the Akka package repository used to resolve implicit dependencies, as well as dependencies on Spark and Hadoop libraries.

The source code for all examples can be compiled with:

```
$ sbt compile
```

Or, it can be packaged into a JAR file with:

```
$ sbt package
```

A helper script to execute compiled classes can be generated with:

```
$ sbt add-start-script-tasks
$ sbt start-script
```

The helper can be invoked as follows:

```
$ target/start <class name> <master> <param1> … <param n>
```

Here, `<master>` is the URI of the master node. An interactive Scala session can be invoked via `sbt` with the following command:

```
$ sbt console
```

This console is not the same as the Spark interactive shell; rather, it is an alternative way to execute code. In order to run Spark code in it we will need to manually import and instantiate a `SparkContext` object. All examples presented in this section expect a `twitter4j.properties` file containing the consumer key and secret and the access tokens to be present in the same directory where `sbt` or `spark-shell` is being invoked:

```
oauth.consumerKey=
oauth.consumerSecret=
oauth.accessToken=
oauth.accessTokenSecret=
```

Running the examples on YARN

To run the examples on a YARN grid, we first build a JAR file using:

```
$ sbt package
```

Then, we ship it to the resource manager using the `spark-submit` command:

```
./bin/spark-submit --class application.to.execute --master yarn-cluster
[options] target/scala-2.10/chapter-4_2.10-1.0.jar [<param1> … <param n>]
```

Unlike the standalone mode, we don't need to specify a `<master>` URI. In YARN, the ResourceManager is selected from the cluster configuration. More information on launching spark in YARN can be found at `http://spark.apache.org/docs/latest/running-on-yarn.html`.

Finding popular topics

Unlike the earlier examples with the Spark shell we initialize a `SparkContext` as part of the program. We pass three arguments to the `SparkContext` constructor: the type of scheduler we want to use, a name for the application, and the directory where Spark is installed:

```
import org.apache.spark.SparkContext._
import org.apache.spark.SparkContext
import scala.util.matching.Regex

object HashtagCount {
  def main(args: Array[String]) {
[…]
  val sc = new SparkContext(master,
"HashtagCount",
System.getenv("SPARK_HOME"))

    val file = sc.textFile(inputFile)
    val pattern = new Regex("(?:\\s|\\A|^)[##]+([A-Za-z0-9-_]+)")

    val counts = file.flatMap(line =>
      (pattern findAllIn line).toList)
        .map(word => (word, 1))
        .reduceByKey((m, n) => m + n)

    counts.saveAsTextFile(outputPath)
  }
}
```

We create an initial RDD from a dataset stored in HDFS - inputFile - and apply logic that is similar to the WordCount example.

For each tweet in the dataset, we extract an array of strings that match the hashtag pattern (`pattern findAllIn line).toArray`, and we count an occurrence of each string using the map operator. This generates a new RDD as a list of tuples in the form:

```
(word, 1), (word2, 1), (word, 1)
```

Finally, we combine together elements of this RDD using the `reduceByKey()` method. We store the RDD generated by this last step back into HDFS with `saveAsTextFile`.

The code for the standalone driver can be found at `https://github.com/ learninghadoop2/book-examples/blob/master/ch5/src/main/scala/com/ learninghadoop2/spark/HashTagCount.scala`.

Assigning a sentiment to topics

The source code of this example can be found at https://github.com/
learninghadoop2/book-examples/blob/master/ch5/src/main/scala/com/
learninghadoop2/spark/HashTagSentiment.scala, and the code is as follows:

```scala
import org.apache.spark.SparkContext._
import org.apache.spark.SparkContext
import scala.util.matching.Regex
import scala.io.Source

object HashtagSentiment {
  def main(args: Array[String]) {
    [...]
    val sc = new SparkContext(master,
"HashtagSentiment",
System.getenv("SPARK_HOME"))

    val file = sc.textFile(inputFile)

    val positive = Source.fromFile(positiveWordsPath)
      .getLines
      .filterNot(_ startsWith ";")
      .toSet
    val negative = Source.fromFile(negativeWordsPath)
      .getLines
      .filterNot(_ startsWith ";")
      .toSet

    val pattern = new Regex("(?:\\s|\\A|^)[##]+([A-Za-z0-9-_]+)")
    val counts = file.flatMap(line => (pattern findAllIn line).map({
    word => (word, sentimentScore(line, positive, negative))
    })).reduceByKey({ (m, n) => (m._1 + n._1, m._2 + n._2) })

    val sentiment = counts.map({hashtagScore =>
    val hashtag = hashtagScore._1
    val score = hashtagScore._2
    val normalizedScore = score._1 / score._2
    (hashtag, normalizedScore)
    })

    sentiment.saveAsTextFile(outputPath)
  }
}
```

First, we read a list of positive and negative words into Scala Set objects and filter
out comments (strings beginning with ;).

When a hashtag is found, we call a function - `sentimentScore` - to estimate the sentiment expressed by that given text. This function implements the same logic we used in *Chapter 3, Processing – MapReduce and Beyond,* to estimate the sentiment of a tweet. It takes as input parameters the tweet's text, `str`, and a list of positive and negative words as `Set[String]` objects. The return value is the difference between the positive and negative scores and the number of words in the tweets. In Spark, we represent this return value as a pair of `Double` and `Integer` objects:

```
def sentimentScore(str: String, positive: Set[String],
        negative: Set[String]): (Double, Int) = {
    var positiveScore = 0; var negativeScore = 0;
    str.split("""\s+""").foreach { w =>
        if (positive.contains(w)) { positiveScore+=1; }
        if (negative.contains(w)) { negativeScore+=1; }
    }
    ((positiveScore - negativeScore).toDouble,
        str.split("""\s+""").length)
}
```

We reduce the map output by aggregating by the key (the hashtag). In this phase, we emit a triple made of the hashtag, the sum of the difference between positive and negative scores, and the number of words per tweet. We use an additional map step to normalize the sentiment score and store the resulting list of hashtag and sentiment pairs to HDFS.

Data processing on streams

The previous example can be easily adjusted to work on a real-time stream of data. In this and the following section, we will use `spark-streaming-twitter` to perform some simple analytics tasks on the real-time firehose:

```
val window = 10
val ssc = new StreamingContext(master, "TwitterStreamEcho",
Seconds(window), System.getenv("SPARK_HOME"))

val stream = TwitterUtils.createStream(ssc, auth)

val tweets = stream.map(tweet => (tweet.getText()))
tweets.print()

ssc.start()
ssc.awaitTermination()
}
```

The Scala source code for this example can be found at `https://github.com/learninghadoop2/book-examples/blob/master/ch5/src/main/scala/com/learninghadoop2/spark/TwitterStreamEcho.scala`.

The two key packages we need to import are:

```
import org.apache.spark.streaming.{Seconds, StreamingContext}
import org.apache.spark.streaming.twitter._
```

We initialize a new `StreamingContext` `ssc` on a local cluster using a 10-second window and use this context to create a `DStream` of tweets whose text we print.

Upon successful execution, Twitter's real-time firehose will be echoed in the terminal in batches of 10 seconds worth of data. Notice that the computation will continue indefinitely but can be interrupted at any moment by pressing *Ctrl + C*.

The `TwitterUtils` object is a wrapper to the `Twitter4j` library (`http://twitter4j.org/en/index.html`) that ships with `spark-streaming-twitter`. A successful call to `TwitterUtils.createStream` will return a DStream of `Twitter4j` objects (`TwitterInputDStream`). In the preceding example, we used the `getText()` method to extract the tweet text; however, notice that the `twitter4j` object exposes the full Twitter API. For instance, we can print a stream of users with the following call:

```
val users = stream.map(tweet => (tweet.getUser().getId(),
tweet.getUser().getName()))
users.print()
```

State management

Spark Streaming provides an ad hoc DStream to keep the state of each key in an RDD and the `updateStateByKey` method to mutate state.

We can reuse the code of the batch example to assign and update sentiment scores on streams:

```
object StreamingHashTagSentiment {
[…]

    val counts = text.flatMap(line => (pattern findAllIn line)
      .toList
      .map(word => (word, sentimentScore(line, positive, negative))))
      .reduceByKey({ (m, n) => (m._1 + n._1, m._2 + n._2) })

    val sentiment = counts.map({hashtagScore =>
        val hashtag = hashtagScore._1
        val score = hashtagScore._2
        val normalizedScore = score._1 / score._2
```

```
            (hashtag, normalizedScore)
        })

        val stateDstream = sentiment
            .updateStateByKey[Double](updateFunc)

        stateDstream.print

        ssc.checkpoint("/tmp/checkpoint")
        ssc.start()
    }
```

A state DStream is created by calling `hashtagSentiment.updateStateByKey`.

The `updateFunc` function implements the state mutation logic, which is a cumulative sum of sentiment scores over a period of time:

```
        val updateFunc = (values: Seq[Double], state: Option[Double]) => {
            val currentScore = values.sum

            val previousScore = state.getOrElse(0.0)

            Some( (currentScore + previousScore) * decayFactor)
        }
```

`decayFactor` is a constant value, less than or equal to zero, that we use to proportionally decrease the score over time. Intuitively, this will fade hashtags if they are not trending anymore. Spark Streaming writes intermediate data for stateful operations to HDFS, so we need to checkpoint the Streaming context with `ssc.checkpoint`.

The source code for this example can be found at `https://github.com/ learninghadoop2/book-examples/blob/master/ch5/src/main/scala/com/ learninghadoop2/spark/StreamingHashTagSentiment.scala`.

Data analysis with Spark SQL

Spark SQL can ease the task of representing and manipulating structured data. We will load a JSON file into a temporary table and calculate simple statistics by blending SQL statements and Scala code:

```
object SparkJson {
    [...]
    val file = sc.textFile(inputFile)

    val sqlContext = new org.apache.spark.sql.SQLContext(sc)
    import sqlContext._
```

```
    val tweets = sqlContext.jsonFile(inFile)
    tweets.printSchema()

    // Register the SchemaRDD as a table
    tweets.registerTempTable("tweets")
    val text = sqlContext.sql("SELECT text, user.id FROM tweets")

    // Find the ten most popular hashtags
    val pattern = new Regex("(?:\\s|\\A|^)[##]+([A-Za-z0-9-_]+)")

    val counts = text.flatMap(sqlRow => (pattern findAllIn
    sqlRow(0).toString).toList)
            .map(word => (word, 1))
            .reduceByKey( (m, n) => m+n)
    counts.registerTempTable("hashtag_frequency")

counts.printSchema

val top10 = sqlContext.sql("SELECT _1 as hashtag, _2 as frequency
FROM hashtag_frequency order by frequency desc limit 10")

top10.foreach(println)
}
```

As with previous examples, we instantiate a `SparkContext` `sc` and load the dataset of JSON tweets. We then create an instance of `org.apache.spark.sql.SQLContext` based on the existing `sc`. The `import sqlContext._` gives access to all functions and implicit conventions for `sqlContext`. We load the tweets' JSON dataset using `sqlContext.jsonFile`. The resulting `tweets` object is an instance of `SchemaRDD`, which is a new type of RDD introduced by Spark SQL. The `SchemaRDD` class is conceptually similar to a table in a relational database; it is composed of `Row` objects and a schema that describes the content in each `Row`. We can see the schema for a tweet by calling `tweets.printSchema()`. Before we're able to manipulate tweets with SQL statements, we need to register `SchemaRDD` as a table in the `SQLContext`. We then extract the text field of a JSON tweet with an SQL query. Note that the output of `sqlContext.sql` is an RDD again. As such, we can manipulate it using Spark core methods. In our case, we reuse the logic used in previous examples to extract hashtags and count their occurrences. Finally, we register the resulting RDD as a table, `hashtag_frequency`, and order hashtags by frequency with a SQL query.

The source code of this example can be found at `https://github.com/learninghadoop2/book-examples/blob/master/ch5/src/main/scala/com/learninghadoop2/spark/SparkJson.scala`.

SQL on data streams

At the time of writing, a `SQLContext` cannot be directly instantiated from a `StreamingContext` object. It is, however, possible to query a DStream by registering a `SchemaRDD` for each RDD in a given stream:

```scala
object SqlOnStream {
[...]

    val ssc = new StreamingContext(sc, Seconds(window))

    val gson = new Gson()

    val dstream = TwitterUtils
    .createStream(ssc, auth)
    .map(gson.toJson(_))

    val sqlContext = new org.apache.spark.sql.SQLContext(sc)
    import sqlContext._

  dstream.foreachRDD( rdd => {
     rdd.foreach(println)
       val jsonRDD = sqlContext.jsonRDD(rdd)
       jsonRDD.registerTempTable("tweets")
       jsonRDD.printSchema

        sqlContext.sql(query)
  })

    ssc.checkpoint("/tmp/checkpoint")
    ssc.start()
    ssc.awaitTermination()
}
```

In order to get the two working together, we first create a `SparkContext` `sc` that we use to initialize both a `StreamingContext` `ssc` and a `sqlContext`. As in previous examples, we use `TwitterUtils.createStream` to create a DStream RDD `dstream`. In this example, we use Google's Gson JSON parser to serialize each `twitter4j` object to a JSON string. To execute Spark SQL queries on the stream, we register a `SchemaRDD` `jsonRDD` within a `dstream.foreachRDD` loop. We use the `sqlContext.jsonRDD` method to create an RDD from a batch of JSON tweets. At this point, we can query the `SchemaRDD` using the `sqlContext.sql` method.

The source code of this example can be found at `https://github.com/learninghadoop2/book-examples/blob/master/ch5/src/main/scala/com/learninghadoop2/spark/SqlOnStream.scala`.

Comparing Samza and Spark Streaming

It is useful to compare Samza and Spark Streaming to help identify the areas in which each can best be applied. As it has been hopefully made clear in this book, these technologies are very much complimentary. Even though Spark Streaming might appear competitive with Samza, we feel both products offer compelling advantages in certain areas.

Samza shines when the input data is truly a stream of discrete events and you wish to build processing that operates on this type of input. Samza jobs running on Kafka can have latencies in the order of milliseconds. This provides a programming model focused on the individual messages and is the better fit for true near real-time processing applications. Though it lacks support to build topologies of collaborating jobs, its simple model allows similar constructs to be built and, perhaps more importantly, be easily reasoned about. Its model of partitioning and scaling also focuses on simplicity, which again makes a Samza application very easy to understand and gives it a significant advantage when dealing with something as intrinsically complex as real-time data.

Spark is much more than a streaming product. Its support for building distributed data structures from existing datasets and using powerful primitives to manipulate these gives it the ability to process large datasets at a higher level of granularity. Other products in the Spark ecosystem build additional interfaces or abstractions upon this common batch processing core. This is very much a different focus to the message stream model of Samza.

This batch model is also demonstrated when we look at Spark Streaming; instead of a per-message processing model, it slices the message stream into a series of RDDs. With a fast execution engine, this means latencies as low as 1 second (`http://www.cs.berkeley.edu/~matei/papers/2012/hotcloud_spark_streaming.pdf`). For workloads that wish to analyze the stream in such a way, this will be a better fit than Samza's per-message model, which requires additional logic to provide such windowing.

Summary

This chapter explored Spark and showed you how it adds iterative processing as a new rich framework upon which applications can be built atop YARN. In particular, we highlighted:

- The distributed data-structure-based processing model of Spark and how it allows very efficient in-memory data processing

- The broader Spark ecosystem and how multiple additional projects are built atop it to specialize the computational model even further

In the next chapter we will explore Apache Pig and its programming language, Pig Latin. We will see how this tool can greatly simplify software development for Hadoop by abstracting away some of the MapReduce and Spark complexity.

6
Data Analysis with Apache Pig

In the previous chapters, we explored a number of APIs for data processing. MapReduce, Spark, Tez and Samza are rather low-level, and writing non-trivial business logic with them often requires significant Java development. Moreover, different users will have different needs. It might be impractical for an analyst to write MapReduce code or build a DAG of inputs and outputs to answer some simple queries. At the same time, a software engineer or a researcher might want to prototype ideas and algorithms using high-level abstractions before jumping into low-level implementation details.

In this chapter and the following one, we will explore some tools that provide a way to process data on HDFS using higher-level abstractions. In this chapter we will explore Apache Pig, and, in particular, we will cover the following topics:

- What Apache Pig is and the dataflow model it provides
- Pig Latin's data types and functions
- How Pig can be easily enhanced using custom user code
- How we can use Pig to analyze the Twitter stream

An overview of Pig

Historically, the Pig toolkit consisted of a compiler that generated MapReduce programs, bundled their dependencies, and executed them on Hadoop. Pig jobs are written in a language called **Pig Latin** and can be executed in both interactive and batch fashions. Furthermore, Pig Latin can be extended using **User Defined Functions (UDFs)** written in Java, Python, Ruby, Groovy, or JavaScript.

Pig use cases include the following:

- Data processing
- Ad hoc analytical queries
- Rapid prototyping of algorithms
- Extract Transform Load pipelines

Following a trend we have seen in previous chapters, Pig is moving towards a general-purpose computing architecture. As of version 0.13 the **ExecutionEngine** interface (`org.apache.pig.backend.executionengine`) acts as a bridge between the frontend and the backend of Pig, allowing Pig Latin scripts to be compiled and executed on frameworks other than MapReduce. At the time of writing, version 0.13 ships with **MRExecutionEngine** (`org.apache.pig.backend.hadoop.executionengine.mapReduceLayer.MRExecutionEngine`) and work on a low-latency backend based on **Tez** (`org.apache.pig.backend.hadoop.executionengine.tez.*`) is expected to be included in version 0.14 (see `https://issues.apache.org/jira/browse/PIG-3446`). Work on integrating Spark is currently in progress in the development branch (see `https://issues.apache.org/jira/browse/PIG-4059`).

Pig 0.13 comes with a number of performance enhancements for the MapReduce backend, in particular two features to reduce latency of small jobs: *direct HDFS access* (`https://issues.apache.org/jira/browse/PIG-3642`) and *auto local mode* (`https://issues.apache.org/jira/browse/PIG-3463`). Direct HDFS, the `opt.fetch` property, is turned on by default. When doing a DUMP in a simple (map-only) script that contains only LIMIT, FILTER, UNION, STREAM, or FOREACH operators, input data is fetched from HDFS, and the query is executed directly in Pig, bypassing MapReduce. With auto local, the `pig.auto.local.enabled` property, Pig will run a query in the Hadoop local mode when the data size is smaller than `pig.auto.local.input.maxbytes`. Auto local is off by default.

Pig will launch MapReduce jobs if both modes are off or if the query is not eligible for either. If both modes are on, Pig will check whether the query is eligible for direct access and, if not, fall back to auto local. Failing that, it will execute the query on MapReduce.

Getting started

We will use the `stream.py` script options to extract JSON data and retrieve a specific number of tweets; we can run this with a command such as the following:

```
$ python stream.py -j -n 10000 > tweets.json
```

The `tweets.json` file will contain one JSON string on each line representing a tweet.

Remember that the Twitter API credentials need to be made available as environment variables or hardcoded in the script itself.

Running Pig

Pig is a tool that translates statements written in Pig Latin and executes them either on a single machine in standalone mode or on a full Hadoop cluster when in distributed mode. Even in the latter, Pig's role is to translate Pig Latin statements into MapReduce jobs and therefore it doesn't require the installation of additional services or daemons. It is used as a command-line tool with its associated libraries.

Cloudera CDH ships with Apache Pig version 0.12. Alternatively, the Pig source code and binary distributions can be obtained at `https://pig.apache.org/releases.html`.

As can be expected, the MapReduce mode requires access to a Hadoop cluster and HDFS installation. MapReduce mode is the default mode executed when running the Pig command at the command-line prompt. Scripts can be executed with the following command:

```
$ pig -f <script>
```

Parameters can be passed via the command line using `-param <param>=<val>`, as follows:

```
$ pig –param input=tweets.txt
```

Parameters can also be specified in a `param` file that can be passed to Pig using the `-param_file <file>` option. Multiple files can be specified. If a parameter is present multiple times in the file, the last value will be used and a warning will be displayed. A parameter file contains one parameter per line. Empty lines and comments (specified by starting a line with #) are allowed. Within a Pig script, parameters are in the form `$<parameter>`. The default value can be assigned using the `default` statement: `%default input tweets.json'`. The `default` command will not work within a Grunt session; we'll discuss Grunt in the next section.

In local mode, all files are installed and run using the local host and filesystem. Specify local mode using the `-x` flag:

```
$ pig -x local
```

In both execution modes, Pig programs can be run either in an interactive shell or in batch mode.

Grunt – the Pig interactive shell

Pig can run in an interactive mode using the Grunt shell, which is invoked when we use the `pig` command at the terminal prompt. In the rest of this chapter, we will assume that examples are executed within a Grunt session. Other than executing Pig Latin statements, Grunt offers a number of utilities and access to shell commands:

- `fs`: allows users to manipulate Hadoop filesystem objects and has the same semantics as the Hadoop CLI
- `sh`: executes commands via the operating system shell
- `exec`: launches a Pig script within an interactive Grunt session
- `kill`: kills a MapReduce job
- `help`: prints a list of all available commands

Elastic MapReduce

Pig scripts can be executed on EMR by creating a cluster with `--applications Name=Pig,Args=--version,<version>`, as follows:

```
$ aws emr create-cluster \
--name "Pig cluster" \
--ami-version <ami version> \
--instance-type <EC2 instance> \
--instance-count <number of nodes> \
--applications Name=Pig,Args=--version,<version>\
--log-uri <S3 bucket> \
--steps Type=PIG,\
Name="Pig script",\
Args=[-f,s3://<script location>,\
-p,input=<input param>,\
-p,output=<output param>]
```

The preceding command will provision a new EMR cluster and execute `s3://<script location>`. Notice that the scripts to be executed and the input (`-p input`) and output (`-p output`) paths are expected to be located on S3.

As an alternative to creating a new EMR cluster, it is possible to add Pig steps to an already-instantiated EMR cluster using the following command:

```
$ aws emr add-steps \
--cluster-id <cluster id>\
--steps Type=PIG,\
Name= "Other Pig script",\
Args=[-f,s3://<script location>,\
-p,input=<input param>,\
-p,output=<output param>]
```

In the preceding command, `<cluster id>` is the ID of the instantiated cluster.

It is also possible to ssh into the master node and run Pig Latin statements within a Grunt session with the following command:

```
$ aws emr ssh --cluster-id <cluster id> --key-pair-file <key pair>
```

Fundamentals of Apache Pig

The primary interface to program Apache Pig is Pig Latin, a procedural language that implements ideas of the dataflow paradigm.

Pig Latin programs are generally organized as follows:

- A LOAD statement reads data from HDFS
- A series of statements aggregates and manipulates data
- A STORE statement writes output to the filesystem
- Alternatively, a DUMP statement displays the output to the terminal

The following example shows a sequence of statements that outputs the top 10 hashtags ordered by the frequency, extracted from the dataset of tweets:

```
tweets = LOAD 'tweets.json'
  USING JsonLoader('created_at:chararray,
    id:long,
    id_str:chararray,
    text:chararray');

hashtags = FOREACH tweets {
  GENERATE FLATTEN(
```

```
        REGEX_EXTRACT(
          text,
          '(?:\\s|\\A|^)[##]+([A-Za-z0-9-_]+)', 1)
        ) as tag;
}

hashtags_grpd = GROUP hashtags BY tag;
hashtags_count = FOREACH hashtags_grpd {
  GENERATE
    group,
    COUNT(hashtags) as occurrencies;
}
hashtags_count_sorted = ORDER hashtags_count BY occurrencies DESC;
top_10_hashtags = LIMIT hashtags_count_sorted 10;
DUMP top_10_hashtags;
```

First, we load the `tweets.json` dataset from HDFS, de-serialize the JSON file, and map it to a four-column schema that contains a tweet's creation time, its ID in numerical and string form, and the text. For each tweet, we extract hashtags from its text using a regular expression. We aggregate on hashtag, count the number of occurrences, and order by frequency. Finally, we limit the ordered records to the top 10 most frequent hashtags.

A series of statements like the previous one is picked up by the Pig compiler, transformed into MapReduce jobs, and executed on a Hadoop cluster. The planner and optimizer will resolve dependencies on input and output relations and parallelize the execution of statements wherever possible.

Statements are the building blocks of processing data with Pig. They take a relation as input and produce another relation as output. In Pig Latin terms, a relation can be defined as a bag of **tuples**, two data types we will use throughout the remainder of this chapter.

Users experienced with SQL and the relational data model might find Pig Latin's syntax somewhat familiar. While there are indeed similarities in the syntax itself, Pig Latin implements an entirely different computational model. Pig Latin is procedural, it specifies the actual data transforms to be performed, whereas SQL is declarative and describes the nature of the problem but does not specify the actual runtime processing. In terms of organizing data, a relation can be thought of as a table in a relational database, where tuples in a bag correspond to the rows in a table. Relations are unordered and therefore easily parallelizable, and they are less constrained than relational tables. Pig relations can contain tuples with different numbers of fields, and those with the same field count can have fields of different types in corresponding positions.

A key difference between SQL and the dataflow model adopted by Pig Latin lies in how splits in a data pipeline are managed. In the relational world, a declarative language such as SQL implements and executes queries that will generate a single result. The dataflow model sees data transformations as a graph where input and output are nodes connected by an operator. For instance, intermediate steps of a query might require the input to be grouped by a number of keys and result in multiple outputs (GROUP BY). Pig has built-in mechanisms to manage multiple data flows in such a graph by executing operators as soon as inputs are readily available and potentially apply different operators to each flow. For instance, Pig's implementation of the GROUP BY operator uses the parallel feature (http://pig.apache.org/docs/r0.12.0/perf.html#parallel) to allow a user to increase the number of reduce tasks for the MapReduce jobs generated and hence increases concurrency. An additional side effect of this property is that when multiple operators can be executed in parallel in the same program, Pig does so (more details on Pig's multi-query implementation can be found at http://pig.apache.org/docs/r0.12.0/perf.html#multi-query-execution). Another consequence of Pig Latin's approach to computation is that it allows the persistence of data at any point in the pipeline. It allows the developer to select specific operator implementations and execution plans when necessary, effectively overriding the optimizer.

Pig Latin allows and even encourages developers to insert their own code almost anywhere in a pipeline by means of **User Defined Functions (UDFs)** as well as by utilizing Hadoop streaming. UDFs allow users to specify custom business logic on how data is loaded, how it is stored, and how it is processed, whereas streaming allows users to launch executables at any point in the data flow.

Programming Pig

Pig Latin comes with a number of built-in functions (the eval, load/store, math, string, bag, and tuple functions) and a number of scalar and complex data types. Additionally, Pig allows function and data-type extension by means of UDFs and dynamic invocation of Java methods.

Pig data types

Pig supports the following scalar data types:

- int: a signed 32-bit integer
- long: a signed 64-bit integer
- float: a 32-bit floating point
- double: a 64-bit floating point

- `chararray`: a character array (string) in Unicode UTF-8 format
- `bytearray`: a byte array (blob)
- `boolean`: a boolean
- `datetime`: a datetime
- `biginteger`: a Java BigInteger
- `bigdecimal`: a Java BigDecimal

Pig supports the following complex data types:

- `map`: an associative array enclosed by `[]`, with the key and value separated by #, and items separated by ,
- `tuple`: an ordered list of data, where elements can be of any scalar or complex type enclosed by `()`, with items separated by ,
- `bag`: an unordered collection of tuples enclosed by `{}` and separated by ,

By default, Pig treats data as untyped. The user can declare the types of data at load time or manually cast it when necessary. If a data type is not declared, but a script implicitly treats a value as a certain type, Pig will assume it is of that type and cast it accordingly. The fields of a bag or tuple can be referred to by the name `tuple.field` or by the position `$<index>`. Pig counts from 0 and hence the first element will be denoted as `$0`.

Pig functions

Built-in functions are implemented in Java, and they try to follow standard Java conventions. There are however a number of differences to keep in mind, which are as follows:

- Function names are case sensitive and uppercase
- If the result value is null, empty, or **not a number** (NaN), Pig returns null
- If Pig is unable to process the expression, it returns an exception

A list of all built-in functions can be found at `http://pig.apache.org/docs/r0.12.0/func.html`.

Load/store

Load/store functions determine how data goes into and comes out of Pig. The `PigStorage`, `TextLoader`, and `BinStorage` functions can be used to read and write UTF-8 delimited, unstructured text, and binary data respectively. Support for compression is determined by the load/store function. The `PigStorage` and `TextLoader` functions support gzip and bzip2 compression for both read (load) and write (store). The `BinStorage` function does not support compression.

As of version 0.12, Pig includes built-in support for loading and storing Avro and JSON data via the `AvroStorage` (load/store), `JsonStorage` (store), and `JsonLoader` (load). At the time of writing, JSON support is still somewhat limited. In particular, Pig expects a schema for the data to be provided as an argument to `JsonLoader`/`JsonStorage`, or it assumes that `.pig_schema` (produced by `JsonStorage`) is present in the directory containing the input data. In practice, this makes it difficult to work with JSON dumps not generated by Pig itself.

As seen in our following example, we can load the JSON dataset with `JsonLoader`:

```
tweets = LOAD 'tweets.json' USING JsonLoader(
'created_at:chararray,
id:long,
id_str:chararray,
text:chararray,
source:chararray');
```

We provide a schema so that the first five elements of a JSON object `created_id`, `id`, `id_str`, `text`, and `source` are mapped. We can look at the schema of tweets by using `describe tweets`, which returns the following:

```
 tweets: {created_at: chararray,id: long,id_str: chararray,text:
chararray,source: chararray}
```

Eval

Eval functions implement a set of operations to be applied on an expression that returns a bag or map data type. The expression result is evaluated within the function context.

- `AVG(expression)`: computes the average of the numeric values in a single-column bag

- `COUNT(expression)`: counts all elements with non-null values in the first position in a bag

- `COUNT_STAR(expression)`: counts all elements in a bag
- `IsEmpty(expression)`: checks whether a bag or map is empty
- `MAX(expression)`, `MIN(expression)`, and `SUM(expression)`: return the max, min, or the sum of elements in a bag
- `TOKENIZE(expression)`: splits a string and outputs a bag of words

The tuple, bag, and map functions

These functions allow conversion from and to the bag, tuple, and map types. They include the following:

- `TOTUPLE(expression)`, `TOMAP(expression)`, and `TOBAG(expression)`: These coerce `expression` to a tuple, map, or bag
- `TOP(n, column, relation)`: This returns the top n tuples from a bag of tuples

The math, string, and datetime functions

Pig exposes a number of functions provided by the `java.lang.Math`, `java.lang. String`, `java.util.Date`, and Joda-Time `DateTime` class (found at `http://www. joda.org/joda-time/`).

Dynamic invokers

Dynamic invokers allow the execution of Java functions without having to wrap them in a UDF. They can be used for any static function that:

- accepts no arguments or accepts a combination of `string`, `int`, `long`, `double`, `float`, or `array` with these same types
- returns a `string`, `int`, `long`, `double`, or `float` value

Only primitives can be used for numbers and Java boxed classes (such as Integer) cannot be used as arguments. Depending on the return type, a specific kind of invoker must be used: `InvokeForString`, `InvokeForInt`, `InvokeForLong`, `InvokeForDouble`, or `InvokeForFloat`. More details regarding dynamic invokers can be found at `http://pig.apache.org/docs/r0.12.0/func.html#dynamic-invokers`.

Macros

As of version 0.9, Pig Latin's preprocessor supports macro expansion. Macros are defined using the DEFINE statement:

```
DEFINE macro_name(param1, ..., paramN) RETURNS output_bag {
  pig_latin_statements
};
```

The macro is expanded inline, and its parameters are referenced in the Pig Latin block within { }.

The macro output relation is given in the RETURNS statements (output_bag). RETURNS void is used for a macro with no output relation.

We can define a macro to count the number of rows in a relation, as follows:

```
DEFINE count_rows(X) RETURNS cnt {
  grpd = group $X all;
  $cnt = foreach grpd generate COUNT($X);
};
```

We can use it in a Pig script or Grunt session to count the number of tweets:

```
tweets_count = count_rows(tweets);
DUMP tweets_count;
```

Macros allow us to make scripts modular by housing code in separate files and importing them where needed. For example, we can save count_rows in a file called count_rows.macro and later on import it with the command import 'count_rows.macro'.

Macros have a number of limitations; in particular, only Pig Latin statements are allowed inside a macro. It is not possible to use REGISTER statements and shell commands, UDFs are not allowed, and parameter substitution inside the macro is not supported.

Working with data

Pig Latin provides a number of relational operators to combine functions and apply transformations on data. Typical operations in a data pipeline consist of filtering relations (FILTER), aggregating inputs based on keys (GROUP), generating transformations based on columns of data (FOREACH), and joining relations (JOIN) based on shared keys.

In the following sections, we will illustrate such operators on a dataset of tweets generated by loading JSON data.

Filtering

The FILTER operator selects tuples from a relation based on an expression, as follows:

```
relation = FILTER relation BY expression;
```

We can use this operator to filter tweets whose text matches the hashtag regular expression, as follows:

```
tweets_with_tag = FILTER tweets BY
    (text
        MATCHES '(?:\\s|\\A|^)[##]+([A-Za-z0-9-_]+)'
);
```

Aggregation

The GROUP operator groups together data in one or more relations based on an expression or a key, as follows:

```
relation = GROUP relation BY expression;
```

We can group tweets by the source field into a new relation grpd, as follows:

```
grpd = GROUP tweets BY source;
```

It is possible to group on multiple dimensions by specifying a tuple as the key, as follows:

```
grpd = GROUP tweets BY (created_at, source);
```

The result of a GROUP operation is a relation that includes one tuple per unique value of the group expression. This tuple contains two fields. The first field is named group and is of the same type as the group key. The second field takes the name of the original relation and is of the type bag. The names of both fields are generated by the system.

Using the ALL keyword, Pig will aggregate across the whole relation. The GROUP tweets ALL scheme will aggregate all tuples in the same group.

As previously mentioned, Pig allows explicit handling of the concurrency level of the GROUP operator using the PARALLEL operator:

```
grpd = GROUP tweets BY (created_at, id) PARALLEL 10;
```

In the preceding example, the MapReduce job generated by the compiler will run 10 concurrent reduce tasks. Pig has a heuristic estimate of how many reducers to use. Another way of globally enforcing the number of reduce tasks is to use the `set default_parallel <n>` command.

Foreach

The `FOREACH` operator applies functions on columns, as follows:

```
relation = FOREACH relation GENERATE transformation;
```

The output of `FOREACH` depends on the transformation applied.

We can use the operator to project the text of all tweets that contain a hashtag, as follows:

```
t = FOREACH tweets_with_tag GENERATE text;
```

We can also apply a function to the projected columns. For instance, we can use the `REGEX_TOKENIZE` function to split each tweet into words, as follows:

```
t = FOREACH tweets_with_tag GENERATE FLATTEN(TOKENIZE(text)) as word;
```

The `FLATTEN` modifier further un-nests the bag generated by `TOKENIZE` into a tuple of words.

Join

The `JOIN` operator performs an inner join of two or more relations based on common field values. Its syntax is as follows:

```
relation = JOIN relation1 BY expression1, relation2 BY expression2;
```

We can use a join operation to detect tweets that contain positive words, as follows:

```
positive = LOAD 'positive-words.txt' USING PigStorage() as
(w:chararray);
```

Filter out the comments, as follows:

```
positive_words = FILTER positive BY NOT w MATCHES '^;.*';
```

`positive_words` is a bag of tuples, each containing a word. We then tokenize the tweets' text and create a new bag of (id_str, word) tuples as follows:

```
id_words = FOREACH tweets {
   GENERATE
      id_str,
      FLATTEN(TOKENIZE(text)) as word;
}
```

We join the two relations on the `word` field and obtain a relation of all tweets that contain one or more positive words, as follows:

```
positive_tweets = JOIN positive_words BY w, id_words BY word;
```

In this statement, we join `positive_words` and `id_words` on the condition that `id_words.word` is a positive word. The `positive_tweets` operator is a bag in the form of {`w:chararray,id_str:chararray, word:chararray`} that contains all elements of `positive_words` and `id_words` that match the join condition.

We can combine the GROUP and FOREACH operator to calculate the number of positive words per tweet (with at least one positive word). First, we group the relation of positive tweets by the tweet ID, and then we count the number of occurrences of each ID in the relation, as follows:

```
grpd = GROUP positive_tweets BY id_str;
score = FOREACH grpd GENERATE FLATTEN(group), COUNT(positive_tweets);
```

The JOIN operator can make use of the parallelize feature as well, as follows:

```
positive_tweets = JOIN positive_words BY w, id_words BY word PARALLEL
10
```

The preceding command will execute the join with 10 reducer tasks.

It is possible to specify the operator's behavior with the USING keyword followed by the ID of a specialized join. More details can be found at `http://pig.apache.org/docs/r0.12.0/perf.html#specialized-joins`.

Extending Pig (UDFs)

Functions can be a part of almost every operator in Pig. There are two main differences between UDFs and built-in functions. First, UDFs need to be registered using the REGISTER keyword in order to make them available to Pig. Secondly, they need to be qualified when used. Pig UDFs can currently be implemented in Java, Python, Ruby, JavaScript, and Groovy. The most extensive support is provided for Java functions, which allow you to customize all parts of the process including data load/store, transformation, and aggregation. Additionally, Java functions are also more efficient because they are implemented in the same language as Pig and because additional interfaces are supported, such as the Algebraic and Accumulator interfaces. On the other hand, Ruby and Python APIs allow more rapid prototyping.

The integration of UDFs with the Pig environment is mainly managed by the following two statements REGISTER and DEFINE:

- REGISTER registers a JAR file so that the UDFs in the file can be used, as follows:

```
REGISTER 'piggybank.jar'
```

- DEFINE creates an alias to a function or a streaming command, as follows:

```
DEFINE MyFunction my.package.uri.MyFunction
```

The version 0.12 of Pig introduced the streaming of UDFs as a mechanism for writing functions using languages with no JVM implementation.

Contributed UDFs

Pig's code base hosts a UDF repository called **Piggybank**. Other popular contributed repositories are **Twitter's Elephant Bird** (found at https://github.com/kevinweil/elephant-bird/) and **Apache DataFu** (found at http://datafu.incubator.apache.org/).

Piggybank

Piggybank is a place for Pig users to share their functions. Shared code is located in the official Pig Subversion repository found at `http://svn.apache.org/viewvc/pig/trunk/contrib/piggybank/java/src/main/java/org/apache/pig/piggybank/`. The API documentation can be found at `http://pig.apache.org/docs/r0.12.0/api/` under the **contrib** section. Piggybank UDFs can be obtained by checking out and compiling the sources from the Subversion repository or by using the JAR file that ships with binary releases of Pig. In Cloudera CDH, `piggybank.jar` is available at `/opt/cloudera/parcels/CDH/lib/pig/piggybank.jar`.

Elephant Bird

Elephant Bird is an open source library of all things Hadoop used in production at Twitter. This library contains a number of serialization tools, custom input and output formats, writables, Pig load/store functions, and more miscellanea.

Elephant Bird ships with an extremely flexible JSON loader function, which at the time of writing, is the go-to resource for manipulating JSON data in Pig.

Apache DataFu

Apache DataFu Pig collects a number of analytical functions developed and contributed by LinkedIn. These include statistical and estimation functions, bag and set operations, sampling, hashing, and link analysis.

Analyzing the Twitter stream

In the following examples, we will use the implementation of JsonLoader provided by Elephant Bird to load and manipulate JSON data. We will use Pig to explore tweet metadata and analyze trends in the dataset. Finally, we will model the interaction between users as a graph and use Apache DataFu to analyze this social network.

Prerequisites

Download the `elephant-bird-pig` (http://central.maven.org/maven2/com/
twitter/elephantbird/elephant-bird-pig/4.5/elephant-bird-pig-4.5.jar),
`elephant-bird-hadoop-compat` (http://central.maven.org/maven2/com/
twitter/elephantbird/elephant-bird-hadoop-compat/4.5/elephant-bird-
hadoop-compat-4.5.jar), and `elephant-bird-core` (http://central.maven.
org/maven2/com/twitter/elephantbird/elephant-bird-core/4.5/elephant-
bird-core-4.5.jar) JAR files from the Maven central repository and copy them
onto HDFS using the following command:

```
$ hdfs dfs -put target/elephant-bird-pig-4.5.jar hdfs:///jar/
$ hdfs dfs -put target/elephant-bird-hadoop-compat-4.5.jar hdfs:///jar/
$ hdfs dfs -put elephant-bird-core-4.5.jar hdfs:///jar/
```

Dataset exploration

Before diving deeper into the dataset, we need to register the dependencies to
Elephant Bird and DataFu, as follows:

```
REGISTER /opt/cloudera/parcels/CDH/lib/pig/datafu-1.1.0-cdh5.0.0.jar
REGISTER /opt/cloudera/parcels/CDH/lib/pig/lib/json-simple-1.1.jar
REGISTER hdfs:///jar/elephant-bird-pig-4.5.jar
REGISTER hdfs:///jar/elephant-bird-hadoop-compat-4.5.jar
REGISTER hdfs:///jar/elephant-bird-core-4.5.jar
```

Then, load the JSON dataset of tweets using `com.twitter.elephantbird.pig.
load.JsonLoader`, as follows:

```
tweets = LOAD 'tweets.json' using  com.twitter.elephantbird.pig.load.
JsonLoader('-nestedLoad');
```

`com.twitter.elephantbird.pig.load.JsonLoader` decodes each line of the
input file to JSON and passes the resulting map of values to Pig as a single-element
tuple. This enables access to elements of the JSON object without having to specify
a schema upfront. The `-nestedLoad` argument instructs the class to load nested
data structures.

Tweet metadata

In the remainder of the chapter, we will use metadata from the JSON dataset to model the tweet stream. One example of metadata attached to a tweet is the `Place` object, which contains geographical information about the user's location. `Place` contains fields that describe its name, ID, country, country code, and more. A full description can be found at `https://dev.twitter.com/docs/platform-objects/places`.

```
place = FOREACH tweets GENERATE (chararray)$0#'place' as place;
```

Entities give information such as structured data from tweets, URLs, hashtags, and mentions, without having to extract them from text. A description of entities can be found at `https://dev.twitter.com/docs/entities`. The hashtag entity is an array of tags extracted from a tweet. Each entity has the following two attributes:

- **Text**: is the hashtag text
- **Indices**: is the character position from which the hashtag was extracted

The following code uses entities:

```
hashtags_bag = FOREACH tweets {
    GENERATE
        FLATTEN($0#'entities'#'hashtags') as tag;
}
```

We then flatten `hashtags_bag` to extract each hashtag's text:

```
hashtags = FOREACH hashtags_bag GENERATE tag#'text' as topic;
```

Entities for user objects contain information that appears in the user profile and description fields. We can extract the tweet author's ID via the `user` field in the tweet map:

```
users = FOREACH tweets GENERATE $0#'user'#'id' as id;
```

Data preparation

The SAMPLE built-in operator selects a set of n tuples with probability p out of the dataset, as follows:

```
sampled = SAMPLE tweets 0.01;
```

The preceding command will select approximately 1 percent of the dataset. Given that SAMPLE is probabilistic (http://en.wikipedia.org/wiki/Bernoulli_sampling), there is no guarantee that the sample size will be exact. Moreover the function samples with replacement, which means that each item might appear more than once.

Apache DataFu implements a number of sampling methods for cases where having an exact sample size and no replacement is desired (SimpleRandomSampling), sampling with replacement (SimpleRandomSampleWithReplacementVote and SimpleRandomSampleWithReplacementElect), when we want to account for sample bias (WeightedRandomSampling), or to sample across multiple relations (SampleByKey).

We can create a sample of exactly 1 percent of the dataset, with each item having the same probability of being selected, using SimpleRandomSample.

The actual guarantee is a sample of size *ceil (p*n)* with a probability of at least 99 percent.

First, we pass a sampling probability 0.01 to the UDF constructor:

```
DEFINE SRS datafu.pig.sampling.SimpleRandomSample('0.01');
```

and the bag, created with (GROUP tweets ALL), to be sampled:

```
sampled = FOREACH (GROUP tweets ALL) GENERATE FLATTEN(SRS(tweets));
```

The SimpleRandomSample UDF selects without replacement, which means that each item will appear only once.

Which sampling method to use depends both on the data we are working with, assumptions on how items are distributed, the size of the dataset, and what we practically want to achieve. In general, when we want to explore a dataset to formulate hypotheses, SimpleRandomSample can be a good choice. However, in several analytics applications, it is common to use methods that assume replacement (for example, bootstrapping).

Note that when working with very large datasets, sampling with replacement and sampling without replacement tend to behave similarly. The probability of an item being selected twice out of a population of billions of items will be low.

Top n statistics

One of the first questions we might want to ask is how frequent certain things are. For instance, we might want to create a histogram of the top 10 topics by the number of mentions. Similarly, we might want to find the top 50 countries or the top 10 users. Before looking at tweets data, we will define a macro so that we can apply the same selection logic to different collections of items:

```
DEFINE top_n(rel, col, n)
  RETURNS top_n_items {
    grpd = GROUP $rel BY $col;
    cnt_items = FOREACH grpd
        GENERATE FLATTEN(group), COUNT($rel) AS cnt;
    cnt_items_sorted = ORDER cnt_items BY cnt DESC;
    $top_n_items = LIMIT cnt_items_sorted $n;
  }
```

The `top_n` method takes a relation `rel`, the column `col` we want to count, and the number of items to return n as parameters. In the Pig Latin block, we first group `rel` by items in `col`, count the number of occurrences of each item, sort them, and select the most frequent n.

To find the top 10 English hashtags, we filter them by language, and extract their text:

```
tweets_en = FILTER tweets by $0#'lang' == 'en';
hashtags_bag = FOREACH tweets {
    GENERATE
        FLATTEN($0#'entities'#'hashtags') AS tag;
}
hashtags = FOREACH hashtags_bag GENERATE tag#'text' AS tag;
```

And apply the `top_n` macro:

```
top_10_hashtags = top_n(hashtags, tag, 10);
```

In order to better characterize what is trending and make this information more relevant to users, we can drill down into the dataset and look at hashtags per geographic location.

First, we generate bag of (`place`, `hashtag`) tuples, as follows:

```
hashtags_country_bag = FOREACH tweets generate {
    0#'place' as place,
    FLATTEN($0#'entities'#'hashtags') as tag;
}
```

And then, we extract the country code and hashtag text, as follows:

```
hashtags_country = FOREACH hashtags_country_bag {
  GENERATE
    place#'country_code' as co,
    tag#'text' as tag;
}
```

Then, we count how many times each country code and hashtag appear together, as follows:

```
hashtags_country_frequency = FOREACH (GROUP hashtags_country ALL) {
  GENERATE
    FLATTEN(group),
    COUNT(hashtags_country) as count;
}
```

Finally, we count the top 10 countries per hashtag with the TOP function, as follows:

```
hashtags_country_regrouped= GROUP hashtags_country_frequency BY cnt;
top_results = FOREACH hashtags_country_regrouped {
    result = TOP(10, 1, hashtags_country_frequency);
    GENERATE FLATTEN(result);
}
```

TOP's parameters are the number of tuples to return, the column to compare, and the relation containing said column:

```
top_results = FOREACH D {
  result = TOP(10, 1, C);
  GENERATE FLATTEN(result);
}
```

The source code for this example can be found at `https://github.com/learninghadoop2/book-examples/blob/master/ch6/topn.pig`.

Datetime manipulation

The `created_at` field in the JSON tweets gives us time-stamped information about when the tweet was posted. Unfortunately, its format is not compatible with Pig's built-in `datetime` type.

Piggybank comes to the rescue with a number of time manipulation UDFs contained in `org.apache.pig.piggybank.evaluation.datetime.convert`. One of them is `CustomFormatToISO`, which converts an arbitrarily formatted timestamp into an ISO 8601 datetime string.

In order to access these UDFs, we first need to register the `piggybank.jar` file, as follows:

```
REGISTER /opt/cloudera/parcels/CDH/lib/pig/piggybank.jar
```

To make our code less verbose, we create an alias for the `CustomFormatToISO` class's fully qualified Java name:

```
DEFINE CustomFormatToISO org.apache.pig.piggybank.evaluation.datetime.
convert.CustomFormatToISO();
```

By knowing how to manipulate timestamps, we can calculate statistics at different time intervals. For instance, we can look at how many tweets are created per hour. Pig has a built-in `GetHour` function that extracts the hour out of a `datetime` type. To use this, we first convert the timestamp string to ISO 8601 with `CustomFormatToISO` and then the resulting `chararray` to `datetime` using the built-in `ToDate` function, as follows:

```
hourly_tweets = FOREACH tweets {
  GENERATE
    GetHour(
      ToDate(
      CustomFormatToISO(
$0#'created_at', 'EEE MMMM d HH:mm:ss Z y')
      )
    ) as hour;
}
```

Now, it is just a matter of grouping `hourly_tweets` by hour and then generating a count of tweets per group, as follows:

```
hourly_tweets_count =  FOREACH (GROUP hourly_tweets BY hour) {
  GENERATE FLATTEN(group), COUNT(hourly_tweets);
}
```

Sessions

DataFu's `Sessionize` class can help us to better capture user activity over time. A session represents the activity of a user within a given period of time. For instance, we can look at each user's tweet stream at intervals of 15 minutes and measure these sessions to determine both network volumes as well as user activity:

```
DEFINE Sessionize datafu.pig.sessions.Sessionize('15m');
users_activity = FOREACH tweets {
    GENERATE
      CustomFormatToISO($0#'created_at',
                  'EEE MMMM d HH:mm:ss Z y') AS dt,
```

```
              (chararray)$0#'user'#'id' as user_id;
    }
    users_activity_sessionized = FOREACH
        (GROUP users_activity BY user_id) {
        ordered = ORDER users_activity BY dt;
        GENERATE FLATTEN(Sessionize(ordered))
                        AS (dt, user_id, session_id);
    }
```

`user_activity` simply records the time `dt` a given `user_id` posted a status update.

`Sessionize` takes the session timeout and a bag as input. The first element of the input bag is an ISO 8601 timestamp, and the bag must be sorted by this timestamp. Events that are within 15 minutes from each other will belong to the same session.

It returns the input bag with a new field, `session_id`, that uniquely identifies a session. With this data, we can calculate the session's length and some other statistics. More examples of `Sessionize` usage can be found at `http://datafu. incubator.apache.org/docs/datafu/guide/sessions.html`.

Capturing user interactions

In the remainder of the chapter, we will look at how to capture patterns from user interactions. As a first step in this direction, we will create a dataset suitable to model a social network. This dataset will contain a timestamp, the ID of the tweet, the user who posted the tweet, the user and tweet she's replying to, and the hashtag in the tweet.

Twitter considers as a reply (`in_reply_to_status_id_str`) any message beginning with the @ character. Such tweets are interpreted as a direct message to that person. Placing an @ character anywhere else in the tweet is interpreted as a mention (`'entities'#'user_mentions'`) and not a reply. The difference is that mentions are immediately broadcast to a person's followers, whereas replies are not. Replies are, however, considered as mentions.

When working with personally identifiable information, it is a good idea to anonymize if not remove entirely sensitive data such as IP addresses, names, and user IDs. A commonly used technique involves a `hash` function that takes as input the data we want to anonymize, concatenated with additional random data called salt. The following code shows an example of such anonymization:

```
DEFINE SHA datafu.pig.hash.SHA();
from_to_bag = FOREACH tweets {
```

```
      dt = $0#'created_at';
      user_id = (chararray)$0#'user'#'id';
      tweet_id = (chararray)$0#'id_str';
      reply_to_tweet = (chararray)$0#'in_reply_to_status_id_str';
      reply_to = (chararray)$0#'in_reply_to_user_id_str';
      place = $0#'place';
      topics = $0#'entities'#'hashtags';

      GENERATE
        CustomFormatToISO(dt, 'EEE MMMM d HH:mm:ss Z y') AS dt,
        SHA((chararray)CONCAT('SALT', user_id)) AS source,
        SHA(((chararray)CONCAT('SALT', tweet_id))) AS tweet_id,
        ((reply_to_tweet IS NULL)
             ? NULL
             : SHA((chararray)CONCAT('SALT', reply_to_tweet)))
                 AS  reply_to_tweet_id,
        ((reply_to IS NULL)
             ? NULL
             : SHA((chararray)CONCAT('SALT', reply_to)))
                  AS destination,
        (chararray)place#'country_code' as country,
        FLATTEN(topics) AS topic;
  }

  -- extract the hashtag text
  from_to = FOREACH from_to_bag {
    GENERATE
       dt,
       tweet_id,
       reply_to_tweet_id,
       source,
       destination,
       country,
       (chararray)topic#'text' AS topic;
  }
```

In this example, we use CONCAT to append a (not so random) salt string to personal data. We then generate a hash of the salted IDs with DataFu's SHA function. The SHA function requires its input parameters to be non null. We enforce this condition using if-then-else statements. In Pig Latin, this is expressed as <condition is true> ? <true branch> : <false branch>. If the string is null, we return NULL, and if not, we return the salted hash. To make code more readable, we use aliases for the tweet JSON fields and reference them in the GENERATE block.

Link analysis

We can redefine our approach to determine trending topics to include users' reactions. A first, naïve, approach could be to consider a topic as important if it caused a number of replies larger than a threshold value.

A problem with this approach is that tweets generate relatively few replies, so the volume of the resulting dataset will be low. Hence, it requires a very large amount of data to contain tweets being replied to and produce any result. In practice, we would likely want to combine this metric with other ones (for example, mentions) in order to perform more meaningful analyses.

To satisfy this query, we will create a new dataset that includes the hashtags extracted from both the tweet and the one a user is replying to:

```
tweet_hashtag = FOREACH from_to GENERATE tweet_id, topic;
from_to_self_joined = JOIN from_to BY reply_to_tweet_id LEFT,
tweet_hashtag BY tweet_id;

twitter_graph = FOREACH from_to_self_joined  {
    GENERATE
        from_to::dt AS dt,
        from_to::tweet_id AS tweet_id,
        from_to::reply_to_tweet_id AS reply_to_tweet_id,
        from_to::source AS source,
        from_to::destination AS destination,
        from_to::topic AS topic,
        from_to::country AS country,
        tweet_hashtag::topic AS topic_replied;
}
```

Note that Pig does not allow a cross join on the same relation, hence we have to create `tweet_hashtag` for the right-hand side of the join. Here, we use the `::` operator to disambiguate from which relation and column we want to select records.

Once again, we can look for the top 10 topics by number of replies using the `top_n` macro:

```
top_10_topics = top_n(twitter_graph, topic_replied, 10);
```

Counting things will only take us so far. We can compute more descriptive statistics on this dataset with DataFu. Using the `Quantile` function, we can calculate the median, the 90th, 95th, and the 99th percentiles of the number of hashtag reactions, as follows:

```
DEFINE Quantile datafu.pig.stats.Quantile('0.5','0.90','0.95','0.99');
```

Since the UDF expects an ordered bag of integer values as input, we first count the frequency of each `topic_replied` entry, as follows.

```
topics_with_replies_grpd = GROUP twitter_graph BY topic_replied;
topics_with_replies_cnt = FOREACH topics_with_replies_grpd {
  GENERATE
COUNT(twitter_graph) as cnt;
}
```

Then, we apply `Quantile` on the bag of frequencies, as follows:

```
quantiles = FOREACH (GROUP topics_with_replies_cnt ALL) {
    sorted = ORDER topics_with_replies_cnt BY cnt;
    GENERATE Quantile(sorted);
}
```

The source code for this example can be found at `https://github.com/learninghadoop2/book-examples/blob/master/ch6/graph.pig`.

Influential users

We will use PageRank, an algorithm developed by Google to rank web pages (`http://ilpubs.stanford.edu:8090/422/1/1999-66.pdf`), to identify influential users in the Twitter graph we generated in the previous section.

This type of analysis has a number of use cases, such as targeted and contextual advertisement, recommendation systems, spam detection, and obviously measuring the importance of web pages. A similar approach, used by Twitter to implement the Who to Follow feature, is described in the research paper *WTF: The Who to Follow service at Twitter* found at `http://stanford.edu/~rezab/papers/wtf_overview.pdf`.

Informally, PageRank determines the importance of a page based on the importance of other pages linking to it and assigns it a score between 0 and 1. A high PageRank score indicates that a lot of pages point to it. Intuitively, being linked by pages with a high PageRank is a quality endorsement. In terms of the Twitter graph, we assume that users receiving a lot of replies are important or influential within the social network. In Twitter's case, we consider an extended definition of PageRank, where the link between two users is given by a direct reply and labeled by any eventual hashtag present in the message. Heuristically, we want to identify influential users on a given topic.

In DataFu's implementation, each graph is represented as a bag of (source, edges) tuples. The source tuple is an integer ID representing the source node. The edges are a bag of (destination, weight) tuples. destination is an integer ID representing the destination node. weight is a double representing how much the edge should be weighted. The output of the UDF is a bag of (source, rank) pairs, where rank is the PageRank value for the source user in the graph. Notice that we talked about nodes, edges, and graphs as abstract concepts. In Google's case, nodes are web pages, edges are links from one page to the other, and graphs are groups of pages connected directly and indirectly.

In our case, nodes represent users, edges represent in_reply_to_user_id_str mentions, and edges are labeled by hashtags in tweets. The output of PageRank should suggest which users are influential on a given topic given their interaction patterns.

In this section, we will write a pipeline to:

- Represent data as a graph where each node is a user and a hashtag labels the edge
- Map IDs and hashtags to integers so that they can be consumed by PageRank
- Apply PageRank
- Store the results into HDFS in an interoperable format (Avro)

We represent the graph as a bag of tuples in the form (source, destination, topic), where each tuple represents the interaction between nodes. The source code for this example can be found at https://github.com/learninghadoop2/book-examples/blob/master/ch6/pagerank.pig.

We will map users' and hashtags' text to numerical IDs. We use the Java String hashCode() method to perform this conversion step and wrap the logic in an Eval UDF.

 The size of an integer is effectively the upper bound for the number of nodes and edges in the graph. For production code, it is recommended that you use a more robust hash function.

The StringToInt class takes a string as input, calls the hashCode() method, and returns the method output to Pig. The UDF code can be found at https://github.com/learninghadoop2/book-examples/blob/master/ch6/udf/com/learninghadoop2/pig/udf/StringToInt.java.

```
package com.learninghadoop2.pig.udf;
import java.io.IOException;
import org.apache.pig.EvalFunc;
```

```
import org.apache.pig.data.Tuple;

public class StringToInt extends EvalFunc<Integer> {
    public Integer exec(Tuple input) throws IOException {
        if (input == null || input.size() == 0)
            return null;
        try {
            String str = (String) input.get(0);
            return str.hashCode();
        } catch(Exception e) {
          throw
            new IOException("Cannot convert String to Int", e);
        }
    }
}
```

We extend `org.apache.pig.EvalFunc` and override the `exec` method to return `str.hashCode()` on the function input. The `EvalFunc<Integer>` class is parameterized with the return type of the UDF (`Integer`).

Next, we compile the class and archive it into a JAR, as follows:

```
$ javac -classpath /opt/cloudera/parcels/CDH/lib/pig/pig.jar:$(hadoop
classpath) com/learninghadoop2/pig/udf/StringToInt.java
$ jar cvf myudfs-pig.jar com/learninghadoop2/pig/udf/StringToInt.class
```

We can now register the UDF in Pig and create an alias to `StringToInt`, as follows:

```
REGISTER myudfs-pig.jar
DEFINE StringToInt com.learninghadoop2.pig.udf.StringToInt();
```

We filter out tweets with no `destination` and no `topic`, as follows:

```
tweets_graph_filtered = FILTER twitter_graph by
(destination IS NOT NULL) AND
(topic IS NOT null);
```

Then, we convert the `source`, `destination`, and `topic` to integer IDs:

```
from_to = foreach tweets_graph_filtered {
  GENERATE
    StringToInt(source) as source_id,
    StringToInt(destination) as destination_id,
    StringToInt(topic) as topic_id;
}
```

Once data is in the appropriate format, we can reuse the implementation of PageRank and the example code (found at `https://github.com/apache/incubator-datafu/blob/master/datafu-pig/src/main/java/datafu/pig/linkanalysis/PageRank.java`) provided by DataFu, as shown in the following code:

```
DEFINE PageRank datafu.pig.linkanalysis.PageRank('dangling_
nodes','true');
```

We begin by creating a bag of (`source_id`, `destination_id`, `topic_id`) tuples, as follows:

```
reply_to = group from_to by (source_id, destination_id, topic_id);
```

We count the occurrences of each tuple, that is, how many times two people talked about a topic, as follows:

```
topic_edges = foreach reply_to {
  GENERATE flatten(group), ((double)COUNT(from_to.topic_id)) as w;
}
```

Remember that topic is the edge of our graph; we begin by creating an association between the source node and the topic edge, as follows:

```
topic_edges_grouped = GROUP topic_edges by (topic_id, source_id);
```

Then we regroup it with the purpose of adding a destination node and the edge weight, as follows:

```
topic_edges_grouped = FOREACH topic_edges_grouped {
  GENERATE
    group.topic_id as topic,
    group.source_id as source,
    topic_edges.(destination_id,w) as edges;
}
```

Once we create the Twitter graph, we calculate the PageRank of all users (`source_id`):

```
topic_rank = FOREACH (GROUP topic_edges_grouped BY topic) {
  GENERATE
    group as topic,
    FLATTEN(PageRank(topic_edges_grouped.(source,edges))) as
(source,rank);
}
topic_rank = FOREACH topic_rank GENERATE topic, source, rank;
```

We store the result in HDFS in Avro format. If Avro dependencies are not present in the classpath, we need to add the Avro MapReduce jar file to our environment before accessing individual fields. Within Pig, for example, on the Cloudera CDH5 VM:

```
REGISTER /opt/cloudera/parcels/CDH/lib/avro/avro.jar
REGISTER /opt/cloudera/parcels/CDH/lib/avro/avro-mapred-hadoop2.jar
STORE topic_rank INTO 'replies-pagerank' using AvroStorage();
```

In these last two sections, we made a number of implicit assumptions on what a Twitter graph might look like and what the concepts of topic and user interaction mean. Given the constraints that we posed, the resulting social network we analyzed will be relatively small and not necessarily representative of the entire Twitter social network. Extrapolating results from this dataset is discouraged. In practice, there are many other factors that should be taken into account to generate a robust model of social interaction.

Summary

In this chapter, we introduced Apache Pig, a platform for large-scale data analysis on Hadoop. In particular, we covered the following topics:

- The goals of Pig as a way of providing a dataflow-like abstraction that does not require hands-on MapReduce development

- How Pig's approach to processing data compares to SQL, where Pig is procedural while SQL is declarative

- Getting started with Pig — an easy task, as it is a library that generates custom code and doesn't require additional services

- An overview of the data types, core functions, and extension mechanisms provided by Pig

- Examples of applying Pig to analyze the Twitter dataset in detail, which demonstrated its ability to express complex concepts in a very concise fashion

- How libraries such as Piggybank, Elephant Bird, and DataFu provide repositories for numerous useful prewritten Pig functions

- In the next chapter, we will revisit the SQL comparison by exploring tools that expose a SQL-like abstraction over data stored in HDFS

7
Hadoop and SQL

MapReduce is a powerful paradigm that enables complex data processing that can reveal valuable insights. As discussed in earlier chapters however, it does require a different mindset and some training and experience on the model of breaking processing analytics into a series of map and reduce steps. There are several products that are built atop Hadoop to provide higher-level or more familiar views of the data held within HDFS, and Pig is a very popular one. This chapter will explore the other most common abstraction implemented atop Hadoop: SQL.

In this chapter, we will cover the following topics:

- What the use cases for SQL on Hadoop are and why it is so popular
- HiveQL, the SQL dialect introduced by Apache Hive
- Using HiveQL to perform SQL-like analysis of the Twitter dataset
- How HiveQL can approximate common features of relational databases such as joins and views
- How HiveQL allows the incorporation of user-defined functions into its queries
- How SQL on Hadoop complements Pig
- Other SQL-on-Hadoop products such as Impala and how they differ from Hive

Why SQL on Hadoop

So far we have seen how to write Hadoop programs using the MapReduce APIs and how Pig Latin provides a scripting abstraction and a wrapper for custom business logic by means of UDFs. Pig is a very powerful tool, but its dataflow-based programming model is not familiar to most developers or business analysts. The traditional tool of choice for such people to explore data is SQL.

Back in 2008 Facebook released Hive, the first widely used implementation of SQL on Hadoop.

Instead of providing a way of more quickly developing map and reduce tasks, Hive offers an implementation of *HiveQL*, a query language based on SQL. Hive takes HiveQL statements and immediately and automatically translates the queries into one or more MapReduce jobs. It then executes the overall MapReduce program and returns the results to the user.

This interface to Hadoop not only reduces the time required to produce results from data analysis, it also significantly widens the net as to who can use Hadoop. Instead of requiring software development skills, anyone who's familiar with SQL can use Hive.

The combination of these attributes is that HiveQL is often used as a tool for business and data analysts to perform ad hoc queries on the data stored on HDFS. With Hive, the data analyst can work on refining queries without the involvement of a software developer. Just as with Pig, Hive also allows HiveQL to be extended by means of User Defined Functions, enabling the base SQL dialect to be customized with business-specific functionality.

Other SQL-on-Hadoop solutions

Though Hive was the first product to introduce and support HiveQL, it is no longer the only one. Later in this chapter, we will also discuss Impala, released in 2013 and already a very popular tool, particularly for low-latency queries. There are others, but we will mostly discuss Hive and Impala as they have been the most successful.

While introducing the core features and capabilities of SQL on Hadoop however, we will give examples using Hive; even though Hive and Impala share many SQL features, they also have numerous differences. We don't want to constantly have to caveat each new feature with exactly how it is supported in Hive compared to Impala. We'll generally be looking at aspects of the feature set that are common to both, but if you use both products, it's important to read the latest release notes to understand the differences.

Prerequisites

Before diving into specific technologies, let's generate some data that we'll use in the examples throughout this chapter. We'll create a modified version of a former Pig script as the main functionality for this. The script in this chapter assumes that the Elephant Bird JARs used previously are available in the /jar directory on HDFS. The full source code is at https://github.com/learninghadoop2/book-examples/blob/master/ch7/extract_for_hive.pig, but the core of extract_for_hive.pig is as follows:

```
-- load JSON data
tweets = load '$inputDir' using  com.twitter.elephantbird.pig.load.
JsonLoader('-nestedLoad');
-- Tweets
tweets_tsv = foreach tweets {
generate
    (chararray)CustomFormatToISO($0#'created_at',
'EEE MMMM d HH:mm:ss Z y') as dt,
    (chararray)$0#'id_str',
(chararray)$0#'text' as text,
    (chararray)$0#'in_reply_to',
(boolean)$0#'retweeted' as is_retweeted,
(chararray)$0#'user'#'id_str' as user_id, (chararray)$0#'place'#'id'
as place_id;
}
store tweets_tsv into '$outputDir/tweets'
using PigStorage('\u0001');
-- Places
needed_fields = foreach tweets {
   generate
(chararray)CustomFormatToISO($0#'created_at',
'EEE MMMM d HH:mm:ss Z y') as dt,
     (chararray)$0#'id_str' as id_str,
$0#'place' as place;
}
place_fields = foreach needed_fields {
generate
    (chararray)place#'id' as place_id,
    (chararray)place#'country_code' as co,
    (chararray)place#'country' as country,
    (chararray)place#'name' as place_name,
    (chararray)place#'full_name' as place_full_name,
    (chararray)place#'place_type' as place_type;
}
filtered_places = filter place_fields by co != '';
```

```
unique_places = distinct filtered_places;
store unique_places into '$outputDir/places'
using PigStorage('\u0001');

-- Users
users = foreach tweets {
   generate
(chararray)CustomFormatToISO($0#'created_at',
'EEE MMMM d HH:mm:ss Z y') as dt,
(chararray)$0#'id_str' as id_str,
$0#'user' as user;
}
user_fields = foreach users {
   generate
     (chararray)CustomFormatToISO(user#'created_at',
'EEE MMMM d HH:mm:ss Z y') as dt,
  (chararray)user#'id_str' as user_id,
  (chararray)user#'location' as user_location,
  (chararray)user#'name' as user_name,
  (chararray)user#'description' as user_description,
  (int)user#'followers_count' as followers_count,
  (int)user#'friends_count' as friends_count,
  (int)user#'favourites_count' as favourites_count,
  (chararray)user#'screen_name' as screen_name,
  (int)user#'listed_count' as listed_count;

}
unique_users = distinct user_fields;
store unique_users into '$outputDir/users'
using PigStorage('\u0001');
```

Run this script as follows:

```
$ pig -f extract_for_hive.pig –param inputDir=<json input> -param
outputDir=<output path>
```

The preceding code writes data into three separate TSV files for the tweet, user, and place information. Notice that in the store command, we pass an argument when calling PigStorage. This single argument changes the default field separator from a tab character to unicode value U0001, or you can also use *Ctrl +C + A*. This is often used as a separator in Hive tables and will be particularly useful to us as our tweet data could contain tabs in other fields.

Overview of Hive

We will now show how you can import data into Hive and run a query against the table abstraction Hive provides over the data. In this example, and in the remainder of the chapter, we will assume that queries are typed into the shell that can be invoked by executing the `hive` command.

Recently a client called Beeline also became available and will likely be the preferred CLI client in the near future.

When importing any new data into Hive, there is generally a three-stage process:

- Create the specification of the table into which the data is to be imported
- Import the data into the created table
- Execute HiveQL queries against the table

Most of the HiveQL statements are direct analogues to similarly named statements in standard SQL. We assume only a passing knowledge of SQL throughout this chapter, but if you need a refresher, there are numerous good online learning resources.

Hive gives a structured query view of our data, and to enable that, we must first define the specification of the table's columns and import the data into the table before we can execute any queries. A table specification is generated using a CREATE statement that specifies the table name, the name and types of its columns, and some metadata about how the table is stored:

```
CREATE table tweets (
created_at string,
tweet_id string,
text string,
in_reply_to string,
retweeted boolean,
user_id string,
place_id string
) ROW FORMAT DELIMITED
FIELDS TERMINATED BY '\u0001'
STORED AS TEXTFILE;
```

The statement creates a new table `tweets` defined by a list of names for columns in the dataset and their data type. We specify that fields are delimited by the Unicode U0001 character and that the format used to store data is TEXTFILE.

Data can be imported from a location in HDFS `tweets/` using the LOAD DATA statement:

```
LOAD DATA INPATH 'tweets' OVERWRITE INTO TABLE tweets;
```

By default, data for Hive tables is stored on HDFS under `/user/hive/warehouse`. If a LOAD statement is given a path to data on HDFS, it will not simply copy the data into `/user/hive/warehouse`, but will move it there instead. If you want to analyze data on HDFS that is used by other applications, then either create a copy or use the EXTERNAL mechanism that will be described later.

Once data has been imported into Hive, we can run queries against it. For instance:

```
SELECT COUNT(*) FROM tweets;
```

The preceding code will return the total number of tweets present in the dataset. HiveQL, like SQL, is not case sensitive in terms of keywords, columns, or table names. By convention, SQL statements use uppercase for SQL language keywords, and we will generally follow this when using HiveQL within files, as will be shown later. However, when typing interactive commands, we will frequently take the line of least resistance and use lowercase.

If you look closely at the time taken by the various commands in the preceding example, you'll notice that loading data into a table takes about as long as creating the table specification, but even the simple count of all rows takes significantly longer. The output also shows that table creation and the loading of data do not actually cause MapReduce jobs to be executed, which explains the very short execution times.

The nature of Hive tables

Although Hive copies the data file into its working directory, it does not actually process the input data into rows at that point.

Both the CREATE TABLE and LOAD DATA statements do not truly create concrete table data as such; instead, they produce the metadata that will be used when Hive generates MapReduce jobs to access the data conceptually stored in the table but actually residing on HDFS. Even though the HiveQL statements refer to a specific table structure, it is Hive's responsibility to generate code that correctly maps this to the actual on-disk format in which the data files are stored.

This might seem to suggest that Hive isn't a *real* database; this is true, it isn't. Whereas a relational database will require a table schema to be defined before data is ingested and then ingest only data that conforms to that specification, Hive is much more flexible. The less concrete nature of Hive tables means that schemas can be defined based on the data as it has already arrived and not on some assumption of how the data should be, which might prove to be wrong. Though changeable data formats are troublesome regardless of technology, the Hive model provides an additional degree of freedom in handling the problem when, not if, it arises.

Hive architecture

Until version 2, Hadoop was primarily a batch system. As we saw in previous chapters, MapReduce jobs tend to have high latency and overhead derived from submission and scheduling. Internally, Hive compiles HiveQL statements into MapReduce jobs. Hive queries have traditionally been characterized by high latency. This has changed with the Stinger initiative and the improvements introduced in Hive 0.13 that we will discuss later.

Hive runs as a client application that processes HiveQL queries, converts them into MapReduce jobs, and submits these to a Hadoop cluster either to native MapReduce in Hadoop 1 or to the MapReduce Application Master running on YARN in Hadoop 2.

Regardless of the model, Hive uses a component called the metastore, in which it holds all its metadata about the tables defined in the system. Ironically, this is stored in a relational database dedicated to Hive's usage. In the earliest versions of Hive, all clients communicated directly with the metastore, but this meant that every user of the Hive CLI tool needed to know the metastore username and password.

HiveServer was created to act as a point of entry for remote clients, which could also act as a single access-control point and which controlled all access to the underlying metastore. Because of limitations in HiveServer, the newest way to access Hive is through the multi-client HiveServer2.

HiveServer2 introduces a number of improvements over its predecessor, including user authentication and support for multiple connections from the same client. More information can be found at `https://cwiki.apache.org/confluence/display/Hive/Setting+Up+HiveServer2`.

Instances of `HiveServer` and `HiveServer2` can be manually executed with the `hive --service hiveserver` and `hive --service hiveserver2` commands, respectively.

In the examples we saw before and in the remainder of this chapter, we implicitly use HiveServer to submit queries via the Hive command-line tool. HiveServer2 comes with Beeline. For compatibility and maturity reasons, Beeline being relatively new, both tools are available on Cloudera and most other major distributions. The Beeline client is part of the core Apache Hive distribution and so is also fully open source. Beeline can be executed in embedded version with the following command:

```
$ beeline -u jdbc:hive2://
```

Data types

HiveQL supports many of the common data types provided by standard database systems. These include primitive types, such as `float`, `double`, `int`, and `string`, through to structured collection types that provide the SQL analogues to types such as `arrays`, `structs`, and `unions` (`structs` with options for some fields). Since Hive is implemented in Java, primitive types will behave like their Java counterparts. We can distinguish Hive data types into the following five broad categories:

- **Numeric**: `tinyint`, `smallint`, `int`, `bigint`, `float`, `double`, and `decimal`
- **Date and time**: `timestamp` and `date`
- **String**: `string`, `varchar`, and `char`
- **Collections**: `array`, `map`, `struct`, and `uniontype`
- **Misc**: `boolean`, `binary`, and `NULL`

DDL statements

HiveQL provides a number of statements to create, delete, and alter databases, tables, and views. The `CREATE DATABASE <name>` statement creates a new database with the given name. A database represents a namespace where table and view metadata is contained. If multiple databases are present, the `USE <database name>` statement specifies which one to use to query tables or create new metadata. If no database is explicitly specified, Hive will run all statements against the `default` database. `SHOW [DATABASES, TABLES, VIEWS]` displays the databases currently available within a data warehouse and which table and view metadata is present within the database currently in use:

```
CREATE DATABASE twitter;
SHOW databases;
USE twitter;
SHOW TABLES;
```

The CREATE TABLE [IF NOT EXISTS] <name> statement creates a table with the given name. As alluded to earlier, what is really created is the metadata representing the table and its mapping to files on HDFS as well as a directory in which to store the data files. If a table or view with the same name already exists, Hive will raise an exception.

Both table and column names are case insensitive. In older versions of Hive (0.12 and earlier), only alphanumeric and underscore characters were allowed in table and column names. As of Hive 0.13, the system supports unicode characters in column names. Reserved words, such as load and create, need to be escaped by backticks (the ` character) to be treated literally.

The EXTERNAL keyword specifies that the table exists in resources out of Hive's control, which can be a useful mechanism to extract data from another source at the beginning of a Hadoop-based **Extract-Transform-Load** (ETL) pipeline. The LOCATION clause specifies where the source file (or directory) is to be found. The EXTERNAL keyword and LOCATION clause have been used in the following code:

```
CREATE EXTERNAL TABLE tweets (
created_at string,
tweet_id string,
text string,
in_reply_to string,
retweeted boolean,
user_id string,
place_id string
) ROW FORMAT DELIMITED
FIELDS TERMINATED BY '\u0001'
STORED AS TEXTFILE
LOCATION '${input}/tweets';
```

This table will be created in the metastore but the data will not be copied into the /user/hive/warehouse directory.

 Note that Hive has no concept of primary key or unique identifier. Uniqueness and data normalization are aspects to be addressed before loading data into the data warehouse.

The `CREATE VIEW <view name>` ... `AS SELECT` statement creates a view with the given name. For example, we can create a view to isolate retweets from other messages, as follows:

```
CREATE VIEW retweets
COMMENT 'Tweets that have been retweeted'
AS SELECT * FROM tweets WHERE retweeted = true;
```

Unless otherwise specified, column names are derived from the defining `SELECT` statement. Hive does not currently support materialized views.

The `DROP TABLE` and `DROP VIEW` statements remove both metadata and data for a given table or view. When dropping an `EXTERNAL` table or a view, only metadata will be removed and the actual data files will not be affected.

Hive allows table metadata to be altered via the `ALTER TABLE` statement, which can be used to change a column type, name, position, and comment or to add and replace columns.

When adding columns, it is important to remember that only metadata will be changed and not the dataset itself. This means that if we were to add a column in the middle of the table which didn't exist in older files, then while selecting from older data, we might get wrong values in the wrong columns. This is because we would be looking at old files with a new format. We will discuss data and schema migrations in *Chapter 8, Data Lifecycle Management*, when discussing Avro.

Similarly, `ALTER VIEW <view name> AS <select statement>` changes the definition of an existing view.

File formats and storage

The data files underlying a Hive table are no different from any other file on HDFS. Users can directly read the HDFS files in the Hive tables using other tools. They can also use other tools to write to HDFS files that can be loaded into Hive through `CREATE EXTERNAL TABLE` or through `LOAD DATA INPATH`.

Hive uses the `Serializer` and `Deserializer` classes, SerDe, as well as `FileFormat` to read and write table rows. A native SerDe is used if `ROW FORMAT` is not specified or `ROW FORMAT DELIMITED` is specified in a `CREATE TABLE` statement. The `DELIMITED` clause instructs the system to read delimited files. Delimiter characters can be escaped using the `ESCAPED BY` clause.

Hive currently uses the following `FileFormat` classes to read and write HDFS files:

- `TextInputFormat` and `HiveIgnoreKeyTextOutputFormat`: will read/write data in plain text file format

- `SequenceFileInputFormat` and `SequenceFileOutputFormat`: classes read/write data in the Hadoop `SequenceFile` format

Additionally, the following SerDe classes can be used to serialize and deserialize data:

- `MetadataTypedColumnsetSerDe`: will read/write delimited records such as CSV or tab-separated records

- `ThriftSerDe`, and `DynamicSerDe`: will read/write Thrift objects

JSON

As of version 0.13, Hive ships with the native `org.apache.hive.hcatalog.data.JsonSerDe`. For older versions of Hive, Hive-JSON-Serde (found at `https://github.com/rcongiu/Hive-JSON-Serde`) is arguably one of the most feature-rich JSON serialization/deserialization modules.

We can use either module to load JSON tweets without any need for preprocessing and just define a Hive schema that matches the content of a JSON document. In the following example, we use Hive-JSON-Serde.

As with any third-party module, we load the SerDe JARs into Hive with the following code:

```
ADD JAR JAR json-serde-1.3-jar-with-dependencies.jar;
```

Then, we issue the usual `CREATE` statement, as follows:

```
CREATE EXTERNAL TABLE tweets (
   contributors string,
   coordinates struct <
      coordinates: array <float>,
      type: string>,
   created_at string,
   entities struct <
      hashtags: array <struct <
            indices: array <tinyint>,
            text: string>>,
   ...
   )
```

```
ROW FORMAT SERDE 'org.openx.data.jsonserde.JsonSerDe'
STORED AS TEXTFILE
LOCATION 'tweets';
```

With this SerDe, we can map nested documents (such as entities or users) to the `struct` or `map` types. We tell Hive that the data stored at `LOCATION 'tweets'` is text (`STORED AS TEXTFILE`) and that each row is a JSON object (`ROW FORMAT SERDE 'org.openx.data.jsonserde.JsonSerDe'`). In Hive 0.13 and later, we can express this property as `ROW FORMAT SERDE 'org.apache.hive.hcatalog.data.JsonSerDe'`.

Manually specifying the schema for complex documents can be a tedious and error-prone process. The `hive-json` module (found at `https://github.com/hortonworks/hive-json`) is a handy utility to analyze large documents and generate an appropriate Hive schema. Depending on the document collection, further refinement might be necessary.

In our example, we used a schema generated with `hive-json` that maps the tweets JSON to a number of `struct` data types. This allows us to query the data using a handy dot notation. For instance, we can extract the screen name and description fields of a user object with the following code:

```
SELECT user.screen_name, user.description FROM tweets_json LIMIT 10;
```

Avro

AvroSerde (`https://cwiki.apache.org/confluence/display/Hive/AvroSerDe`) allows us to read and write data in Avro format. Starting from 0.14, Avro-backed tables can be created using the `STORED AS AVRO` statement, and Hive will take care of creating an appropriate Avro schema for the table. Prior versions of Hive are a bit more verbose.

As an example, let's load into Hive the PageRank dataset we generated in *Chapter 6, Data Analysis with Apache Pig*. This dataset was created using Pig's `AvroStorage` class, and has the following schema:

```
{
  "type":"record",
  "name":"record",
  "fields": [
    {"name":"topic","type":["null","int"]},
    {"name":"source","type":["null","int"]},
    {"name":"rank","type":["null","float"]}
  ]
}
```

The table structure is captured in an Avro record, which contains header information (a name and optional namespace to qualify the name) and an array of the fields. Each field is specified with its name and type as well as an optional documentation string.

For a few of the fields, the type is not a single value, but instead a pair of values, one of which is null. This is an Avro union, and this is the idiomatic way of handling columns that might have a null value. Avro specifies null as a concrete type, and any location where another type might have a null value needs to be specified in this way. This will be handled transparently for us when we use the following schema.

With this definition, we can now create a Hive table that uses this schema for its table specification, as follows:

```
CREATE EXTERNAL TABLE tweets_pagerank
ROW FORMAT SERDE
    'org.apache.hadoop.hive.serde2.avro.AvroSerDe'
WITH SERDEPROPERTIES ('avro.schema.literal'='{
    "type":"record",
    "name":"record",
    "fields": [
        {"name":"topic","type":["null","int"]},
        {"name":"source","type":["null","int"]},
        {"name":"rank","type":["null","float"]}
    ]
}')
STORED AS INPUTFORMAT
    'org.apache.hadoop.hive.ql.io.avro.AvroContainerInputFormat'
OUTPUTFORMAT
    'org.apache.hadoop.hive.ql.io.avro.AvroContainerOutputFormat'
LOCATION '${data}/ch5-pagerank';
```

Then, look at the following table definition from within Hive (note also that HCatalog, which we'll introduce in *Chapter 8*, *Data Life Cycle Management*, also supports such definitions):

```
DESCRIBE tweets_pagerank;
OK
topic                   int                    from deserializer
source                  int                    from deserializer
rank                    float                  from deserializer
```

In the DDL, we told Hive that data is stored in Avro format using `AvroContainerInputFormat` and `AvroContainerOutputFormat`. Each row needs to be serialized and deserialized using `org.apache.hadoop.hive.serde2.avro.AvroSerDe`. The table schema is inferred by Hive from the Avro schema embedded in `avro.schema.literal`.

Alternatively, we can store a schema on HDFS and have Hive read it to determine the table structure. Create the preceding schema in a file called `pagerank.avsc` — this is the standard file extension for Avro schemas. Then place it on HDFS; we prefer to have a common location for schema files such as `/schema/avro`. Finally, define the table using the `avro.schema.url` SerDe property `WITH SERDEPROPERTIES ('avro.schema.url'='hdfs://<namenode>/schema/avro/pagerank.avsc')`.

If Avro dependencies are not present in the classpath, we need to add the Avro `MapReduce` JAR to our environment before accessing individual fields. Within Hive, on the Cloudera CDH5 VM:

```
ADD JAR /opt/cloudera/parcels/CDH/lib/avro/avro-mapred-hadoop2.jar;
```

We can also use this table like any other. For instance, we can query the data to select the user and topic pairs with a high PageRank:

```
SELECT source, topic from tweets_pagerank WHERE rank >= 0.9;
```

In *Chapter 8, Data Lifecycle Management*, we will see how Avro and `avro.schema.url` play an instrumental role in enabling schema migrations.

Columnar stores

Hive can also take advantage of columnar storage via the ORC (`https://cwiki.apache.org/confluence/display/Hive/LanguageManual+ORC`) and Parquet (`https://cwiki.apache.org/confluence/display/Hive/Parquet`) formats.

If a table is defined with very many columns, it is not unusual for any given query to only process a small subset of these columns. But even in a SequenceFile each full row and all its columns will be read from disk, decompressed, and processed. This consumes a lot of system resources for data that we know in advance is not of interest.

Traditional relational databases also store data on a row basis, and a type of database called **columnar** changed this to be column-focused. In the simplest model, instead of one file for each table, there would be one file for each column in the table. If a query only needed to access five columns in a table with 100 columns in total, then only the files for those five columns will be read. Both ORC and Parquet use this principle as well as other optimizations to enable much faster queries.

Queries

Tables can be queried using the familiar `SELECT ... FROM` statement. The `WHERE` statement allows the specification of filtering conditions, `GROUP BY` aggregates records, `ORDER BY` specifies sorting criteria, and `LIMIT` specifies the number of records to retrieve. Aggregate functions, such as `count` and `sum`, can be applied to aggregated records. For instance, the following code returns the top 10 most prolific users in the dataset:

```
SELECT user_id, COUNT(*) AS cnt FROM tweets GROUP BY user_id ORDER BY
cnt DESC LIMIT 10
```

This returns the top 10 most prolific users in the dataset:

2263949659 4

1332188053 4

959468857 3

1367752118 3

362562944 3

58646041 3

2375296688 3

1468188529 3

37114209 3

2385040940 3

We can improve the readability of the `hive` output by setting the following:

```
SET hive.cli.print.header=true;
```

This will instruct `hive`, though not `beeline`, to print column names as part of the output.

 You can add the command to the .hiverc file usually found in the root of the executing user's home directory to have it apply to all hive CLI sessions.

HiveQL implements a JOIN operator that enables us to combine tables together. In the *Prerequisites* section, we generated separate datasets for the user and place objects. Let's now load them into hive using external tables.

We first create a user table to store user data, as follows:

```
CREATE EXTERNAL TABLE user (
created_at string,
user_id string,
`location` string,
name string,
description string,
followers_count bigint,
friends_count bigint,
favourites_count bigint,
screen_name string,
listed_count bigint
) ROW FORMAT DELIMITED
FIELDS TERMINATED BY '\u0001'
STORED AS TEXTFILE
LOCATION '${input}/users';
```

We then create a place table to store location data, as follows:

```
CREATE EXTERNAL TABLE place (
place_id string,
country_code string,
country string,
`name` string,
full_name string,
place_type string
) ROW FORMAT DELIMITED
FIELDS TERMINATED BY '\u0001'
STORED AS TEXTFILE
LOCATION '${input}/places';
```

We can use the JOIN operator to display the names of the 10 most prolific users, as follows:

```
SELECT tweets.user_id, user.name, COUNT(tweets.user_id) AS cnt
FROM tweets
JOIN user ON user.user_id  = tweets.user_id
GROUP BY tweets.user_id, user.user_id, user.name
ORDER BY cnt DESC LIMIT 10;
```

Only equality, outer, and left (semi) joins are supported in Hive.

Notice that there might be multiple entries with a given user ID but different values for the `followers_count`, `friends_count`, and `favourites_count` columns. To avoid duplicate entries, we count only `user_id` from the `tweets` table.

We can rewrite the previous query as follows:

```
SELECT tweets.user_id, u.name, COUNT(*) AS cnt
FROM tweets
join (SELECT user_id, name FROM user GROUP BY user_id, name) u
ON u.user_id = tweets.user_id
GROUP BY tweets.user_id, u.name
ORDER BY cnt DESC LIMIT 10;
```

Instead of directly joining the `user` table, we execute a subquery, as follows:

```
SELECT user_id, name FROM user GROUP BY user_id, name;
```

The subquery extracts unique user IDs and names. Note that Hive has limited support for subqueries, historically only permitting a subquery in the `FROM` clause of a `SELECT` statement. Hive 0.13 has added limited support for subqueries within the `WHERE` clause also.

HiveQL is an ever-evolving rich language, a full exposition of which is beyond the scope of this chapter. A description of its query and ddl capabilities can be found at `https://cwiki.apache.org/confluence/display/Hive/LanguageManual`.

Structuring Hive tables for given workloads

Often Hive isn't used in isolation, instead tables are created with particular workloads in mind or needs invoked in ways that are suitable for inclusion in automated processes. We'll now explore some of these scenarios.

Partitioning a table

With columnar file formats, we explained the benefits of excluding unneeded data as early as possible when processing a query. A similar concept has been used in SQL for some time: table partitioning.

When creating a partitioned table, a column is specified as the partition key. All values with that key are then stored together. In Hive's case, different subdirectories for each partition key are created under the table directory in the warehouse location on HDFS.

It's important to understand the cardinality of the partition column. With too few distinct values, the benefits are reduced as the files are still very large. If there are too many values, then queries might need a large number of files to be scanned to access all the required data. Perhaps the most common partition key is one based on date. We could, for example, partition our `user` table from earlier based on the `created_at` column, that is, the date the user was first registered. Note that since partitioning a table by definition affects its file structure, we create this table now as a non-external one, as follows:

```
CREATE TABLE partitioned_user (
created_at string,
user_id string,
`location` string,
name string,
description string,
followers_count bigint,
friends_count bigint,
favourites_count bigint,
screen_name string,
listed_count bigint
)  PARTITIONED BY (created_at_date string)
ROW FORMAT DELIMITED
FIELDS TERMINATED BY '\u0001'
STORED AS TEXTFILE;
```

To load data into a partition, we can explicitly give a value for the partition into which to insert the data, as follows:

```
INSERT INTO TABLE partitioned_user
PARTITION( created_at_date = '2014-01-01')
SELECT
created_at,
user_id,
location,
name,
description,
followers_count,
friends_count,
```

```
favourites_count,
screen_name,
listed_count
FROM user;
```

This is at best verbose, as we need a statement for each partition key value; if a single LOAD or INSERT statement contains data for multiple partitions, it just won't work. Hive also has a feature called dynamic partitioning, which can help us here. We set the following three variables:

```
SET hive.exec.dynamic.partition = true;
SET hive.exec.dynamic.partition.mode = nonstrict;
SET hive.exec.max.dynamic.partitions.pernode=5000;
```

The first two statements enable all partitions (nonstrict option) to be dynamic. The third one allows 5,000 distinct partitions to be created on each mapper and reducer node.

We can then simply use the name of the column to be used as the partition key, and Hive will insert data into partitions depending on the value of the key for a given row:

```
INSERT INTO TABLE partitioned_user
PARTITION( created_at_date )
SELECT
created_at,
user_id,
location,
name,
description,
followers_count,
friends_count,
favourites_count,
screen_name,
listed_count,
to_date(created_at) as created_at_date
FROM user;
```

Even though we use only a single partition column here, we can partition a table by multiple column keys; just have them as a comma-separated list in the PARTITIONED BY clause.

Note that the partition key columns need to be included as the last columns in any statement being used to insert into a partitioned table. In the preceding code we use Hive's `to_date` function to convert the `created_at` timestamp to a YYYY-MM-DD formatted string.

Partitioned data is stored in HDFS as `/path/to/warehouse/<database>/<table>/key=<value>`. In our example, the `partitioned_user` table structure will look like `/user/hive/warehouse/default/partitioned_user/created_at=2014-04-01`.

If data is added directly to the filesystem, for instance by some third-party processing tool or by `hadoop fs -put`, the metastore won't automatically detect the new partitions. The user will need to manually run an `ALTER TABLE` statement such as the following for each newly added partition:

```
ALTER TABLE <table_name> ADD PARTITION <location>;
```

To add metadata for all partitions not currently present in the metastore we can use: `MSCK REPAIR TABLE <table_name>;` statement. On EMR, this is equivalent to executing the following statement:

```
ALTER TABLE <table_name> RECOVER PARTITIONS;
```

Notice that both statements will work also with `EXTERNAL` tables. In the following chapter, we will see how this pattern can be exploited to create flexible and interoperable pipelines.

Overwriting and updating data

Partitioning is also useful when we need to update a portion of a table. Normally a statement of the following form will replace all the data for the destination table:

```
INSERT OVERWRITE INTO <table>…
```

If `OVERWRITE` is omitted, then each `INSERT` statement will add additional data to the table. Sometimes, this is desirable, but often, the source data being ingested into a Hive table is intended to fully update a subset of the data and keep the rest untouched.

If we perform an `INSERT OVERWRITE` statement (or a `LOAD OVERWRITE` statement) into a partition of a table, then only the specified partition will be affected. Thus, if we were inserting user data and only wanted to affect the partitions with data in the source file, we could achieve this by adding the `OVERWRITE` keyword to our previous `INSERT` statement.

We can also add caveats to the SELECT statement. Say, for example, we only wanted to update data for a certain month:

```
INSERT INTO TABLE partitioned_user
PARTITION (created_at_date)
SELECT created_at ,
user_id,
location,
name,
description,
followers_count,
friends_count,
favourites_count,
screen_name,
listed_count,
to_date(created_at) as created_at_date
FROM user
WHERE to_date(created_at) BETWEEN '2014-03-01' and '2014-03-31';
```

Bucketing and sorting

Partitioning a table is a construct that you take explicit advantage of by using the partition column (or columns) in the WHERE clause of queries against the tables. There is another mechanism called bucketing that can further segment how a table is stored and does so in a way that allows Hive itself to optimize its internal query plans to take advantage of the structure.

Let's create bucketed versions of our tweets and user tables; note the following additional CLUSTER BY and SORT BY statements in the CREATE TABLE statements:

```
CREATE table bucketed_tweets (
tweet_id string,
text string,
in_reply_to string,
retweeted boolean,
user_id string,
place_id string
)  PARTITIONED BY (created_at string)
CLUSTERED BY(user_ID) into 64 BUCKETS
ROW FORMAT DELIMITED
FIELDS TERMINATED BY '\u0001'
STORED AS TEXTFILE;

CREATE TABLE bucketed_user (
user_id string,
```

```
`location` string,
name string,
description string,
followers_count bigint,
friends_count bigint,
favourites_count bigint,
screen_name string,
listed_count bigint
)  PARTITIONED BY (created_at string)
CLUSTERED BY(user_ID) SORTED BY(name) into 64 BUCKETS
ROW FORMAT DELIMITED
FIELDS TERMINATED BY '\u0001'
STORED AS TEXTFILE;
```

Note that we changed the tweets table to also be partitioned; you can only bucket a table that is partitioned.

Just as we need to specify a partition column when inserting into a partitioned table, we must also take care to ensure that data inserted into a bucketed table is correctly clustered. We do this by setting the following flag before inserting the data into the table:

```
SET hive.enforce.bucketing=true;
```

Just as with partitioned tables, you cannot apply the bucketing function when using the LOAD DATA statement; if you wish to load external data into a bucketed table, first insert it into a temporary table, and then use the INSERT...SELECT... syntax to populate the bucketed table.

When data is inserted into a bucketed table, rows are allocated to a bucket based on the result of a hash function applied to the column specified in the CLUSTERED BY clause.

One of the greatest advantages of bucketing a table comes when we need to join two tables that are similarly bucketed, as in the previous example. So, for example, any query of the following form would be vastly improved:

```
SET hive.optimize.bucketmapjoin=true;
SELECT ...
FROM bucketed_user u JOIN bucketed_tweet t
ON u.user_id = t.user_id;
```

With the join being performed on the column used to bucket the table, Hive can optimize the amount of processing as it knows that each bucket contains the same set of user_id columns in both tables. While determining which rows against which to match, only those in the bucket need to be compared against, and not the whole table. This does require that the tables are both clustered on the same column and that the bucket numbers are either identical or one is a multiple of the other. In the latter case, with say one table clustered into 32 buckets and another into 64, the nature of the default hash function used to allocate data to a bucket means that the IDs in bucket 3 in the first table will cover those in both buckets 3 and 35 in the second.

Sampling data

Bucketing a table can also help while using Hive's ability to sample data in a table. Sampling allows a query to gather only a specified subset of the overall rows in the table. This is useful when you have an extremely large table with moderately consistent data patterns. In such a case, applying a query to a small fraction of the data will be much faster and will still give a broadly representative result. Note, of course, that this only applies to queries where you are looking to determine table characteristics, such as pattern ranges in the data; if you are trying to count anything, then the result needs to be scaled to the full table size.

For a non-bucketed table, you can sample in a mechanism similar to what we saw earlier by specifying that the query should only be applied to a certain subset of the table:

```
SELECT max(friends_count)
FROM user TABLESAMPLE(BUCKET 2 OUT OF 64 ON name);
```

In this query, Hive will effectively hash the rows in the table into 64 buckets based on the name column. It will then only use the second bucket for the query. Multiple buckets can be specified, and if RAND() is given as the ON clause, then the entire row is used by the bucketing function.

Though successful, this is highly inefficient as the full table needs to be scanned to generate the required subset of data. If we sample on a bucketed table and ensure the number of buckets sampled is equal to or a multiple of the buckets in the table, then Hive will only read the buckets in question. For example:

```
SELECT MAX(friends_count)
FROM bucketed_user TABLESAMPLE(BUCKET 2 OUT OF 32 on user_id);
```

In the preceding query against the `bucketed_user` table, which is created with 64 buckets on the `user_id` column, the sampling, since it is using the same column, will only read the required buckets. In this case, these will be buckets 2 and 34 from each partition.

A final form of sampling is block sampling. In this case, we can specify the required amount of the table to be sampled, and Hive will use an approximation of this by only reading enough source data blocks on HDFS to meet the required size. Currently, the data size can be specified as either a percentage of the table, as an absolute data size, or as a number of rows (in each block). The syntax for `TABLESAMPLE` is as follows, which will sample 0.5 percent of the table, 1 GB of data or 100 rows per split, respectively:

```
TABLESAMPLE(0.5 PERCENT)
TABLESAMPLE(1G)
TABLESAMPLE(100 ROWS)
```

If these latter forms of sampling are of interest, then consult the documentation, as there are some specific limitations on the input format and file formats that are supported.

Writing scripts

We can place Hive commands in a file and run them with the `-f` option in the `hive` CLI utility:

```
$ cat show_tables.hql

show tables;

$ hive -f show_tables.hql
```

We can parameterize HiveQL statements by means of the `hiveconf` mechanism. This allows us to specify an environment variable name at the point it is used rather than at the point of invocation. For example:

```
$ cat show_tables2.hql

show tables like '${hiveconf:TABLENAME}';

$ hive -hiveconf TABLENAME=user -f show_tables2.hql
```

The variable can also be set within the Hive script or an interactive session:

```
SET TABLE_NAME='user';
```

The preceding `hiveconf` argument will add any new variables in the same namespace as the Hive configuration options. As of Hive 0.8, there is a similar option called `hivevar` that adds any user variables into a distinct namespace. Using `hivevar`, the preceding command would be as follows:

```
$ cat show_tables3.hql
show tables like '${hivevar:TABLENAME}';
$ hive -hivevar TABLENAME=user -f show_tables3.hql
```

Or we can write the command interactively:

```
SET hivevar:TABLE_NAME='user';
```

Hive and Amazon Web Services

With Elastic MapReduce as the AWS Hadoop-on-demand service, it is of course possible to run Hive on an EMR cluster. But it is also possible to use Amazon storage services, particularly S3, from any Hadoop cluster be it within EMR or your own local cluster.

Hive and S3

As mentioned in *Chapter 2, Storage*, it is possible to specify a default filesystem other than HDFS for Hadoop and S3 is one option. But, it doesn't have to be an all-or-nothing thing; it is possible to have specific tables stored in S3. The data for these tables will be retrieved into the cluster to be processed, and any resulting data can either be written to a different S3 location (the same table cannot be the source and destination of a single query) or onto HDFS.

We can take a file of our tweet data and place it onto a location in S3 with a command such as the following:

```
$ aws s3 put tweets.tsv s3://<bucket-name>/tweets/
```

We firstly need to specify the access key and secret access key that can access the bucket. This can be done in three ways:

- Set `fs.s3n.awsAccessKeyId` and `fs.s3n.awsSecretAccessKey` to the appropriate values in the Hive CLI
- Set the same values in `hive-site.xml` though note this limits use of S3 to a single set of credentials
- Specify the table location explicitly in the table URL, that is, `s3n://<access key>:<secret access key>@<bucket>/<path>`

Then we can create a table referencing this data, as follows:

```
CREATE table remote_tweets (
created_at string,
tweet_id string,
text string,
in_reply_to string,
retweeted boolean,
user_id string,
place_id string
)  CLUSTERED BY(user_ID) into 64 BUCKETS
ROW FORMAT DELIMITED
FIELDS TERMINATED BY '\t'
LOCATION 's3n://<bucket-name>/tweets'
```

This can be an incredibly effective way of pulling S3 data into a local Hadoop cluster for processing.

 In order to use AWS credentials in the URI of an S3 location regardless of how the parameters are passed, the secret and access keys must not contain /, +, =, or \ characters. If necessary, a new set of credentials can be generated from the IAM console at https://console.aws.amazon.com/iam/.

In theory, you can just leave the data in the external table and refer to it when needed to avoid WAN data transfer latencies (and costs), even though it often makes sense to pull the data into a local table and do future processing from there. If the table is partitioned, then you might find yourself retrieving a new partition each day, for example.

Hive on Elastic MapReduce

On one level, using Hive within Amazon Elastic MapReduce is just the same as everything discussed in this chapter. You can create a persistent cluster, log in to the master node, and use the Hive CLI to create tables and submit queries. Doing all this will use the local storage on the EC2 instances for the table data.

Not surprisingly, jobs on EMR clusters can also refer to tables whose data is stored on S3 (or DynamoDB). And also not surprisingly, Amazon has made extensions to its version of Hive to make all this very seamless. It is quite simple from within an EMR job to pull data from a table stored in S3, process it, write any intermediate data to the EMR local storage, and then write the output results into S3, DynamoDB, or one of a growing list of other AWS services.

The pattern mentioned earlier where new data is added to a new partition directory for a table each day has proved very effective in S3; it is often the storage location of choice for large and incrementally growing datasets. There is a syntax difference when using EMR; instead of the MSCK command mentioned earlier, the command to update a Hive table with new data added to a partition directory is as follows:

```
ALTER TABLE <table-name> RECOVER PARTITIONS;
```

Consult the EMR documentation for the latest enhancements at http://docs. aws.amazon.com/ElasticMapReduce/latest/DeveloperGuide/emr-hive-additional-features.html. Also, consult the broader EMR documentation. In particular, the integration points with other AWS services is an area of rapid growth.

Extending HiveQL

The HiveQL language can be extended by means of plugins and third-party functions. In Hive, there are three types of functions characterized by the number of rows they take as input and produce as output:

- **User Defined Functions (UDFs)**: are simpler functions that act on one row at a time.

- **User Defined Aggregate Functions (UDAFs)**: take multiple rows as input and generate multiple rows as output. These are aggregate functions to be used in conjunction with a GROUP BY statement (similar to COUNT(), AVG(), MIN(), MAX(), and so on).

- **User Defined Table Functions (UDTFs)**: take multiple rows as input and generate a logical table comprised of multiple rows that can be used in join expressions.

 These APIs are provided only in Java. For other languages, it is possible to stream data through a user-defined script using the TRANSFORM, MAP, and REDUCE clauses that act as a frontend to Hadoop's streaming capabilities.

Two APIs are available to write UDFs. A simple API org.apache.hadoop.hive.
ql.exec.UDF can be used for functions that take and return basic writable types. A
richer API, which provides support for data types other than writable is available in
the org.apache.hadoop.hive.ql.udf.generic.GenericUDF package. We'll now
illustrate how org.apache.hadoop.hive.ql.exec.UDF can be used to implement
a string to ID function similar to the one we used in *Chapter 5, Iterative Computation
with Spark*, to map hashtags to integers in Pig. Building a UDF with this API only
requires extending the UDF class and writing an evaluate() method,
as follows:

```
public class StringToInt extends UDF {
    public Integer evaluate(Text input) {
        if (input == null)
            return null;

        String str = input.toString();
        return str.hashCode();
    }
}
```

The function takes a Text object as input and maps it to an integer value
with the hashCode() method. The source code of this function can be found
at https://github.com/learninghadoop2/book-examples/blob/master/ch7/
udf/com/learninghadoop2/hive/udf/StringToInt.java.

As noted in *Chapter 6, Data Analysis with Apache Pig*, a more robust
hash function should be used in production.

We compile the class and archive it into a JAR file, as follows:

```
$ javac -classpath $(hadoop classpath):/opt/cloudera/parcels/CDH/lib/
hive/lib/* com/learninghadoop2/hive/udf/StringToInt.java
$ jar cvf myudfs-hive.jar com/learninghadoop2/hive/udf/StringToInt.class
```

Before being able to use it, a UDF must be registered in Hive with the
following commands:

```
ADD JAR myudfs-hive.jar;
CREATE TEMPORARY FUNCTION string_to_int AS 'com.learninghadoop2.hive.
udf.StringToInt';
```

The ADD JAR statement adds a JAR file to the distributed cache. The CREATE TEMPORARY FUNCTION <function> AS <class> statement registers a function in Hive that implements a given Java class. The function will be dropped once the Hive session is closed. As of Hive 0.13, it is possible to create permanent functions whose definition is kept in the metastore using CREATE FUNCTION ... .

Once registered, StringToInt can be used in a query just like any other function. In the following example, we first extract a list of hashtags from the tweet's text by applying regexp_extract. Then, we use string_to_int to map each tag to a numerical ID:

```
SELECT unique_hashtags.hashtag, string_to_int(unique_hashtags.hashtag)
AS tag_id FROM
    (
        SELECT regexp_extract(text,
            '(?:\\s|\\A|^)[##]+([A-Za-z0-9-_]+)') as hashtag
        FROM tweets
        GROUP BY regexp_extract(text,
        '(?:\\s|\\A|^)[##]+([A-Za-z0-9-_]+)')
    ) unique_hashtags GROUP BY unique_hashtags.hashtag, string_to_
int(unique_hashtags.hashtag);
```

Just as we did in the previous chapter, we can use the preceding query to create a lookup table:

```
CREATE TABLE lookuptable (tag string, tag_id bigint);
INSERT OVERWRITE TABLE lookuptable
SELECT unique_hashtags.hashtag,
    string_to_int(unique_hashtags.hashtag) as tag_id
FROM
  (
    SELECT regexp_extract(text,
        '(?:\\s|\\A|^)[##]+([A-Za-z0-9-_]+)') AS hashtag
        FROM tweets
        GROUP BY regexp_extract(text,
            '(?:\\s|\\A|^)[##]+([A-Za-z0-9-_]+)')
  ) unique_hashtags
GROUP BY unique_hashtags.hashtag, string_to_int(unique_hashtags.
hashtag);
```

Programmatic interfaces

In addition to the `hive` and `beeline` command-line tools, it is possible to submit HiveQL queries to the system via the JDBC and Thrift programmatic interfaces. Support for ODBC was bundled in older versions of Hive, but as of Hive 0.12, it needs to be built from scratch. More information on this process can be found at `https://cwiki.apache.org/confluence/display/Hive/HiveODBC`.

JDBC

A Hive client written using JDBC APIs looks exactly the same as a client program written for other database systems (for example MySQL). The following is a sample Hive client program using JDBC APIs. The source code for this example can be found at `https://github.com/learninghadoop2/book-examples/blob/master/ch7/clients/com/learninghadoop2/hive/client/HiveJdbcClient.java`.

```java
public class HiveJdbcClient {
    private static String driverName = " org.apache.hive.jdbc.
HiveDriver";

    // connection string
    public static String URL = "jdbc:hive2://localhost:10000";

    // Show all tables in the default database
    public static String QUERY = "show tables";

    public static void main(String[] args) throws SQLException {
        try {
            Class.forName (driverName);
        }
        catch (ClassNotFoundException e) {
            e.printStackTrace();
            System.exit(1);
        }
        Connection con = DriverManager.getConnection (URL);
        Statement stmt = con.createStatement();

        ResultSet resultSet = stmt.executeQuery(QUERY);
        while (resultSet.next()) {
            System.out.println(resultSet.getString(1));
        }
    }
}
```

The URL part is the JDBC URI that describes the connection end point. The format for establishing a remote connection is `jdbc:hive2:<host>:<port>/<database>`. Connections in embedded mode can be established by not specifying a host or port, like `jdbc:hive2://`.

`hive` and `hive2` are the drivers to be used when connecting to `HiveServer` and `HiveServer2`. `QUERY` contains the HiveQL query to be executed.

> Hive's JDBC interface exposes only the default database. In order to access other databases, you need to reference them explicitly in the underlying queries using the `<database>.<table>` notation.

First we load the `HiveServer2` JDBC driver `org.apache.hive.jdbc.HiveDriver`.

> Use `org.apache.hadoop.hive.jdbc.HiveDriver` to connect to HiveServer.

Then, like with any other JDBC program, we establish a connection to `URL` and use it to instantiate a `Statement` class. We execute `QUERY`, with no authentication, and store the output dataset into the `ResultSet` object. Finally, we scan `resultSet` and print its content to the command line.

Compile and execute the example with the following commands:

```
$ javac HiveJdbcClient.java
```

```
$ java -cp $(hadoop classpath):/opt/cloudera/parcels/CDH/lib/hive/lib/*:/
opt/cloudera/parcels/CDH/lib/hive/lib/hive-jdbc.jar: com.learninghadoop2.
hive.client.HiveJdbcClient
```

Thrift

Thrift provides lower-level access to Hive and has a number of advantages over the JDBC implementation of HiveServer. Primarily, it allows multiple connections from the same client, and it allows programming languages other than Java to be used with ease. With HiveServer2, it is a less commonly used option but still worth mentioning for compatibility. A sample Thrift client implemented using the Java API can be found at `https://github.com/learninghadoop2/book-examples/blob/master/ch7/clients/com/learninghadoop2/hive/client/HiveThriftClient.java`. This client can be used to connect to HiveServer, but due to protocol differences, the client won't work with HiveServer2.

In the example we define a `getClient()` method that takes as input the host and port of a HiveServer service and returns an instance of `org.apache.hadoop.hive.service.ThriftHive.Client`.

A client is obtained by first instantiating a socket connection, `org.apache.thrift.transport.TSocket`, to the HiveServer service, and by specifying a protocol, `org.apache.thrift.protocol.TBinaryProtocol`, to serialize and transmit data, as follows:

```
TSocket transport = new TSocket(host, port);
transport.setTimeout(TIMEOUT);
transport.open();
TBinaryProtocol protocol = new TBinaryProtocol(transport);
client = new ThriftHive.Client(protocol);
```

We call `getClient()` from the main method and use the client to execute a query against an instance of HiveServer running on localhost on port `11111`, as follows:

```
public static void main(String[] args) throws Exception {
    Client client = getClient("localhost", 11111);
    client.execute("show tables");
    List<String> results = client.fetchAll();
for (String result : results) {
System.out.println(result);
}
    }
```

Make sure that HiveServer is running on port `11111`, and if not, start an instance with the following command:

```
$ sudo hive --service hiveserver -p 11111
```

Compile and execute the `HiveThriftClient.java` example with:

```
$ javac $(hadoop classpath):/opt/cloudera/parcels/CDH/lib/hive/lib/* com/
learninghadoop2/hive/client/HiveThriftClient.java
```

```
$ java -cp $(hadoop classpath):/opt/cloudera/parcels/CDH/lib/hive/lib/*:
com.learninghadoop2.hive.client.HiveThriftClient
```

Stinger initiative

Hive has remained very successful and capable since its earliest releases, particularly in its ability to provide SQL-like processing on enormous datasets. But other technologies did not stand still, and Hive acquired a reputation of being relatively slow, particularly in regard to lengthy startup times on large jobs and its inability to give quick responses to conceptually simple queries.

These perceived limitations were less due to Hive itself and more a consequence of how translation of SQL queries into the MapReduce model has much built-in inefficiency when compared to other ways of implementing a SQL query. Particularly in regard to very large datasets, MapReduce saw lots of I/O (and consequently time) spent writing out the results of one MapReduce job just to have them read by another. As discussed in *Chapter 3*, *Processing – MapReduce and Beyond*, this is a major driver in the design of Tez, which can schedule jobs on a Hadoop cluster as a graph of tasks that does not require inefficient writes and reads between them.

The following is a query on the MapReduce framework versus Tez:

```
SELECT a.country, COUNT(b.place_id) FROM place a JOIN tweets b ON (a.
place_id = b.place_id) GROUP BY a.country;
```

The following figure contrasts the execution plan for the preceding query on the MapReduce framework versus Tez:

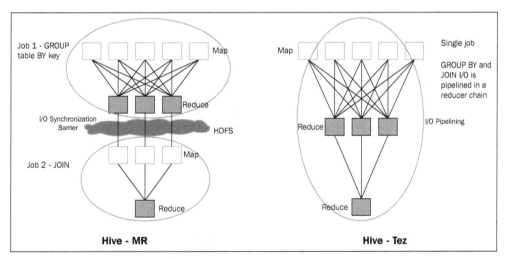

Hive on MapReduce versus Tez

In plain MapReduce, two jobs are created for the GROUP BY and JOIN clauses. The first job is composed of a set of MapReduce tasks that read data from the disk to carry out grouping. The reducers write intermediate results to the disk so that output can be synchronized. The mappers in the second job read the intermediate results from the disk as well as data from table b. The combined dataset is then passed to the reducer where shared keys are joined. Were we to execute an ORDER BY statement, this would have resulted in a third job and further MapReduce passes. The same query is executed on Tez as a single job by a single set of Map tasks that read data from the disk. I/O grouping and joining are pipelined across reducers.

Alongside these architectural limitations, there were quite a few areas around SQL language support that could also provide better efficiency, and in early 2013, the Stinger initiative was launched with an explicit goal of making Hive over 100 times as fast and with much richer SQL support. Hive 0.13 has all the features of the three phases of Stinger, resulting in a much more complete SQL dialect. Also, Tez is offered as an execution framework in addition to a MapReduce-based implementation atop YARN which is more efficient than previous implementations on Hadoop 1 MapReduce.

With Tez as the execution engine, Hive is no longer limited to a series of linear MapReduce jobs and can instead build a processing graph where any given step can, for example, stream results to multiple sub-steps.

To take advantage of the Tez framework, there is a new `hive` variable setting:

```
set hive.execution.engine=tez;
```

This setting relies on Tez being installed on the cluster; it is available in source form from `http://tez.apache.org` or in several distributions, though at the time of writing, not Cloudera.

The alternative value is `mr`, which uses the classic MapReduce model (atop YARN), so it is possible in a single installation to compare with the performance of Hive using Tez.

Impala

Hive is not the only product providing SQL-on-Hadoop capability. The second most widely used is likely Impala, announced in late 2012 and released in spring 2013. Though originally developed internally within Cloudera, its source code is periodically pushed to an open source Git repository (`https://github.com/cloudera/impala`).

Impala was created out of the same perception of Hive's weaknesses that led to the Stinger initiative.

Impala also took some inspiration from Google Dremel (`http://static.googleusercontent.com/media/research.google.com/en//pubs/archive/36632.pdf`) which was first openly described by a paper published in 2009. Dremel was built at Google to address the gap between the need for very fast queries on very large datasets and the high latency inherent in the existing MapReduce model underpinning Hive at the time. Dremel was a sophisticated approach to this problem that, rather than building mitigations atop MapReduce such as implemented by Hive, instead created a new service that accessed the same data stored in HDFS. Dremel also benefited from significant work to optimize the storage format of the data in a way that made it more amenable to very fast analytic queries.

The architecture of Impala

The basic architecture has three main components; the Impala daemons, the state store, and the clients. Recent versions have added additional components that improve the service, but we'll focus on the high-level architecture.

The Impala daemon (`impalad`) should be run on each host where a DataNode process is managing HDFS data. Note that `impalad` does not access the filesystem blocks through the full HDFS FileSystem API; instead, it uses a feature called short-circuit reads to make data access more efficient.

When a client submits a query, it can do so to any of the running `impalad` processes, and this one will become the coordinator for the execution of that query. The key aspect of Impala's performance is that for each query, it generates custom native code, which is then pushed to and executed by all the `impalad` processes on the system. This highly optimized code performs the query on the local data, and each `impalad` then returns its subset of the result set to the coordinator node, which performs the final data consolidation to produce the final result. This type of architecture should be familiar to anyone who has worked with any of the (usually commercial and expensive) **Massively Parallel Processing** (**MPP**) (the term used for this type of shared scale-out architecture) data warehouse solutions available today. As the cluster runs, the state store daemon ensures that each `impalad` process is aware of all the others and provides a view of the overall cluster health.

Co-existing with Hive

Impala, as a newer product, tends to have a more restricted set of SQL data types and supports a more constrained dialect of SQL than Hive. It is, however, expanding this support with each new release. Refer to the Impala documentation (`http://www.cloudera.com/content/cloudera-content/cloudera-docs/CDH5/latest/Impala/impala.html`) to get an overview of the current level of support.

Impala supports the Hive metastore mechanism used by Hive to persistently store the metadata surrounding its table structure and storage. This means that on a cluster with an existing Hive setup, it should be immediately possible to use Impala as it will access the same metastore and therefore provide access to the same tables available in Hive.

But be warned that the differences in SQL dialect and data types might cause unexpected results when working in a combined Hive and Impala environment. Some queries might work on one but not the other, they might show very different performance characteristics (more on this later), or they might actually give different results. This last point might become apparent when using data types such as float and double that are simply treated differently in the underlying systems (Hive is implemented on Java while Impala is written in C++).

As of version 1.2, it supports UDFs written both in C++ and Java, although C++ is strongly recommended as a much faster solution. Keep this in mind if you are looking to share custom functions between Hive and Impala.

A different philosophy

When Impala was first released, its greatest benefit was in how it truly enabled what is often called *speed of thought* analysis. Queries could be returned sufficiently fast that an analyst could explore a thread of analysis in a completely interactive fashion without having to wait for minutes at a time for each query to complete. It's fair to say that most adopters of Impala were at times stunned by its performance, especially when compared to the version of Hive shipping at the time.

The Impala focus has remained mostly on these shorter queries, and this does impose some limitations on the system. Impala tends to be quite memory-heavy as it relies on in-memory processing to achieve much of its performance. If a query requires a dataset to be held in memory rather than being available on the executing node, then that query will simply fail in versions of Impala before 2.0.

Comparing the work on Stinger to Impala, it could be argued that Impala has a much stronger focus on excelling in the shorter (and arguably more common) queries that support interactive data analysis. Many business intelligence tools and services are now certified to directly run on Impala. The Stinger initiative has put less effort into making Hive just as fast in the area where Impala excels but has instead improved Hive (to varying degrees) for all workloads. Impala is still developing at a fast pace and Stinger has put additional momentum into Hive, so it is most likely wise to consider both products and determine which best meets the performance and functionality requirements of your projects and workflows.

It should also be kept in mind that there are competitive commercial pressures shaping the direction of Impala and Hive. Impala was created and is still driven by Cloudera, the most popular vendor of Hadoop distributions. The Stinger initiative, though contributed to by many companies as diverse as Microsoft (yes, really!) and Intel, was lead by Hortonworks, probably the second largest vendor of Hadoop distributions. The fact is that if you are using the Cloudera distribution of Hadoop, then some of the core features of Hive might be slower to arrive, whereas Impala will always be up-to-date. Conversely, if you use another distribution, you might get the latest Hive release, but that might either have an older Impala or, as is currently the case, you might have to download and install it yourself.

A similar situation has arisen with the Parquet and ORC file formats mentioned earlier. Parquet is preferred by Impala and developed by a group of companies led by Cloudera, while ORC is preferred by Hive and is championed by Hortonworks.

Unfortunately, the reality is that Parquet support is often very quick to arrive in the Cloudera distribution but less so in say the Hortonworks distribution, where the ORC file format is preferred.

These themes are a little concerning since, although competition in this space is a good thing, and arguably the announcement of Impala helped energize the Hive community, there is a greater risk that your choice of distribution might have a larger impact on the tools and file formats that will be fully supported, unlike in the past. Hopefully, the current situation is just an artifact of where we are in the development cycles of all these new and improved technologies, but do consider your choice of distribution carefully in relation to your SQL-on-Hadoop needs.

Drill, Tajo, and beyond

You should also consider that SQL on Hadoop no longer only refers to Hive or Impala. Apache Drill (`http://drill.apache.org`) is a fuller implementation of the Dremel model first described by Google. Although Impala implements the Dremel architecture across HDFS data, Drill looks to provide similar functionality across multiple data sources. It is still in its early stages, but if your needs are broader than what Hive or Impala provides, it might be worth considering.

Tajo (`http://tajo.apache.org`) is another Apache project that seeks to be a full data warehouse system on Hadoop data. With an architecture similar to that of Impala, it offers a much richer system with components such as multiple optimizers and ETL tools that are commonplace in traditional data warehouses but less frequently bundled in the Hadoop world. It has a much smaller user base but has been used by certain companies very successfully for a significant length of time, and might be worth considering if you need a fuller data warehousing solution.

Other products are also emerging in this space, and it's a good idea to do some research. Hive and Impala are awesome tools, but if you find that they don't meet your needs, then look around — something else might.

Summary

In its early days, Hadoop was sometimes erroneously seen as the latest supposed relational database killer. Over time, it has become more apparent that the more sensible approach is to view it as a complement to RDBMS technologies and that, in fact, the RDBMS community has developed tools such as SQL that are also valuable in the Hadoop world.

HiveQL is an implementation of SQL on Hadoop and was the primary focus of this chapter. In regard to HiveQL and its implementations, we covered the following topics:

- How HiveQL provides a logical model atop data stored in HDFS in contrast to relational databases where the table structure is enforced in advance

- How HiveQL supports many standard SQL data types and commands including joins and views

- The ETL-like features offered by HiveQL, including the ability to import data into tables and optimize the table structure through partitioning and similar mechanisms

- How HiveQL offers the ability to extend its core set of operators with user-defined code and how this contrasts to the Pig UDF mechanism

- The recent history of Hive developments, such as the Stinger initiative, that have seen Hive transition to an updated implementation that uses Tez

- The broader ecosystem around HiveQL that now includes products such as Impala, Tajo and Drill and how each of these focuses on specific areas in which to excel

With Pig and Hive, we've introduced alternative models to process MapReduce data, but so far we've not looked at another question: what approaches and tools are required to actually allow this massive dataset being collected in Hadoop to remain useful and manageable over time? In the next chapter, we'll take a slight step up the abstraction hierarchy and look at how to manage the life cycle of this enormous data asset.

8

Data Lifecycle Management

Our previous chapters were quite technology focused, describing particular tools or techniques and how they can be used. In this and the next chapter, we are going to take a more top-down approach whereby we will describe a problem space you are likely to encounter and then explore how to address it. In particular, we'll cover the following topics:

- What we mean by the term data life cycle management
- Why data life cycle management is something to think about
- The categories of tools that can be used to address the problem
- How to use these tools to build the first half of a Twitter sentiment analysis pipeline

What data lifecycle management is

Data doesn't exist only at a point in time. Particularly for long-running production workflows, you are likely to acquire a significant quantity of data in a Hadoop cluster. Requirements rarely stay static for long, so alongside new logic you might also see the format of that data change or require multiple data sources to be used to provide the dataset processed in your application. We use the term **data lifecycle management** to describe an approach to handling the collection, storage, and transformation of data that ensures that data is where it needs to be, in the format it needs to be in, in a way that allows data and system evolution over time.

Importance of data lifecycle management

If you build data processing applications, you are by definition reliant on the data that is processed. Just as we consider the reliability of applications and systems, it becomes necessary to ensure that the data is also production-ready.

Data at some point needs to be ingested into Hadoop. It is one part of an enterprise and often has multiple points of integration with external systems. If the ingest of data coming from those systems is not reliable, then the impact on the jobs that process that data is often as disruptive as a major system failure. Data ingest becomes a critical component in its own right. And when we say the ingest needs to be reliable, we don't just mean that data is arriving; it also has to be arriving in a format that is usable and through a mechanism that can handle evolution over time.

The problem with many of these issues is that they do not arise in a significant fashion until the flows are large, the system is critical, and the business impact of any problems is non-trivial. Ad hoc approaches that worked for a less critical dataflow often will simply not scale, but will be very painful to replace on a live system.

Tools to help

But don't panic! There are a number of categories of tools that can help with the data life cycle management problem. We'll give examples of the following three broad categories in this chapter:

- **Orchestration services**: building an ingest pipeline usually has multiple discrete stages, and we will use an orchestration tool to allow these to be described, executed, and managed

- **Connectors**: given the importance of integration with external systems, we will look at how we can use connectors to simplify the abstractions provided by Hadoop storage

- **File formats**: how we store the data impacts how we manage format evolution over time, and several rich storage formats have ways of supporting this

Building a tweet analysis capability

In earlier chapters, we used various implementations of Twitter data analysis to describe several concepts. We will take this capability to a deeper level and approach it as a major case study.

In this chapter, we will build a data ingest pipeline, constructing a production-ready dataflow that is designed with reliability and future evolution in mind.

We'll build out the pipeline incrementally throughout the chapter. At each stage, we'll highlight what has changed but can't include full listings at each stage without trebling the size of the chapter. The source code for this chapter, however, has every iteration in its full glory.

Getting the tweet data

The first thing we need to do is get the actual tweet data. As in previous examples, we can pass the -j and -n arguments to stream.py to dump JSON tweets to stdout:

```
$ stream.py -j -n 10000 > tweets.json
```

Since we have this tool that can create a batch of sample tweets on demand, we could start our ingest pipeline by having this job run on a periodic basis. But how?

Introducing Oozie

We could, of course, bang rocks together and use something like cron for simple job scheduling, but recall that we want an ingest pipeline that is built with reliability in mind. So, we really want a scheduling tool that we can use to detect failures and otherwise respond to exceptional situations.

The tool we will use here is Oozie (http://oozie.apache.org), a workflow engine and scheduler built with a focus on the Hadoop ecosystem.

Oozie provides a means to define a workflow as a series of nodes with configurable parameters and controlled transition from one node to the next. It is installed as part of the Cloudera QuickStart VM, and the main command-line client is, not surprisingly, called oozie.

We've tested the workflows in this chapter against version 5.0 of the Cloudera QuickStart VM, and at the time of writing Oozie in the latest version, 5.1, has some issues. There's nothing particularly version-specific in our workflows, however, so they should be compatible with any correctly working Oozie v4 implementation.

Though powerful and flexible, Oozie can take a little getting used to, so we'll give some examples and describe what we are doing along the way.

The most common node in an Oozie workflow is an action. It is within action nodes that the steps of the workflow are actually executed; the other node types handle management of the workflow in terms of decisions, parallelism, and failure detection. Oozie has multiple types of actions that it can perform. One of these is the shell action, which can be used to execute any command on the system, such as native binaries, shell scripts, or any other command-line utility. Let's create a script to generate a file of tweets and copy this to HDFS:

```
set -e
source twitter.keys
python stream.py -j -n 500 > /tmp/tweets.out
hdfs dfs -put /tmp/tweets.out /tmp/tweets/tweets.out
rm -f /tmp/tweets.out
```

Note that the first line will cause the entire script to fail should any of the included commands fail. We use an environment file to provide the Twitter keys to our script in `twitter.keys`, which is of the following form:

```
export TWITTER_CONSUMER_KEY=<value>
export TWITTER_CONSUMER_SECRET=<value>
export TWITTER_ACCESS_KEY=<value>
export TWITTER_ACCESS_SECRET=<value>
```

Oozie uses XML to describe its workflows, usually stored in a file called `workflow.xml`. Let's walk through the definition for an Oozie workflow that calls a shell command.

The schema for an Oozie workflow is called **workflow-app**, and we can give the workflow a specific name. This is useful when viewing job history in the CLI or Oozie web UI. In the examples in this book, we'll use an increasing version number to allow us to more easily separate the iterations within the source repository. This is how we give the workflow-app a specific name:

```
<workflow-app xmlns="uri:oozie:workflow:0.4" name="v1">
```

Oozie workflows are made up of a series of connected nodes, each of which represents a step in the process, and which are represented by XML nodes in the workflow definition. Oozie has a number of nodes that deal with the transition of the workflow from one step to the next. The first of these is the start node, which simply states the name of the first node to be executed as part of the workflow, as follows:

```
<start to="fs-node"/>
```

We then have the definition for the named start node. In this case, it is an action node, which is the generic node type for most Oozie nodes that actually perform some processing, as follows:

```
<action name="fs-node">
```

Action is a broad category of nodes, and we will typically then specialize it with the particular processing for this given node. In this case, we are using the fs node type, which allows us to perform filesystem operations:

```
<fs>
```

We want to ensure that the directory on HDFS to which we wish to copy the file of tweet data, exists, is empty, and has suitable permissions. We do this by trying to delete the directory if it exists, then creating it, and finally applying the required permissions, as follows:

```
<delete path="${nameNode}/tmp/tweets"/>
<mkdir path="${nameNode}/tmp/tweets"/>
<chmod path="${nameNode}/tmp/tweets" permissions="777"/>
</fs>
```

We'll see an alternative way of setting up directories later. After performing the functionality of the node, Oozie needs know how to proceed with the workflow. In most cases, this will comprise moving to another action node if this node was successful and aborting the workflow otherwise. This is specified by the next elements. The ok node gives the name of the node to which to transition if the execution was successful; the error node names the destination node for failure scenarios. Here's how the ok and fail nodes are used:

```
<ok to="shell-node"/>
<error to="fail"/>
</action>
<action name="shell-node">
```

The second action node is again specialized with its specific processing type; in this case, we have a shell node:

```
<shell xmlns="uri:oozie:shell-action:0.2">
```

The shell action then has the Hadoop JobTracker and NameNode locations specified. Note that the actual values are given by variables; we'll explain where they come from later. The JobTracker and NameNode are specified as follows:

```
<job-tracker>${jobTracker}</job-tracker>
<name-node>${nameNode}</name-node>
```

As mentioned in *Chapter 3, Processing – MapReduce and Beyond*, MapReduce uses multiple queues to provide support for different approaches to resource scheduling. The next element specifies the MapReduce queue to which the workflow should be submitted:

```
<configuration>
    <property>
        <name>mapred.job.queue.name</name>
        <value>${queueName}</value>
    </property>
</configuration>
```

Now that the shell node is fully configured, we can specify the command to invoke, again via a variable, as follows:

```
<exec>${EXEC}</exec>
```

The various steps of Oozie workflows are executed as MapReduce jobs. This shell action will, therefore, be executed as a specific task instance on a particular TaskTracker. We, therefore, need to specify which files need to be copied to the local working directory on the TaskTracker machine before the action can be performed. In this case, we need to copy the main shell script, the Python tweet generator, and the Twitter config file, as follows:

```
<file>${workflowRoot}/${EXEC}</file>
<file>${workflowRoot}/twitter.keys</file>
<file>${workflowRoot}/stream.py</file>
```

After closing the shell element, we again specify what to do depending on whether the action completed successfully or not. Because MapReduce is used for job execution, the majority of node types by definition have built-in retry and recovery logic, though this is not the case for shell nodes:

```
        </shell>
        <ok to="end"/>
        <error to="fail"/>
    </action>
```

If the workflow fails, let's just kill it in this case. The `kill` node type does exactly that— terminate the workflow from proceeding to any further steps, usually logging error messages along the way. Here's how the `kill` node type is used:

```
<kill name="fail">
    <message>Shell action failed, error
        message[${wf:errorMessage(wf:lastErrorNode())}]</message>
</kill>
```

The `end` node on the other hand simply halts the workflow and logs it as a successful completion within Oozie:

```
    <end name="end"/>
</workflow-app>
```

The obvious question is what the preceding variables represent and from where they get their concrete values. The preceding variables are examples of the Oozie Expression Language often referred to as EL.

Alongside the workflow definition file (`workflow.xml`), which describes the steps in the flow, we also need to create a configuration file that gives the specific values for a given execution of the workflow. This separation of functionality and configuration allows us to write workflows that can be used on different clusters, on different file locations, or with different variable values without having to recreate the workflow itself. By convention, this file is usually named `job.properties`. For the preceding workflow, here's a sample `job.properties` file.

Firstly, we specify the location of the JobTracker, the NameNode, and the MapReduce queue to which to submit the workflow. The following should work on the Cloudera 5.0 QuickStart VM, though in v 5.1 the hostname has been changed to `quickstart.cloudera`. The important thing is that the specified NameNode and JobTracker addresses need to be in the Oozie whitelist—the local services on the VM are added automatically:

```
jobTracker=localhost.localdomain:8032
nameNode=hdfs://localhost.localdomain:8020
queueName=default
```

Next, we set some values for where the workflow definitions and associated files can be found on the HDFS filesystem. Note the use of a variable representing the username running the job. This allows a single workflow to be applied to different paths depending on the submitting user, as follows:

```
tasksRoot=book
workflowRoot=${nameNode}/user/${user.name}/${tasksRoot}/v1
oozie.wf.application.path=${nameNode}/user/${user.name}/${tasksRoot}/
v1
```

Next, we name the command to be executed in the workflow as `${EXEC}`:

```
EXEC=gettweets.sh
```

More complex workflows will require additional entries in the `job.properties` file; the preceding workflow is as simple as it gets.

The `oozie` command-line tool needs to know where the Oozie server is running. This can be added as an argument to every Oozie shell command, but that gets unwieldy very quickly. Instead, you can set the shell environment variable, as follows:

```
$ export OOZIE_URL='http://localhost:11000/oozie'
```

After all that work, we can now actually run an Oozie workflow. Create a directory on HDFS as specified in the values in the `job.properties` file. In the preceding command, we'd be creating this as `book/v1` under our home directory on HDFS. Copy the `stream.py`, `gettweets.sh` and `twitter.properties` files to that directory; these are the files required to perform the actual execution of the shell command. Then, add the `workflow.xml` file to the same directory.

To run the workflow then, we do the following:

```
$ oozie job -run -config <path-to-job.properties>
```

If submitted successfully, Oozie will print the job name to the screen. You can see the current status of this workflow with:

```
$ oozie job -info <job-id>
```

You can also check the logs for the job:

```
$ oozie job -log <job-id>
```

In addition, all current and recent jobs can be viewed with:

```
$ oozie jobs
```

A note on HDFS file permissions

There is a subtle aspect in the shell command that can catch the unwary. As an alternative to having the `fs` node, we could instead include a preparation element within the shell node to create the directory we need on the filesystem. It would look like the following:

```
<prepare>
    <mkdir path="${nameNode}/tmp/tweets"/>
</prepare>
```

The prepare stage is executed by the user who submitted the workflow, but since the actual script execution is performed on YARN, it is usually executed as the yarn user. You might hit a problem where the script generates the tweets, the `/tmp/tweets` directory is created on HDFS, but the script then fails to have permission to write to that directory. You can either resolve this through assigning permissions more precisely or, as shown earlier, you add a filesystem node to encapsulate the needed operations. We'll use a mixture of both techniques in this chapter; for non-shell nodes, we'll use prepare elements, particularly if the needed directory is manipulated only by that node. For cases where a shell node is involved or where the created directories will be used across multiple nodes, we'll be safe and use the more explicit `fs` node.

Making development a little easier

It can sometimes get awkward to manage the files and resources for an Oozie job during development. Some need to be on HDFS, while some need to be local, and changes to some files require changes to others. The easiest approach is often to develop or make changes in a complete clone of the workflow directory on the local filesystem and push changes from there to the similarly named directory in HDFS, not forgetting, of course, to ensure that all changes are under revision control! For operational execution of the workflow, the `job.properties` file is the only thing that needs to be on the local filesystem and, conversely, all the other files need to be on HDFS. Always remember this: it's all too easy to make changes to a local copy of a workflow, forget to push the changes to HDFS, and then be confused as to why the workflow isn't reflecting the changes.

Extracting data and ingesting into Hive

With our data on HDFS, we can now extract the separate datasets for tweets and users, and place data as in previous chapters. We can reuse `extract_for_hive.pig` to parse the raw tweet JSON into separate files, store them again on HDFS, and then follow up with a Hive step that ingests these new files into Hive tables for tweets, users, and places.

To do this within Oozie, we'll need to add two new nodes to our workflow, a Pig action for the first step and a Hive action for the second.

For our Hive action, we'll just create three external tables that point to the files generated by Pig. This would then allow us to follow our previously described model of ingesting into temporary or external tables and using HiveQL INSERT statements from there to insert into the operational, and often partitioned, tables. This `create.hql` script can be found at `https://github.com/learninghadoop2/book-examples/blob/master/ch8/v2/hive/create.hql` but is simply of the following form:

```
CREATE DATABASE IF NOT EXISTS twttr ;
USE twttr;
DROP TABLE IF EXISTS tweets;
CREATE EXTERNAL TABLE tweets (
...
) ROW FORMAT DELIMITED
FIELDS TERMINATED BY '\u0001'
STORED AS TEXTFILE
LOCATION '${ingestDir}/tweets';

DROP TABLE IF EXISTS user;
CREATE EXTERNAL TABLE user (
```

```
. . .
) ROW FORMAT DELIMITED
FIELDS TERMINATED BY '\u0001'
STORED AS TEXTFILE
LOCATION '${ingestDir}/users';

DROP TABLE IF EXISTS place;
CREATE EXTERNAL TABLE place (
. . .
) ROW FORMAT DELIMITED
FIELDS TERMINATED BY '\u0001'
STORED AS TEXTFILE
LOCATION '${ingestDir}/places';
```

Note that the file separator on each table is also explicitly set to match what we are outputting from Pig. In addition to this, locations in both scripts are specified by variables for which we will provide concrete values in our `job.properties` file.

With the preceding statements, we can create the Pig node for our workflow found in the source code as v2 of the pipeline. Much of the node definition looks similar to the shell node used previously, as we set the same configuration elements; also notice our use of the `prepare` element to create the needed output directory. We can create the Pig node for our workflow as shown in the following `action`:

```
<action name="pig-node">
    <pig>
        <job-tracker>${jobTracker}</job-tracker>
        <name-node>${nameNode}</name-node>
        <prepare>
            <delete path="${nameNode}/${outputDir}"/>
            <mkdir path="${nameNode}/${outputDir}"/>
        </prepare>
        <configuration>
            <property>
                <name>mapred.job.queue.name</name>
                <value>${queueName}</value>
            </property>
        </configuration>
```

Similarly as with the shell command, we need to tell the Pig action the location of the actual Pig script. This is specified in the following `script` element:

```
<script>${workflowRoot}/pig/extract_for_hive.pig</script>
```

We also need to modify the command line used to invoke the Pig script to add several parameters. The following elements do this; note the construction pattern wherein one element adds the actual parameter name and the next its value (we'll see an alternative mechanism for passing arguments in the next section):

```
<argument>-param</argument>
<argument>inputDir=${inputDir}</argument>
<argument>-param</argument>
<argument>outputDir=${outputDir}</argument>
</pig>
```

Because we want to move from this step to the Hive node, we need to set the following elements appropriately:

```
<ok to="hive-node"/>
<error to="fail"/>
</action>
```

The Hive action itself is a little different than the previous nodes; even though it starts in a similar fashion, it specifies the Hive action-specific namespace, as follows:

```
<action name="hive-node">
    <hive xmlns="uri:oozie:hive-action:0.2">
    <job-tracker>${jobTracker}</job-tracker>
    <name-node>${nameNode}</name-node>
```

The Hive action needs many of the configuration elements used by Hive itself and, in most cases, we copy the `hive-site.xml` file into the workflow directory and specify its location, as shown in the following xml; note that this mechanism is not Hive-specific and can also be used for custom actions:

```
<job-xml>${workflowRoot}/hive-site.xml</job-xml>
```

In addition, we might need to override some MapReduce default configuration properties, as shown in the following xml, where we specify that intermediate compression should be used for our job:

```
<configuration>
    <property>
        <name>mapred.compress.map.output</name>
        <value>true</value>
    </property>
</configuration>
```

After configuring the Hive environment, we now specify the location of the Hive script:

```
<script>${workflowRoot}/hive/create.hql</script>
```

We also have to provide the mechanism to pass arguments to the Hive script. But instead of building out the command line one component at a time, we'll add the `param` elements that map the name of a configuration element in the `job.properties` file to variables specified in the Hive script; this mechanism is also supported with Pig actions:

```
<param>dbName=${dbName}</param>
<param>ingestDir=${ingestDir}</param>
</hive>
```

The Hive node then closes as the others, as follows:

```
<ok to="end"/>
<error to="fail"/>
</action>
```

We now need to put all this together to run the multistage workflow in Oozie. The full `workflow.xml` file can be found at `https://github.com/learninghadoop2/book-examples/tree/master/ch8/v2` and the workflow is visualized in the following diagram:

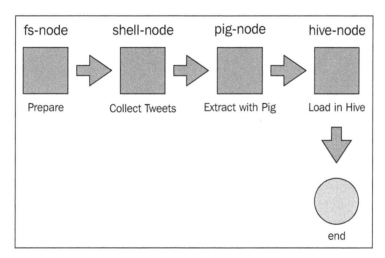

Data ingestion workflow v2

This workflow performs all the steps discussed before; it generates tweet data, extracts subsets of data via Pig, and then ingests these into Hive.

A note on workflow directory structure

We now have quite a few files in our workflow directory and it is best to adopt some structure and naming conventions. For the current workflow, our directory on HDFS looks like the following:

```
/hive/
/hive/create.hql
/lib/
/pig/
/pig/extract_for_hive.pig
/scripts/
/scripts/gettweets.sh
/scripts/stream-json-batch.py
/scripts/twitter-keys
/hive-site.xml
/job.properties
/workflow.xml
```

The model we follow is to keep configuration files in the top-level directory but to keep files related to a given action type in dedicated subdirectories. Note that it is useful to have a `lib` directory even if empty, as some node types look for it.

With the preceding structure, the `job.properties` file for our combined job is now the following:

```
jobTracker=localhost.localdomain:8032
nameNode=hdfs://localhost.localdomain:8020
queueName=default
tasksRoot=book

workflowRoot=${nameNode}/user/${user.name}/${tasksRoot}/v2
oozie.wf.application.path=${nameNode}/user/${user.name}/${tasksRoot}/
v2
oozie.use.system.libpath=true
EXEC=gettweets.sh
inputDir=/tmp/tweets
outputDir=/tmp/tweetdata
ingestDir=/tmp/tweetdata
dbName=twttr
```

In the preceding code, we've fully updated the `workflow.xml` definition to include all the steps described so far—including an initial `fs` node to create the required directory without worrying about user permissions.

Introducing HCatalog

If we look at our current workflow, there is inefficiency in how we use HDFS as the interface between Pig and Hive. We need to output the result of our Pig script onto HDFS, where the Hive script can then use it as the location of some new tables. What this highlights is that it is often very useful to have data stored in Hive, but this is limited, as few tools (primarily Hive) can access the Hive metastore and hence read and write such data. If we think about it, Hive has two main layers: its tools for accessing and manipulating its data plus the execution framework to run queries on that data.

The HCatalog subproject of Hive effectively provides an independent implementation of the first of these layers—the means to access and manipulate data in the Hive metastore. HCatalog provides mechanisms for other tools, such as Pig and MapReduce, to natively read and write table-structured data that is stored on HDFS.

Remember, of course, that the data is stored on HDFS in one format or another. The Hive metastore provides the models to abstract these files into the relational table structure familiar from Hive. So when we say we are storing data in HCatalog, what we really mean is that we are storing data on HDFS in such a way that this data can then be exposed by table structures specified within the Hive metastore. Conversely, when we refer to Hive data, what we really mean is data whose metadata is stored in the Hive metastore, and which can be accessed by any metastore-aware tool, such as HCatalog.

Using HCatalog

The HCatalog command-line tool is called **hcat** and will be preinstalled on the Cloudera QuickStart VM—it is installed, in fact, with any version of Hive later than 0.11 inclusive.

The hcat utility doesn't have an interactive mode, so generally you will use it with explicit command-line arguments or by pointing it at a file of commands, as follows:

```
$ hcat -e "use default; show tables"
$ hcat -f commands.hql
```

Though the hcat tool is useful and can be incorporated into scripts, the more interesting element of HCatalog for our purposes here is its integration with Pig. HCatalog defines a new Pig loader called HCatLoader and a storer called HCatStorer. As the names suggest, these allow Pig scripts to read from or write to Hive tables directly. We can use this mechanism to replace our previous Pig and Hive actions in our Oozie workflow with a single HCatalog-based Pig action that writes the output of the Pig job directly into our tables in Hive.

For clarity, we'll create new tables named `tweets_hcat`, `places_hcat`, and `users_hcat` into which we'll insert this data; note that these are no longer external tables:

```
CREATE TABLE tweets_hcat…
CREATE TABLE places_hcat …
CREATE TABLE users_hcat …
```

Note that if we had these commands in a script file, we could use the hcat CLI tool to execute them, as follows:

```
$ hcat -f create.hql
```

The HCat CLI tool does not, however, offer an interactive shell akin to the Hive CLI. We can now use our previous Pig script and need to only change the store commands, replacing the use of `PigStorage` with `HCatStorer`. Our updated Pig script, `extract_to_hcat.pig`, therefore includes `store` commands such as the following:

```
store tweets_tsv into 'twttr.tweets_hcat' using org.apache.hive.
hcatalog.pig.HCatStorer();
```

Note that the package name for the `HCatStorer` class has the `org.apache.hive.hcatalog` prefix; when HCatalog was in the Apache incubator, it used `org.apache.hcatalog` for its package prefix. This older form is now deprecated, and the new form that explicitly shows HCatalog as a subproject of Hive should be used instead.

With this new Pig script, we can now replace our previous Pig and Hive action with an updated Pig action using HCatalog. This also requires the first usage of the Oozie sharelib, which we'll discuss in the next section. In our workflow definition, the `pig` element of this action will be defined as shown in the following xml and can be found as v3 of the pipeline in the source bundle; in v3, we've also added a utility Hive node to run before the Pig node to ensure that all necessary tables exist before the Pig script that requires them is executed.

```
<pig>
    <job-tracker>${jobTracker}</job-tracker>
    <name-node>${nameNode}</name-node>
    <job-xml>${workflowRoot}/hive-site.xml</job-xml>
     <configuration>
            <property>
                <name>mapred.job.queue.name</name>
                <value>${queueName}</value>
            </property>
            <property>
                <name>oozie.action.sharelib.for.pig</name>
                <value>pig,hcatalog</value>
```

```
            </property>
        </configuration>
        <script>${workflowRoot}/pig/extract_to_hcat.pig
        </script>
        <argument>-param</argument>
        <argument>inputDir=${inputDir}</argument>
    </pig>
```

The two changes of note are the addition of the explicit reference to the
`hive-site.xml` file; this is required by HCatalog, and the new configuration
element that tells Oozie to include the required `HCatalog` JARs.

The Oozie sharelib

That last addition touched on an important aspect of Oozie we've not mentioned
thus far: the Oozie `sharelib`. When Oozie runs all its various action types, it requires
multiple JARs to access Hadoop and to invoke various tools, such as Hive and Pig. As
part of the Oozie installation, a large number of dependent JARs have been placed on
HDFS to be used by Oozie and its various action types: this is the Oozie `sharelib`.

For most usages of Oozie, it's enough to know the `sharelib` exists, usually under
`/user/oozie/share/lib on HDFS`, and when, as in the previous example, some
explicit configuration values need to be added. When using a Pig action, the Pig
JARs will automatically get picked up, but when the Pig script uses something like
HCatalog, then this dependency will not be explicitly known to Oozie.

The Oozie CLI allows manipulation of the `sharelib`, though the scenarios where this
will be required are outside of the scope of this book. The following command can be
useful though to see which components are included in the Oozie `sharelib`:

`$ oozie admin -shareliblist`

The following command is useful to see the individual JARs comprising a particular
component within the `sharelib`, in this case HCatalog:

`$ oozie admin -shareliblist hcat`

These commands can be useful to verify that the required JARs are being included
and to see which specific versions are being used.

HCatalog and partitioned tables

If you rerun the previous workflow a second time, it will fail; dig into the logs, and you will see HCatalog complaining that it cannot write to a table that already contains data. This is a current limitation of HCatalog; it views tables and partitions within tables as immutable by default. Hive, on the other hand, will add new data to a table or partition; its default view of a table is that it is mutable.

Upcoming changes to Hive and HCatalog will see the support of a new table property that will control this behavior in either tool; for example, the following added to a table definition would allow table appends as supported in Hive today:

```
TBLPROPERTIES("immutable"="false")
```

This is currently not available in the shipping version of Hive and HCatalog, however. For us to have a workflow that adds more and more data into our tables, we therefore need to create a new partition for each new run of the workflow. We've made these changes in v4 of our pipeline, where we first recreate the tables with an integer partition key, as follows:

```
CREATE  TABLE tweets_hcat (
...)
PARTITIONED BY (partition_key int)
ROW FORMAT DELIMITED
  FIELDS TERMINATED BY '\u0001'
STORED AS SEQUENCEFILE;

CREATE  TABLE `places_hcat`(
... )
partitioned by(partition_key int)
ROW FORMAT DELIMITED
  FIELDS TERMINATED BY '\u0001'
STORED AS SEQUENCEFILE
TBLPROPERTIES("immutable"="false") ;

CREATE  TABLE `users_hcat`(
...)
partitioned by(partition_key int)
ROW FORMAT DELIMITED
  FIELDS TERMINATED BY '\u0001'
STORED AS SEQUENCEFILE
TBLPROPERTIES("immutable"="false") ;
```

The Pig `HCatStorer` takes an optional partition definition and we modify the `store` statements in our Pig script accordingly; for example:

```
store tweets_tsv into 'twttr.tweets_hcat'
using org.apache.hive.hcatalog.pig.HCatStorer(
'partition_key=$partitionKey');
```

We then modify our Pig action in the `workflow.xml` file to include this additional parameter:

```
<script>${workflowRoot}/pig/extract_to_hcat.pig</script>
        <param>inputDir=${inputDir}</param>
        <param>partitionKey=${partitionKey}</param>
```

The question is then how we pass this partition key to the workflow. We could specify it in the `job.properties` file, but by doing so we would hit the same problem with trying to write to an existing partition on the next re-run.

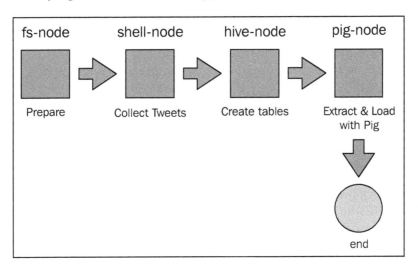

Ingestion workflow v4

For now, we'll pass this as an explicit argument to the invocation of the Oozie CLI and explore better ways to do this later:

```
$ oozie job -run -config v4/job.properties -DpartitionKey=12345
```

Note that a consequence of this behavior is that rerunning an HCat workflow with the same arguments will fail. Be aware of this when testing workflows or playing with the sample code from this book.

Producing derived data

Now that we have our main data pipeline established, there is most likely a series of actions that we wish to take after we add each new additional dataset. As a simple example, note that with our previous mechanism of adding each set of user data to a separate partition, the users_hcat table will contain users multiple times. Let's create a new table for unique users and regenerate this each time we add new user data.

Note that given the aforementioned limitations of HCatalog, we'll use a Hive action for this purpose, as we need to replace the data in a table.

First, we'll create a new table for unique user information, as follows:

```
CREATE TABLE IF NOT EXISTS `unique_users`(
  `user_id` string ,
  `name` string ,
  `description` string ,
  `screen_name` string )
ROW FORMAT DELIMITED
  FIELDS TERMINATED BY '\t'
STORED AS sequencefile ;
```

In this table, we'll only store the attributes of a user that either never change (ID) or change rarely (the screen name, and so on). We can then write a simple Hive statement to populate this table from the full users_hcat table:

```
USE twttr;
INSERT OVERWRITE TABLE unique_users
SELECT DISTINCT user_id, name, description, screen_name
FROM users_hcat;
```

We can then add an additional Hive action node that comes after our previous Pig node in the workflow. When doing this, we discover that our pattern of simply giving nodes names such as hive-node is a really bad idea, as we now have two Hive-based nodes. In v5 of the workflow, we add this new node and also change our nodes to have more descriptive names:

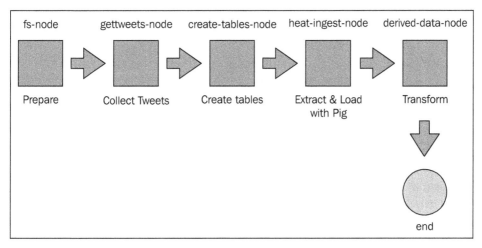

Ingestion workflow v5

Performing multiple actions in parallel

Our workflow has two types of activity: initial setup with the nodes that initialize the filesystem and Hive tables, and the functional nodes that perform actual processing. If we look at the two setup nodes we have been using, it is obvious that they are quite distinct and not interdependent. We can therefore take advantage of an Oozie feature called `fork` and `join` nodes to execute these actions in parallel. The start of our `workflow.xml` file now becomes:

```
<start to="setup-fork-node"/>
```

The Oozie `fork` node contains a number of `path` elements, each of which specifies a starting node. Each of these will be launched in parallel:

```
<fork name="setup-fork-node">
   <path start="setup-filesystem-node" />
   <path start="create-tables-node" />
</fork>
```

Each of the specified action nodes is no different from any we have used previously. An action node can link to a series of other nodes; the only requirement is that each parallel series of actions must end with a transition to the `join` node associated with the `fork` node, as follows:

```
<action name="setup-filesystem-node">
...
    <ok to="setup-join-node"/>
    <error to="fail"/>
</action>
<action name="create-tables-node">
...
    <ok to="setup-join-node"/>
    <error to="fail"/>
</action>
```

The `join` node itself acts as the point of coordination; any workflow that has completed will wait until all the paths specified in the `fork` node reach this point. At that point, the workflow continues at the node specified within the `join` node. Here's how the `join` node is used:

```
<join name="create-join-node" to="gettweets-node"/>
```

In the preceding code we omitted the action definitions for space purposes, but the full workflow definition is in v6:

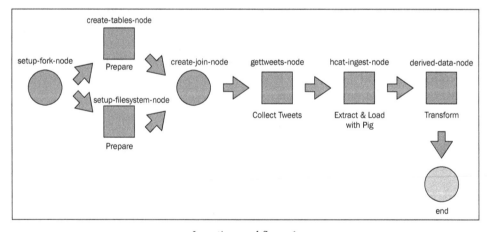

Ingestion workflow v6

Calling a subworkflow

Though the `fork/join` mechanism makes the process of parallel actions more efficient, it does still add significant verbosity if we include it in our main `workflow.xml` definition. Conceptually, we have a series of actions that are performing related tasks required by our workflow but not necessarily part of it. For this and similar cases, Oozie offers the ability to invoke a subworkflow. The parent workflow will execute the child and wait for it to complete, with the ability to pass configuration elements from one workflow to the other.

The child workflow will be a full workflow in its own right, usually stored in a directory on HDFS with all the usual structure we expect for a workflow, the main `workflow.xml` file, and any required Hive, Pig, or similar files.

We can create a new directory on HDFS called setup-workflow, and in this create the files required only for our filesystem and Hive creation actions. The subworkflow configuration file will look like the following:

```
<workflow-app xmlns="uri:oozie:workflow:0.4" name="create-workflow">
    <start to="setup-fork-node"/>
    <fork name="setup-fork-node">
        <path start="setup-filesystem-node" />
      <path start="create-tables-node" />
    </fork>
    <action name="setup-filesystem-node">
    ...
    </action>
    <action name="create-tables-node">
    ...
    </action>
    <join name="create-join-node" to="end"/>
    <kill name="fail">
        <message>Action failed, error
          message[${wf:errorMessage(wf:lastErrorNode())}]</message>
    </kill>
    <end name="end"/>
</workflow-app>
```

With this subworkflow defined, we then modify the first nodes of our main workflow to use a subworkflow node, as in the following:

```
<start to="create-subworkflow-node"/>
<action name="create-subworkflow-node">
    <sub-workflow>
        <app-path>${subWorkflowRoot}</app-path>
        <propagate-configuration/>
    </sub-workflow>
    <ok to="gettweets-node"/>
    <error to="fail"/>
</action>
```

We will specify the `subWorkflowPath` in the `job.properties` of our parent workflow, and the `propagate-configuration` element will pass the configuration of the parent workflow to the child.

Adding global settings

By extracting utility nodes into subworkflows, we can significantly reduce clutter and complexity in our main workflow definition. In v7 of our ingest pipeline, we'll make one additional simplification and add a global configuration section, as in the following:

```
<workflow-app xmlns="uri:oozie:workflow:0.4" name="v7">
    <global>
            <job-tracker>${jobTracker}</job-tracker>
            <name-node>${nameNode}</name-node>
            <job-xml>${workflowRoot}/hive-site.xml</job-xml>
            <configuration>
                <property>
                    <name>mapred.job.queue.name</name>
                    <value>${queueName}</value>
                </property>
            </configuration>
    </global>
</global>
<start to="create-subworkflow-node"/>
```

By adding this global configuration section, we remove the need to specify any of these values in the Hive and Pig nodes in the remaining workflow (note that currently the shell node does not support the global configuration mechanism). This can dramatically simplify some of our nodes; for example, our Pig node is now as follows:

```
<action name="hcat-ingest-node">
    <pig>
```

```
        <configuration>
          <property>
            <name>oozie.action.sharelib.for.pig</name>
            <value>pig,hcatalog</value>
            </property>
          </configuration>
          <script>${workflowRoot}/pig/extract_to_hcat.pig</script>
            <param>inputDir=${inputDir}</param>
            <param>dbName=${dbName}</param>
            <param>partitionKey=${partitionKey}</param>
      </pig>
      <ok to="derived-data-node"/>
      <error to="fail"/>
    </action>
```

As can be seen, we can add additional configuration elements, or indeed override those specified in the global section, resulting in a much clearer action definition that focuses only on the information specific to the action in question. Our workflow v7 has had both a global section added as well as the addition of the subworkflow, and this makes a significant improvement in the workflow readability:

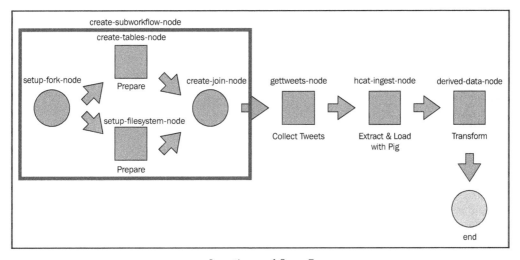

Ingestion workflow v7

Challenges of external data

When we rely on external data to drive our application, we are implicitly dependent on the quality and stability of that data. This is, of course, true for any data, but when the data is generated by an external source over which we do not have control, the risks are most likely higher. Regardless, when building what we expect to be reliable applications on top of such data feeds, and especially when our data volumes grow, we need to think about how to mitigate these risks.

Data validation

We use the general term data validation to refer to the act of ensuring that incoming data complies with our expectations and potentially applying normalization to modify it accordingly or to even delete malformed or corrupt input. What this actually involves will be very application-specific. In some cases, the important thing is ensuring the system only ingests data that conforms to a given definition of accurate or clean. For our tweet data, we don't care about every single record and could very easily adopt a policy such as dropping records that don't have values in particular fields we care about. For other applications, however, it is imperative to capture every input record, and this might drive the implementation of logic to reformat every record to make sure it complies with the requirements. In yet other cases, only correct records will be ingested, but the rest, instead of being discarded, might be stored elsewhere for later analysis.

The bottom line is that trying to define a generic approach to data validation is vastly beyond the scope of this chapter.

However, we can offer some thoughts on where in the pipeline to incorporate various types of validation logic.

Validation actions

Logic to do any necessary validation or cleanup can be incorporated directly into other actions. A shell node running a script to gather data can have commands added to handle malformed records differently. Pig and Hive actions that load data into tables can either perform filtering on ingest (easier done in Pig) or add caveats when copying data from an ingest table to the operational store.

There is an argument though for the addition of a validation node into the workflow, even if initially it performs no actual logic. This could, for instance, be a Pig action that reads the data, applies the validation, and writes the validated data to a new location to be read by follow-on nodes. The advantage here is that we can later update the validation logic without altering our other actions, which should reduce the risk of accidentally breaking the rest of the pipeline and also make nodes more cleanly defined in terms of responsibilities. The natural extension of this train of thought is that a new subworkflow for validation is most likely a good model as well, as it not only provides separation of responsibilities, but also makes the validation logic easier to test and update.

The obvious disadvantage of this approach is that it adds additional processing and another cycle of reading the data and writing it all again. This is, of course, directly working against one of the advantages we highlighted when considering the use of HCatalog from Pig.

In the end, it will come down to a trade-off of performance against workflow complexity and maintainability. When considering how to perform validation and just what that means for your workflow, take all these elements into account before deciding on an implementation.

Handling format changes

We can't declare victory just because we have data flowing into our system and are confident the data is sufficiently validated. Particularly when the data comes from an external source we have to think about how the structure of the data might change over time.

Remember that systems such as Hive only apply the table schema when the data is being read. This is a huge benefit in enabling flexible data storage and ingest, but can lead to user-facing queries or workloads failing suddenly when the ingested data no longer matches the queries being executed against it. A relational database, which applies schemas on write, would not even allow such data to be ingested into the system.

The obvious approach to handling changes made to the data format would be to reprocess existing data into the new format. Though this is tractable on smaller datasets, it quickly becomes infeasible on the sort of volumes seen in large Hadoop clusters.

Handling schema evolution with Avro

Avro has some features with respect to its integration with Hive that help us with this problem. If we take our table for tweets data, we could represent the structure of a tweet record by the following Avro schema:

```
{
 "namespace": "com.learninghadoop2.avrotables",
 "type":"record",
 "name":"tweets_avro",
 "fields":[
   {"name": "created_at", "type": ["null" ,"string"]},
   {"name": "tweet_id_str", "type": ["null","string"]},
   {"name": "text","type":["null","string"]},
   {"name": "in_reply_to", "type": ["null","string"]},
   {"name": "is_retweeted", "type": ["null","string"]},
   {"name": "user_id", "type": ["null","string"]},
  {"name": "place_id", "type": ["null","string"]}
   ]
}
```

Create the preceding schema in a file called `tweets_avro.avsc`—this is the standard file extension for Avro schemas. Then, place it on HDFS; we like to have a common location for schema files such as `/schema/avro`.

With this definition, we can now create a Hive table that uses this schema for its table specification, as follows:

```
CREATE TABLE tweets_avro
PARTITIONED BY ( `partition_key` int)
ROW FORMAT SERDE
  'org.apache.hadoop.hive.serde2.avro.AvroSerDe'
WITH SERDEPROPERTIES (
'avro.schema.url'='hdfs://localhost.localdomain:8020/schema/avro/
tweets_avro.avsc'
)
STORED AS INPUTFORMAT
  'org.apache.hadoop.hive.ql.io.avro.AvroContainerInputFormat'
OUTPUTFORMAT
  'org.apache.hadoop.hive.ql.io.avro.AvroContainerOutputFormat';
```

Then, look at the table definition from within Hive (or HCatalog, which also supports such definitions):

```
describe tweets_avro
OK
created_at              string                  from deserializer
tweet_id_str            string                  from deserializer
text                    string                  from deserializer
in_reply_to             string                  from deserializer
is_retweeted            string                  from deserializer
user_id                 string                  from deserializer
place_id                string                  from deserializer
partition_key           int                     None
```

We can also use this table like any other, for example, to copy the data from partition 3 from the non-Avro table into the Avro table, as follows:

```
SET hive.exec.dynamic.partition.mode=nonstrict
INSERT INTO TABLE tweets_avro
PARTITION (partition_key)
SELECT  FROM tweets_hcat
```

 Just as in previous examples, if Avro dependencies are not present in the classpath, we need to add the Avro MapReduce JAR to our environment before being able to select from the table.

We now have a new tweets table specified by an Avro schema; so far it just looks like other tables. But the real benefits for our purposes in this chapter are in how we can use the Avro mechanism to handle schema evolution. Let's add a new field to our table schema, as follows:

```
{
  "namespace": "com.learninghadoop2.avrotables",
  "type":"record",
  "name":"tweets_avro",
  "fields":[
```

```
    {"name": "created_at", "type": ["null" ,"string"]},
    {"name": "tweet_id_str", "type": ["null","string"]},
    {"name": "text","type":["null","string"]},
    {"name": "in_reply_to", "type": ["null","string"]},
    {"name": "is_retweeted", "type": ["null","string"]},
    {"name": "user_id", "type": ["null","string"]},
   {"name": "place_id", "type": ["null","string"]},
   {"name": "new_feature", "type": "string", "default": "wow!"}
   ]
}
```

With this new schema in place, we can validate that the table definition has also been updated, as follows:

```
describe tweets_avro;
OK
created_at              string              from deserializer
tweet_id_str            string              from deserializer
text                    string              from deserializer
in_reply_to             string              from deserializer
is_retweeted            string              from deserializer
user_id                 string              from deserializer
place_id                string              from deserializer
new_feature             string              from deserializer
partition_key           int                 None
```

Without adding any new data, we can run queries on the new field that will return the default value for our existing data, as follows:

```
SELECT new_feature FROM tweets_avro LIMIT 5;
...
OK
wow!
wow!
wow!
wow!
wow!
```

Even more impressive is the fact that the new column doesn't need to be added at the end; it can be anywhere in the record. With this mechanism, we can now update our Avro schemas to represent the new data structure and see these changes automatically reflected in our Hive table definitions. Any queries that refer to the new column will retrieve the default value for all our existing data that does not have that field present.

Note that the default mechanism we are using here is core to Avro and is not specific to Hive. Avro is a very powerful and flexible format that has applications in many areas and is definitely worth deeper examination than we are giving it here.

Technically, what this provides us with is forward compatibility. We can make changes to our table schema and have all our existing data remain automatically compliant with the new structure we can't, however, continue to ingest data of the old format into the updated tables since the mechanism does not provide backward compatibility:

```
INSERT INTO TABLE tweets_avro
PARTITION (partition_key)
SELECT * FROM tweets_hcat;
FAILED: SemanticException [Error 10044]: Line 1:18 Cannot insert into
target table because column number/types are different 'tweets_avro':
Table insclause-0 has 8 columns, but query has 7 columns.
```

Supporting schema evolution with Avro allows data changes to be something that is handled as part of normal business instead of the firefighting emergency they all too often turn into. But plainly, it's not for free; there is still a need to make the changes in the pipeline and roll these into production. Having Hive tables that provide forward compatibility does, however, allow the process to be performed in more manageable steps; otherwise, you would need to synchronize changes across every stage of the pipeline. If the changes are made from ingest up to the point they are inserted into Avro-backed Hive tables, then all users of those tables can remain unchanged (as long as they don't do things like `select *`, which is usually a terrible idea anyway) and continue to run existing queries against the new data. These applications can then be changed on a different timetable to the ingestion mechanism. In our v8 of the ingest pipeline, we show how to fully use Avro tables for all of our existing functionality.

 Note that Hive 0.14, currently unreleased at the time of writing this, will likely include more built-in support for Avro that might simplify the process of schema evolution even further. If Hive 0.14 is available when you read this, then do check out the final implementation.

Final thoughts on using Avro schema evolution

With this discussion of Avro, we have touched on some aspects of much broader topics, in particular of data management on a broader scale and policies around data versioning and retention. Much of this area becomes very specific to an organization, but here are a few parting thoughts that we feel are more broadly applicable.

Only make additive changes

We discussed adding columns in the preceding example. Sometimes, though more rarely, your source data drops columns or you discover you no longer need a new column. Avro doesn't really provide tools to help with this, and we feel it is often undesirable. Instead of dropping old columns, we tend to maintain the old data and simply do not use the empty columns in all the new data. This is much easier to manage if you control the data format; if you are ingesting external sources, then to follow this approach you will either need to reprocess data to remove the old column or change the ingest mechanism to add a default value for all new data.

Manage schema versions explicitly

In the preceding examples, we had a single schema file to which we made changes directly. This is likely a very bad idea, as it removes our ability to track schema changes over time. In addition to treating schemas as artifacts to be kept under version control (your schemas are in Git too, aren't they?) it is often useful to tag each schema with an explicit version. This is particularly useful when the incoming data is also explicitly versioned. Then, instead of overwriting the existing schema file, you can add the new file and use an ALTER TABLE statement to point the Hive table definition at the new schema. We are, of course, assuming here that you don't have the option of using a different query for the old data with the different format. Though there is no automatic mechanism for Hive to select schema, there might be cases where you can control this manually and sidestep the evolution question.

Think about schema distribution

When using a schema file, think about how it will be distributed to the clients. If, as in the previous example, the file is on HDFS, then it likely makes sense to give it a high replication factor. The file will be retrieved by each mapper in every MapReduce job that queries the table.

The Avro URL can also be specified as a local filesystem location (file://), which is useful for development and also as a web resource (http://). Though the latter is very useful as it is a convenient mechanism to distribute the schema to non-Hadoop clients, remember that the load on the web server might be high. With modern hardware and efficient web servers, this is most likely not a huge concern, but if you have a cluster of thousands of machines running many parallel jobs where each mapper needs to hit the web server, then be careful.

Collecting additional data

Many data processing systems don't have a single data ingest source; often, one primary source is enriched by other secondary sources. We will now look at how to incorporate the retrieval of such reference data into our data warehouse.

At a high level, the problem isn't very different from our retrieval of the raw tweet data, as we wish to pull data from an external source, possibly do some processing on it, and store it somewhere where it can be used later. But this does highlight an aspect we need to consider; do we really want to retrieve this data every time we ingest new tweets? The answer is certainly no. The reference data changes very rarely, and we could easily fetch it much less frequently than new tweet data. This raises a question we've skirted until now: just how do we schedule Oozie workflows?

Scheduling workflows

Until now, we've run all our Oozie workflows on demand from the CLI. Oozie also has a scheduler that allows jobs to be started either on a timed basis or when external criteria such as data appearing in HDFS are met. It would be a good fit for our workflows to have our main tweet pipeline run, say, every 10 minutes but the reference data only refreshed daily.

 Regardless of when data is retrieved, think carefully how to handle datasets that perform a delete/replace operation. In particular, don't do the delete before retrieving and validating the new data; otherwise, any jobs that require the reference data will fail until the next run of the retrieval succeeds. It could be a good option to include the destructive operations in a subworkflow that is only triggered after successful completion of the retrieval steps.

Oozie actually defines two types of applications that it can run: workflows such as we've used so far and coordinators, which schedule workflows to be executed based on various criteria. A coordinator job is conceptually similar to our other workflows; we push an XML configuration file onto HDFS and use a parameterized properties file to configure it at runtime. In addition, coordinator jobs have the facility to receive additional parameterization from the events that trigger their execution.

This is possibly best described by an example. Let's say, we wish to do as previously mentioned and create a coordinator that executes v7 of our ingest workflow every 10 minutes. Here's the `coordinator.xml` file (the standard name for the coordinator XML definition):

```
<coordinator-app name="tweets-10min-coordinator" frequency="${freq}"
start="${startTime}" end="${endTime}" timezone="UTC" xmlns="uri:oozie
:coordinator:0.2">
```

The main action node in a coordinator is the workflow, for which we need to specify its root location on HDFS and all required properties, as follows:

```
<action>
    <workflow>
        <app-path>${workflowPath}</app-path>
            <configuration>
                <property>
                    <name>workflowRoot</name>
                    <value>${workflowRoot}</value>
                </property>
...
```

We also need to include any properties required by any action in the workflow or by any subworkflow it triggers; in effect, this means that any user-defined variables present in any of the workflows to be triggered need to be included here, as follows:

```
<property>
    <name>dbName</name>
    <value>${dbName}</value>
</property>
<property>
    <name>partitionKey</name>
  <value>${coord:formatTime(coord:nominalTime(),
    'yyyyMMddhhmm')}
    </value>
</property>
<property>
    <name>exec</name>
    <value>gettweets.sh</value>
</property>
<property>
    <name>inputDir</name>
    <value>/tmp/tweets</value>
</property>
<property>
```

```
            <name>subWorkflowRoot</name>
            <value>${subWorkflowRoot}</value>
         </property>
      </configuration>
   </workflow>
  </action>
</coordinator-app>
```

We used a few coordinator-specific features in the preceding xml. Note the specification of the starting and ending time of the coordinator and also its frequency (in minutes). We are using the simplest form here; Oozie also has a set of functions to allow quite rich specifications of the frequency.

We use coordinator EL functions in our definition of the `partitionKey` variable. Earlier, when running workflows from the CLI, we specified these explicitly but mentioned there was a better way—this is it. The following expression generates a formatted output containing the year, month, day, hour, and minute:

```
${coord:formatTime(coord:nominalTime(), 'yyyyMMddhhmm')}
```

If we then use this as the value for our partition key, we can ensure that each invocation of the workflow correctly creates a unique partition in our `HCatalog` tables.

The corresponding `job.properties` for the coordinator job looks much like our previous config files with the usual entries for the NameNode and similar variables as well as having values for the application-specific variables, such as `dbName`. In addition, we need to specify the root of the coordinator location on HDFS, as follows:

```
oozie.coord.application.path=${nameNode}/user/${user.
name}/${tasksRoot}/tweets_10min
```

Note the `oozie.coord` namespace prefix instead of the previously used `oozie.wf`. With the coordinator definition on HDFS, we can submit the file to Oozie just as with the previous jobs. But in this case, the job will only run for a given time period. Specifically, it will run every five minutes (the frequency is variable) when the system clock is between `startTime` and `endTime`.

We've included the full configuration in the `tweets_10min` directory in the source code for this chapter.

Other Oozie triggers

The preceding coordinator has a very simple trigger; it starts periodically within a specified time range. Oozie has an additional capability called datasets, where it can be triggered by the availability of new data.

This isn't a great fit for how we've defined our pipeline until now, but imagine that, instead of our workflow collecting tweets as its first step, an external system was pushing new files of tweets onto HDFS on a continuous basis. Oozie can be configured to either look for the presence of new data based on a directory pattern or to specifically trigger when a ready file appears on HDFS. This latter configuration provides a very convenient mechanism with which to integrate the output of MapReduce jobs, which by default, write a _SUCCESS file into their output directory.

Oozie datasets are arguably one of the most powerful parts of the whole system, and we cannot do them justice here for space reasons. But we do strongly recommend that you consult the Oozie home page for more information.

Pulling it all together

Let's review what we've discussed until now and how we can use Oozie to build a sophisticated series of workflows that implement an approach to data life cycle management by putting together all the discussed techniques.

First, it's important to define clear responsibilities and implement parts of the system using good design and separation of concern principles. By applying this, we end up with several different workflows:

- A subworkflow to ensure the environment (mainly HDFS and Hive metadata) is correctly configured
- A subworkflow to perform data validation
- The main workflow that triggers both the preceding subworkflows and then pulls new data through a multistep ingest pipeline
- A coordinator that executes the preceding workflows every 10 minutes
- A second coordinator that ingests reference data that will be useful to the application pipeline

We also define all our tables with Avro schemas and use them wherever possible to help manage schema evolution and changing data formats over time.

We present the full source code of these components in the final version of the workflow in the source code of this chapter.

Other tools to help

Though Oozie is a very powerful tool, sometimes it can be somewhat difficult to correctly write workflow definition files. As pipelines get sizeable, managing complexity becomes a challenge even with good functional partitioning into multiple workflows. At a simpler level, XML is just never fun for a human to write! There are a few tools that can help. Hue, the tool calling itself the Hadoop UI (`http://gethue.com/`), provides some graphical tools to help compose, execute, and manage Oozie workflows. Though powerful, Hue is not a beginner tool; we'll mention it a little more in *Chapter 11, Where to Go Next*.

A new Apache project called Falcon (`http://falcon.incubator.apache.org`) might also be of interest. Falcon uses Oozie to build a range of much higher-level data flows and actions. For example, Falcon provides recipes to enable and ensure cross-site replication across multiple Hadoop clusters. The Falcon team is working on much better interfaces to build their workflows, so the project might well be worth watching.

Summary

Hopefully, this chapter presented the topic of data life cycle management as something other than a dry abstract concept. We covered a lot, particularly:

- The definition of data life cycle management and how it covers a number of issues and techniques that usually become important with large data volumes

- The concept of building a data ingest pipeline along good data life cycle management principles that can then be utilized by higher-level analytic tools

- Oozie as a Hadoop-focused workflow manager and how we can use it to compose a series of actions into a unified workflow

- Various Oozie tools, such as subworkflows, parallel action execution, and global variables, that allow us to apply true design principles to our workflows

- HCatalog and how it provides the means for tools other than Hive to read and write table-structured data; we showed its great promise and integration with tools such as Pig but also highlighted some current weaknesses

- Avro as our tool of choice to handle schema evolution over time

- Using Oozie coordinators to build scheduled workflows based either on time intervals or data availability to drive the execution of multiple ingest pipelines

- Some other tools that can make these tasks easier, namely, Hue and Falcon

In the next chapter, we'll look at several of the higher-level analytic tools and frameworks that can build sophisticated application logic upon the data collected in an ingest pipeline.

9
Making Development Easier

In this chapter, we will look at how, depending on use cases and end goals, application development in Hadoop can be simplified using a number of abstractions and frameworks built on top of the Java APIs. In particular, we will learn about the following topics:

- How the streaming API allows us to write MapReduce jobs using dynamic languages such as Python and Ruby

- How frameworks such as Apache Crunch and Kite Morphlines allow us to express data transformation pipelines using higher-level abstractions

- How Kite Data, a promising framework developed by Cloudera, provides us with the ability to apply design patterns and boilerplate to ease integration and interoperability of different components within the Hadoop ecosystem

Choosing a framework

In the previous chapters, we looked at the MapReduce and Spark programming APIs to write distributed applications. Although very powerful and flexible, these APIs come with a certain level of complexity and possibly require significant development time.

In an effort to reduce verbosity, we introduced the Pig and Hive frameworks, which compile domain-specific languages, Pig Latin and Hive QL, into a number of MapReduce jobs or Spark DAGs, effectively abstracting the APIs away. Both languages can be extended with UDFs, which is a way of mapping complex logic to the Pig and Hive data models.

At times when we need a certain degree of flexibility and modularity, things can get tricky. Depending on the use case and developer needs, the Hadoop ecosystem presents a vast choice of APIs, frameworks, and libraries. In this chapter, we identify four categories of users and match them with the following relevant tools:

- Developers that want to avoid Java in favor of scripting MapReduce jobs using dynamic languages, or use languages not implemented on the JVM. A typical use case would be upfront analysis and rapid prototyping: Hadoop streaming

- Java developers that need to integrate components of the Hadoop ecosystem and could benefit from codified design patterns and boilerplate: Kite Data

- Java developers who want to write modular data pipelines using a familiar API: Apache Crunch

- Developers who would rather configure chains of data transformations. For instance, a data engineer that wants to embed existing code in an ETL pipeline: Kite Morphlines

Hadoop streaming

We have mentioned previously that MapReduce programs don't have to be written in Java. There are several reasons why you might want or need to write your map and reduce tasks in another language. Perhaps you have existing code to leverage or need to use third-party binaries — the reasons are varied and valid.

Hadoop provides a number of mechanisms to aid non-Java development, primary amongst which are Hadoop pipes that provide a native C++ interface and Hadoop streaming that allows any program that uses standard input and output to be used for map and reduce tasks. With the MapReduce Java API, both map and reduce tasks provide implementations for methods that contain the task functionality. These methods receive the input to the task as method arguments and then output results via the Context object. This is a clear and type-safe interface, but it is by definition Java-specific.

Hadoop streaming takes a different approach. With streaming, you write a map task that reads its input from standard input, one line at a time, and gives the output of its results to standard output. The reduce task then does the same, again using only standard input and output for its data flow.

Any program that reads and writes from standard input and output can be used in streaming, such as compiled binaries, Unix shell scripts, or programs written in a dynamic language such as Python or Ruby. The biggest advantage to streaming is that it can allow you to try ideas and iterate them more quickly than using Java. Instead of a compile/JAR/submit cycle, you just write the scripts and pass them as arguments to the streaming JAR file. Especially when doing initial analysis on a new dataset or trying out new ideas, this can significantly speed up development.

The classic debate regarding dynamic versus static languages balances the benefits of swift development against runtime performance and type checking. These dynamic downsides also apply when using streaming. Consequently, we favor the use of streaming for upfront analysis and Java for the implementation of jobs that will be executed on the production cluster.

Streaming word count in Python

We'll demonstrate Hadoop streaming by re-implementing our familiar word count example using Python. First, we create a script that will be our mapper. It consumes UTF-8 encoded rows of text from standard input with a `for` loop, splits this into words, and uses the `print` function to write each word to standard output, as follows:

```python
#!/bin/env python
import sys

for line in sys.stdin:
    # skip empty lines
    if line == '\n':
        continue

    # preserve utf-8 encoding
    try:
        line = line.encode('utf-8')
    except UnicodeDecodeError:
        continue
    # newline characters can appear within the text
    line = line.replace('\n', '')

    # lowercase and tokenize
    line = line.lower().split()
```

```
    for term in line:
        if not term:
          continue
        try:
            print(
                u"%s" % (
                    term.decode('utf-8')))
        except UnicodeEncodeError:
            continue
```

The reducer counts the number of occurrences of each word from standard input, and gives the output as the final value to standard output, as follows:

```
#!/bin/env python
import sys

count = 1
current = None

for word in sys.stdin:
    word = word.strip()

    if word == current:
        count += 1
    else:
        if current:
            print "%s\t%s" % (current.decode('utf-8'), count)
        current = word
        count = 1
if current == word:
    print "%s\t%s" % (current.decode('utf-8'), count)
```

> In both cases, we are implicitly using Hadoop input and output formats discussed in the earlier chapters. It is the TextInputFormat that processes the source file and provides each line one at a time to the map script. Conversely, the TextOutputFormat will ensure that the output of reduce tasks is also correctly written as text.

Copy map.py and reduce.py to HDFS, and execute the scripts as a streaming job using the sample data from the previous chapters, as follows:

**$ hadoop jar /opt/cloudera/parcels/CDH/lib/hadoop-mapreduce/hadoop-streaming.jar **

**-file map.py **

```
-mapper "python map.py" \
-file reduce.py \
-reducer "python reduce.py" \
-input sample.txt \
-output output.txt
```

 Tweets are UTF-8 encoded. Make sure that PYTHONIOENCODING is set accordingly in order to pipe data in a UNIX terminal:
`$ export PYTHONIOENCODING='UTF-8'`

The same code can be executed from the command-line prompt:

`$ cat sample.txt | python map.py| python reduce.py > out.txt`

The mapper and reducer code can be found at `https://github.com/ learninghadoop2/book-examples/blob/master/ch9/streaming/wc/python/ map.py`.

Differences in jobs when using streaming

In Java, we know that our `map()` method will be invoked once for each input key/value pair and our `reduce()` method will be invoked for each key and its set of values.

With streaming, we don't have the concept of the map or reduce methods anymore; instead we have written scripts that process streams of received data. This changes how we need to write our reducer. In Java, the grouping of values to each key was performed by Hadoop; each invocation of the reduce method would receive a single, tab separated key and all its values. In streaming, each instance of the reduce task is given the individual ungathered values one at a time.

Hadoop streaming does sort the keys, for example, if a mapper emitted the following data:

```
First 1
Word 1
Word 1
A 1
First 1
```

The streaming reducer would receive it in the following order:

```
A 1
First 1
First 1
Word 1
Word 1
```

Hadoop still collects the values for each key and ensures that each key is passed only to a single reducer. In other words, a reducer gets all the values for a number of keys, and they are grouped together; however, they are not packaged into individual executions of the reducer, that is, one per key, as with the Java API. Since Hadoop streaming uses the stdin and stdout channels to exchange data between tasks, debug and error messages should not be printed to standard output. In the following example, we will use the Python logging (https://docs.python.org/2/library/logging.html) package to log warning statements to a file.

Finding important words in text

We will now implement a metric, **Term Frequency-Inverse Document Frequency (TF-IDF)**, that will help us to determine the importance of words based on how frequently they appear across a set of documents (tweets, in our case).

Intuitively, if a word appears frequently in a document it is important and should be given a high score. However, if a word appears in many documents, we should penalize it with a lower score, as it is a common word and its frequency is not unique to this document.

Therefore, common words such as *the*, and *for*, which appear in many documents, will be scaled down. Words that appear frequently in a single tweet will be scaled up. Uses of TF-IDF, often in combination with other metrics and techniques, include stop word removal and text classification. Note that this technique will have shortcomings when dealing with short documents, such as tweets. In such cases, the term frequency component will tend to become one. Conversely, one could exploit this property to detect outliers.

The definition of TF-IDF we will use in our example is the following:

```
tf = # of times term appears in a document (raw frequency)
idf = 1+log(#  of documents / # documents with term in it)
tf-idf = tf * idf
```

We will implement the algorithm in Python using three MapReduce jobs:

- The first one calculates term frequency
- The second one calculates document frequency (the denominator of IDF)
- The third one calculates per-tweet TF-IDF

Calculate term frequency

The term frequency part is very similar to the word count example. The main difference is that we will be using a multi-field, tab-separated, key to keep track of co-occurrences of terms and document IDs. For each tweet—in JSON format—the mapper extracts the `id_str` and `text` fields, tokenizes `text`, and emits a `term`, `doc_id` tuple:

```python
for tweet in sys.stdin:
    # skip empty lines
    if tweet == '\n':
        continue
    try:
        tweet = json.loads(tweet)
    except:
        logger.warn("Invalid input %s " % tweet)
        continue
    # In our example one tweet corresponds to one document.
    doc_id = tweet['id_str']
    if not doc_id:
        continue

    # preserve utf-8 encoding
    text = tweet['text'].encode('utf-8')
    # newline characters can appear within the text
    text = text.replace('\n', '')

    # lowercase and tokenize
    text = text.lower().split()

    for term in text:
        try:
            print(
                u"%s\t%s" % (
                    term.decode('utf-8'), doc_id.decode('utf-8'))
                )
        except UnicodeEncodeError:
            logger.warn("Invalid term %s " % term)
```

In the reducer, we emit the frequency of each term in a document as a tab-separated string:

```
freq = 1
cur_term, cur_doc_id = sys.stdin.readline().split()
for line in sys.stdin:
    line = line.strip()
    try:
        term, doc_id = line.split('\t')
    except:
        logger.warn("Invalid record %s " % line)

    # the key is a (doc_id, term) pair
    if (doc_id == cur_doc_id) and (term == cur_term):
        freq += 1

    else:
        print(
            u"%s\t%s\t%s" % (
                cur_term.decode('utf-8'), cur_doc_id.decode('utf-8'),
freq))
        cur_doc_id = doc_id
        cur_term = term
        freq = 1

print(
    u"%s\t%s\t%s" % (
        cur_term.decode('utf-8'), cur_doc_id.decode('utf-8'), freq))
```

For this implementation to work, it is crucial that the reducer input is sorted by term. We can test both scripts from the command line with the following pipe:

```
$ cat tweets.json | python map-tf.py | sort -k1,2 | \
python reduce-tf.py
```

Whereas at the command line we use the `sort` utility, in MapReduce we will use `org.apache.hadoop.mapreduce.lib.KeyFieldBasedComparator`. This comparator implements a subset of features provided by the `sort` command. In particular, ordering by field can be specified with the `-k<position>` option. To filter by term, the first field of our key, we set `-D mapreduce.text.key.comparator.options=-k1`:

```
/usr/bin/hadoop jar /opt/cloudera/parcels/CDH/lib/hadoop-mapreduce/
hadoop-streaming.jar \

-D map.output.key.field.separator=\t \

-D stream.num.map.output.key.fields=2 \

-Dmapreduce.output.key.comparator.class=\

org.apache.hadoop.mapreduce.lib.KeyFieldBasedComparator \

-D mapreduce.text.key.comparator.options=-k1,2 \

-input tweets.json \

-output /tmp/tf-out.tsv \

-file map-tf.py \

-mapper "python map-tf.py" \

-file reduce-tf.py \

-reducer "python reduce-tf.py"
```

 We specify which fields belong to the key (for shuffling) in the comparator options.

The mapper and reducer code can be found at `https://github.com/learninghadoop2/book-examples/blob/master/ch9/streaming/tf-idf/python/map-tf.py`.

Calculate document frequency

The main logic to calculate document frequency is in the reducer, while the mapper is just an identity function that loads and pipes the (ordered by term) output of the TF job. In the reducer, for each term, we count how many times it occurs across all documents. For each term, we keep a buffer `key_cache` of (`term`, `doc_id`, `tf`) tuples, and when a new term is found we flush the buffer to standard output, together with the accumulated document frequency `df`:

```
# Cache the (term,doc_id, tf) tuple.
key_cache = []

line = sys.stdin.readline().strip()
cur_term, cur_doc_id, cur_tf = line.split('\t')
cur_tf = int(cur_tf)
cur_df = 1
```

```
for line in sys.stdin:
    line = line.strip()

    try:
        term, doc_id, tf = line.strip().split('\t')
        tf = int(tf)
    except:
        logger.warn("Invalid record: %s " % line)
        continue

    # term is the only key for this input
    if (term == cur_term):
        # increment document frequency
        cur_df += 1

        key_cache.append(
            u"%s\t%s\t%s" % (term.decode('utf-8'), doc_
id.decode('utf-8'), tf))

    else:
        for key in key_cache:
            print("%s\t%s" % (key, cur_df))

        print (
            u"%s\t%s\t%s\t%s" % (
                cur_term.decode('utf-8'),
                cur_doc_id.decode('utf-8'),
                cur_tf, cur_df)
            )

        # flush the cache
        key_cache = []
        cur_doc_id = doc_id
        cur_term = term
        cur_tf = tf
        cur_df = 1

for key in key_cache:
    print(u"%s\t%s" % (key.decode('utf-8'), cur_df))
print(
    u"%s\t%s\t%s\t%s\n" % (
        cur_term.decode('utf-8'),
        cur_doc_id.decode('utf-8'),
        cur_tf, cur_df))
```

We can test the scripts from the command line with:

```
$ cat /tmp/tf-out.tsv  |  python map-df.py  |  python reduce-df.py > /tmp/
df-out.tsv
```

And we can test the scripts on Hadoop streaming with:

```
/usr/bin/hadoop jar /opt/cloudera/parcels/CDH/lib/hadoop-mapreduce/
hadoop-streaming.jar \
-D map.output.key.field.separator=\t \
-D stream.num.map.output.key.fields=3 \
-D mapreduce.output.key.comparator.class=\
org.apache.hadoop.mapreduce.lib.KeyFieldBasedComparator \
-D mapreduce.text.key.comparator.options=-k1 \
-input /tmp/tf-out.tsv/part-00000 \
-output /tmp/df-out.tsv \
-mapper org.apache.hadoop.mapred.lib.IdentityMapper \
-file reduce-df.py \
-reducer "python reduce-df.py"
```

On Hadoop we use `org.apache.hadoop.mapred.lib.IdentityMapper`, which provides the same logic as the `map-df.py` script.

The mapper and reducer code can be found at `https://github.com/learninghadoop2/book-examples/blob/master/ch9/streaming/tf-idf/python/map-df.py`.

Putting it all together – TF-IDF

To calculate TF-IDF, we only need a mapper that consumes the output of the previous step:

```
num_doc = sys.argv[1]

for line in sys.stdin:
    line = line.strip()

    try:
        term, doc_id, tf, df = line.split('\t')

        tf = float(tf)
```

```
        df = float(df)
        num_doc = float(num_doc)
    except:
        logger.warn("Invalid record %s" % line)

    # idf = num_doc / df
    tf_idf = tf * (1+math.log(num_doc / df))
    print("%s\t%s\t%s" % (term, doc_id, tf_idf))
```

The number of documents in the collection is passed as a parameter to `tf-idf.py`:

```
/usr/bin/hadoop jar /opt/cloudera/parcels/CDH/lib/hadoop-mapreduce/
hadoop-streaming.jar \

-D mapreduce.reduce.tasks=0 \

-input /tmp/df-out.tsv/part-00000 \

-output /tmp/tf-idf.out \

-file tf-idf.py \

-mapper "python tf-idf.py 15578"
```

To calculate the total number of tweets, we can use the `cat` and `wc` Unix utilities in combination with Hadoop streaming:

```
/usr/bin/hadoop jar /opt/cloudera/parcels/CDH/lib/hadoop-mapreduce/
hadoop-streaming.jar \

-input tweets.json \

-output tweets.cnt \

-mapper /bin/cat \

-reducer /usr/bin/wc
```

The mapper source code can be found at https://github.com/learninghadoop2/book-examples/blob/master/ch9/streaming/tf-idf/python/tf-idf.py.

Kite Data

The Kite SDK (http://www.kitesdk.org) is a collection of classes, command-line tools, and examples that aims at easing the process of building applications on top of Hadoop.

In this section we will look at how Kite Data, a subproject of Kite, can ease integration with several components of a Hadoop data warehouse. Kite examples can be found at https://github.com/kite-sdk/kite-examples.

On Cloudera's QuickStart VM, Kite JARs can be found at `/opt/cloudera/parcels/CDH/lib/kite/`.

Kite Data is organized in a number of subprojects, some of which we'll describe in the following sections.

Data Core

As the name suggests, the core is the building block for all capabilities provided in the Data module. Its principal abstractions are datasets and repositories.

The `org.kitesdk.data.Dataset` interface is used to represent an immutable set of data:

```
@Immutable
public interface Dataset<E> extends RefinableView<E> {
  String getName();
  DatasetDescriptor getDescriptor();
  Dataset<E> getPartition(PartitionKey key, boolean autoCreate);
  void dropPartition(PartitionKey key);
  Iterable<Dataset<E>> getPartitions();
  URI getUri();
}
```

Each dataset is identified by a name and an instance of the `org.kitesdk.data.DatasetDescriptor` interface, that is the structural description of a dataset and provides its schema (`org.apache.avro.Schema`) and partitioning strategy.

Implementations of the `Reader<E>` interface are used to read data from an underlying storage system and produce deserialized entities of type `E`. The `newReader()` method can be used to get an appropriate implementation for a given dataset:

```
public interface DatasetReader<E> extends Iterator<E>, Iterable<E>,
Closeable {
  void open();

  boolean hasNext();

  E next();
    void remove();
    void close();
    boolean isOpen();
}
```

An instance of `DatasetReader` will provide methods to read and iterate over streams of data. Similarly, `org.kitesdk.data.DatasetWriter` provides an interface to write streams of data to the `Dataset` objects:

```
public interface DatasetWriter<E> extends Flushable, Closeable {
    void open();
    void write(E entity);
    void flush();
    void close();
    boolean isOpen();
}
```

Like readers, writers are use-once objects. They serialize instances of entities of type `E` and write them to the underlying storage system. Writers are usually not instantiated directly; rather, an appropriate implementation can be created by the `newWriter()` factory method. Implementations of `DatasetWriter` will hold resources until `close()` is called and expect the caller to invoke `close()` in a `finally` block when the writer is no longer in use. Finally, note that implementations of `DatasetWriter` are typically not thread-safe. The behavior of a writer being accessed from multiple threads is undefined.

A particular case of a dataset is the `View` interface, which is as follows:

```
public interface View<E> {
    Dataset<E> getDataset();
    DatasetReader<E> newReader();
    DatasetWriter<E> newWriter();
    boolean includes(E entity);
    public boolean deleteAll();
}
```

Views carry subsets of the keys and partitions of an existing dataset; they are conceptually similar to the notion of "view" in the relational model.

A `View` interface can be created from ranges of data, or ranges of keys, or as a union between other views.

Data HCatalog

Data HCatalog is a module that enables the accessing of HCatalog repositories. The core abstractions of this module are `org.kitesdk.data.hcatalog.HCatalogAbstractDatasetRepository` and its concrete implementation, `org.kitesdk.data.hcatalog.HCatalogDatasetRepository`.

They describe a `DatasetRepository` that uses HCatalog to manage metadata and HDFS for storage, as follows:

```java
public class HCatalogDatasetRepository extends
HCatalogAbstractDatasetRepository {
    HCatalogDatasetRepository(Configuration conf) {
      super(conf, new HCatalogManagedMetadataProvider(conf));
  }
    HCatalogDatasetRepository(Configuration conf, MetadataProvider
provider) {
      super(conf, provider);
  }
    public <E> Dataset<E> create(String name, DatasetDescriptor
descriptor) {
      getMetadataProvider().create(name, descriptor);
      return load(name);
  }
   public boolean delete(String name) {
      return getMetadataProvider().delete(name);
  }
   public static class Builder {
      ...
  }
}
```

 As of Kite 0.17, Data HCatalog is deprecated in favor of the new Data Hive module.

The location of the data directory is either chosen by `Hive/HCatalog` (so-called "managed tables"), or specified when creating an instance of this class by providing a filesystem and a root directory in the constructor (external tables).

Data Hive

The kite-data-module exposes Hive schemas via the `Dataset` interface. As of Kite 0.17, this package supersedes Data HCatalog.

Data MapReduce

The `org.kitesdk.data.mapreduce` package provides interfaces to read and write data to and from a Dataset with MapReduce.

Data Spark

The `org.kitesdk.data.spark` package provides interfaces for reading and writing data to and from a Dataset with Apache Spark.

Data Crunch

The `org.kitesdk.data.crunch.CrunchDatasets` package is a helper class to expose datasets and views as Crunch `ReadableSource` or `Target` classes:

```
public class CrunchDatasets {
public static <E> ReadableSource<E> asSource(View<E> view, Class<E>
type) {
    return new DatasetSourceTarget<E>(view, type);
  }
public static <E> ReadableSource<E> asSource(URI uri, Class<E> type) {
    return new DatasetSourceTarget<E>(uri, type);
  }
public static <E> ReadableSource<E> asSource(String uri, Class<E>
type) {
    return asSource(URI.create(uri), type);
  }

public static <E> Target asTarget(View<E> view) {
    return new DatasetTarget<E>(view);
  }
 public static Target asTarget(String uri) {
    return asTarget(URI.create(uri));
  }
public static Target asTarget(URI uri) {
    return new DatasetTarget<Object>(uri);
  }
}
```

Apache Crunch

Apache Crunch (`http://crunch.apache.org`) is a Java and Scala library to create pipelines of MapReduce jobs. It is based on Google's FlumeJava (`http://dl.acm.org/citation.cfm?id=1806638`) paper and library. The project goal is to make the task of writing MapReduce jobs as straightforward as possible for anybody familiar with the Java programming language by exposing a number of patterns that implement operations such as aggregating, joining, filtering, and sorting records.

Similar to tools such as Pig, Crunch pipelines are created by composing immutable, distributed data structures and running all processing operations on such structures; they are expressed and implemented as user-defined functions. Pipelines are compiled into a DAG of MapReduce jobs, whose execution is managed by the library's planner. Crunch allows us to write iterative code and abstracts away the complexity of thinking in terms of map and reduce operations, while at the same time avoiding the need of an ad hoc programming language such as PigLatin. In addition, Crunch offers a highly customizable type system that allows us to work with, and mix, Hadoop Writables, HBase, and Avro serialized objects.

FlumeJava's main assumption is that MapReduce is the wrong level of abstraction for several classes of problems, where computations are often made up of multiple, chained jobs. Frequently, we need to compose logically independent operations (for example, filtering, projecting, grouping, and other transformations) into a single physical MapReduce job for performance reasons. This aspect also has implications for code testability. Although we won't cover this aspect in this chapter, the reader is encouraged to look further into it by consulting Crunch's documentation.

Getting started

Crunch JARs are already installed on the QuickStart VM. By default, the JARs are found in `/opt/cloudera/parcels/CDH/lib/crunch`.

Alternatively, recent Crunch libraries can be downloaded from `https://crunch.apache.org/download.html`, from Maven Central or Cloudera-specific repositories.

Concepts

Crunch pipelines are created by composing two abstractions: `PCollection` and `PTable`.

The `PCollection<T>` interface is a distributed, immutable collection of objects of type `T`. The `PTable<Key, Value>` interface is a distributed, immutable hashtable—a sub-interface of PCollection—of keys of the `Key` type and values of the `Value` type that exposes methods to work with the key-value pairs.

These two abstractions support the following four primitive operations:

- `parallelDo`: applies a user-defined function, `DoFn`, to a given `PCollection` and returns a new `PCollection`
- `union`: merges two or more `PCollection`s into a single virtual `PCollection`

- groupByKey: sorts and groups the elements of a PTable by their keys

- combineValues: aggregates the values from a groupByKey operation

The https://github.com/learninghadoop2/book-examples/blob/master/ch9/
crunch/src/main/java/com/learninghadoop2/crunch/HashtagCount.java
implements a Crunch MapReduce pipeline that counts hashtag occurrences:

```
Pipeline pipeline = new MRPipeline(HashtagCount.class, getConf());

pipeline.enableDebug();

PCollection<String> lines = pipeline.readTextFile(args[0]);

PCollection<String> words = lines.parallelDo(new DoFn<String,
String>() {
  public void process(String line, Emitter<String> emitter) {
    for (String word : line.split("\\s+")) {
        if (word.matches("(?:\\s|\\A|^)[##]+([A-Za-z0-9-_]+)")) {
            emitter.emit(word);
        }
    }
  }
}, Writables.strings());

PTable<String, Long> counts = words.count();

pipeline.writeTextFile(counts, args[1]);
// Execute the pipeline as a MapReduce.
pipeline.done();
```

In this example, we first create a MRPipeline pipeline and use it to first read the
content of sample.txt created with stream.py -t into a collection of strings, where
each element of the collection represents a tweet. We tokenize each tweet into words
with tweet.split("\\s+"), and we emit each word that matches the hashtag
regular expression, serialized as Writable. Note that the tokenizing and filtering
operations are executed in parallel by MapReduce jobs created by the parallelDo
call. We create a PTable that associates each hashtag, represented as a string, with
the number of times it occurred in the datasets. Finally, we write the PTable counts
into HDFS as a textfile. The pipeline is executed with pipeline.done().

To compile and execute the pipeline, we can use Gradle to manage the needed dependencies, as follows:

```
$ ./gradlew jar
$ ./gradlew copyJars
```

Add the Crunch and Avro dependencies downloaded with `copyJars` to the `LIBJARS` environment variable:

```
$ export CRUNCH_DEPS=build/libjars/crunch-example/lib
$ export LIBJARS=${LIBJARS},${CRUNCH_DEPS}/crunch-core-0.9.0-
cdh5.0.3.jar,${CRUNCH_DEPS}/avro-1.7.5-cdh5.0.3.jar,${CRUNCH_DEPS}/avro-
mapred-1.7.5-cdh5.0.3-hadoop2.jar
```

Then, run the example on Hadoop:

```
$ hadoop jar build/libs/crunch-example.jar \
com.learninghadoop2.crunch.HashtagCount \
tweets.json count-out \
-libjars $LIBJARS
```

Data serialization

One of the framework's goals is to make it easy to process complex records containing nested and repeated data structures, such as protocol buffers and Thrift records.

The `org.apache.crunch.types.PType` interface defines the mapping between a data type that is used in a Crunch pipeline and a serialization and storage format that is used to read/write data from/to HDFS. Every `PCollection` has an associated `PType` that tells Crunch how to read/write data.

The `org.apache.crunch.types.PTypeFamily` interface provides an abstract factory to implement instances of `PType` that share the same serialization format. Currently, Crunch supports two type families: one based on the Writable interface and the other on Apache Avro.

> Although Crunch permits mixing and matching `PCollection` interfaces that use different instances of `PType` in the same pipeline, each `PCollection` interfaces's `PType` must belong to a unique family. For instance, it is not possible to have a `PTable` with a key serialized as Writable and its value serialized using Avro.

Both type families support a common set of primitive types (strings, longs, integers, floats, doubles, booleans, and bytes) as well as more complex PType interfaces that can be constructed out of other PTypes. These include tuples and collections of other PType. A particularly important, complex, PType is tableOf, which determines whether the return type of paralleDo will be a PCollection or PTable.

New PTypes can be created by inheriting and extending the built-ins of the Avro and Writable families. This requires implementing input MapFn<S, T> and output MapFn<T, S> classes. We are implementing PType for instances where S is the original type and T is the new type .

Derived PTypes can be found in the PTypes class. These include serialization support for protocol buffers, Thrift records, Java Enums, BigInteger, and UUIDs. The Elephant Bird library we discussed in *Chapter 6, Data Analysis with Apache Pig,* contains additional examples.

Data processing patterns

org.apache.crunch.lib implements a number of design patterns for common data manipulation operations.

Aggregation and sorting

Most of the data processing patterns provided by org.apache.crunch.lib rely on the PTable's groupByKey method. The method has three different overloaded forms:

- groupByKey(): lets the planner determine the number of partitions
- groupByKey(int numPartitions): is used to set the number of partitions specified by the developer
- groupByKey(GroupingOptions options): allows us to specify custom partitions and comparators for shuffling

The org.apache.crunch.GroupingOptions class takes instances of Hadoop's Partitioner and RawComparator classes to implement custom partitioning and sorting operations.

The groupByKey method returns an instance of PGroupedTable, Crunch's representation of a grouped table. It corresponds to the output of the shuffle phase of a MapReduce job and allows values to be combined with the combineValue method.

The `org.apache.crunch.lib.Aggregate` package exposes methods to perform simple aggregations (count, max, top, and length) on the `PCollection` instances.

Sort provides an API to sort `PCollection` and `PTable` instances whose contents implement the `Comparable` interface.

By default, Crunch sorts data using one reducer. This behavior can be modified by passing the number of partitions required to the `sort` method. The `Sort.Order` method signals the order in which a sort should be done.

The following are how different sort options can be specified for collections:

```
public static <T> PCollection<T> sort(PCollection<T> collection)
public static <T> PCollection<T> sort(PCollection<T> collection,
Sort.Order order)
public static <T> PCollection<T> sort(PCollection<T> collection,
int numReducers,                                        Sort.Order
order)
```

The following are how different sort options can be specified for tables:

```
public static <K,V> PTable<K,V> sort(PTable<K,V> table)

public static <K,V> PTable<K,V> sort(PTable<K,V> table,
Sort.Order key)
public static <K,V> PTable<K,V> sort(PTable<K,V> table,
int numReducers, Sort.Order key)
```

Finally, `sortPairs` sorts the `PCollection` of pairs using the specified column order in `Sort.ColumnOrder`:

```
sortPairs(PCollection<Pair<U,V>> collection,
Sort.ColumnOrder... columnOrders)
```

Joining data

The `org.apache.crunch.lib.Join` package is an API to join `PTables` based on a common key. The following four join operations are supported:

- `fullJoin`
- `join` (defaults to `innerJoin`)
- `leftJoin`
- `rightJoin`

The methods have a common return type and signature. For reference, we will describe the commonly used `join` method that implements an inner join:

```
public static <K,U,V> PTable<K,Pair<U,V>> join(PTable<K,U> left,
PTable<K,V> right)
```

The `org.apache.crunch.lib.Join.JoinStrategy` package provides an interface to define custom join strategies. Crunch's default strategy (`defaultStrategy`) is to join data reduce-side.

Pipelines implementation and execution

Crunch comes with three implementations of the pipeline interface. The oldest one, implicitly used in this chapter, is `org.apache.crunch.impl.mr.MRPipeline`, which uses Hadoop's MapReduce as its execution engine. `org.apache.crunch.impl.mem.MemPipeline` allows all operations to be performed in memory, with no serialization to disk performed. Crunch 0.10 introduced `org.apache.crunch.impl.spark.SparkPipeline` which compiles and runs a DAG of `PCollections` to Apache Spark.

SparkPipeline

With SparkPipeline, Crunch delegates much of the execution to Spark and does relatively little of the planning tasks, with the following exceptions:

- Multiple inputs
- Multiple outputs
- Data serialization
- Checkpointing

At the time of writing, SparkPipeline is still heavily under development and might not handle all of the use cases of a standard MRPipeline. The Crunch community is actively working to ensure complete compatibility between the two implementations.

MemPipeline

MemPipeline executes in-memory on a client. Unlike MRPipeline, MemPipeline is not explicitly created but referenced by calling the static method `MemPipeline.getInstance()`. All operations are in memory, and the use of PTypes is minimal.

Crunch examples

We will now use Apache Crunch to reimplement some of the MapReduce code written so far in a more modular fashion.

Word co-occurrence

In *Chapter 3, Processing – MapReduce and Beyond*, we showed a MapReduce job, BiGramCount, to count co-occurrences of words in tweets. That same logic can be implemented as a `DoFn`. Instead of emitting a multi-field key and having to parse it at a later stage, with Crunch we can use a complex type `Pair<String, String>`, as follows:

```
class BiGram extends DoFn<String, Pair<String, String>> {
    @Override
    public void process(String tweet,
Emitter<Pair<String, String>> emitter) {
        String[] words = tweet.split(" ") ;

        Text bigram = new Text();
        String prev = null;

        for (String s : words) {
          if (prev != null) {
             emitter.emit(Pair.of(prev, s));
           }
           prev = s;
        }
    }
}
```

Notice how, compared to MapReduce, the `BiGram` Crunch implementation is a standalone class, easily reusable in any other codebase. The code for this example is included in `https://github.com/learninghadoop2/book-examples/blob/master/ch9/crunch/src/main/java/com/learninghadoop2/crunch/DataPreparationPipeline.java`.

TF-IDF

We can implement the TF-IDF chain of jobs with a `MRPipeline`, as follows:

```
public class CrunchTermFrequencyInvertedDocumentFrequency
        extends Configured implements Tool, Serializable {
```

```
        private Long numDocs;

        @SuppressWarnings("deprecation")

        public static class TF {
            String term;
            String docId;
            int frequency;

            public TF() {}

            public TF(String term,
                    String docId, Integer frequency) {
                this.term = term;
                this.docId = docId;
                this.frequency = (int) frequency;


            }
        }

        public int run(String[] args) throws Exception {
            if(args.length != 2) {
                System.err.println();
                System.err.println("Usage: " + this.getClass().getName() + "
[generic options] input output");

                return 1;
            }
            // Create an object to coordinate pipeline creation and
execution.
            Pipeline pipeline =
new MRPipeline(TermFrequencyInvertedDocumentFrequency.class,
getConf());

            // enable debug options
            pipeline.enableDebug();

            // Reference a given text file as a collection of Strings.
            PCollection<String> tweets = pipeline.readTextFile(args[0]);
            numDocs = tweets.length().getValue();
```

```
        // We use Avro reflections to map the TF POJO to avsc
        PTable<String, TF> tf = tweets.parallelDo(new
TermFrequencyAvro(), Avros.tableOf(Avros.strings(), Avros.reflects(TF.
class)));


        // Calculate DF
        PTable<String, Long> df = Aggregate.count(tf.parallelDo( new
DocumentFrequencyString(), Avros.strings()));



        // Finally we calculate TF-IDF
        PTable<String, Pair<TF, Long>> tfDf = Join.join(tf, df);
        PCollection<Tuple3<String, String, Double>> tfIdf =
tfDf.parallelDo(new TermFrequencyInvertedDocumentFrequency(),
                Avros.triples(
                        Avros.strings(),
                        Avros.strings(),
                        Avros.doubles()));



        // Serialize as avro
        tfIdf.write(To.avroFile(args[1]));

        // Execute the pipeline as a MapReduce.
        PipelineResult result = pipeline.done();
        return result.succeeded() ? 0 : 1;
    }
    ...
}
```

The approach that we follow here has a number of advantages compared to streaming. First of all, we don't need to manually chain MapReduce jobs using a separate script. This task is Crunch's main purpose. Secondly, we can express each component of the metric as a distinct class, making it easier to reuse in future applications.

To implement term frequency, we create a DoFn class that takes as input a tweet and emits Pair<String, TF>. The first element is a term, and the second is an instance of the POJO class that will be serialized using Avro. The TF part contains three variables: term, documentId, and frequency. In the reference implementation, we expect input data to be a JSON string that we deserialize and parse. We also include tokenizing as a subtask of the process method.

Depending on the use cases, we could abstract both operations in separate DoFns, as follows:

```
class TermFrequencyAvro extends DoFn<String,Pair<String, TF>> {
    public void process(String JSONTweet,
Emitter<Pair <String, TF>> emitter) {
        Map<String, Integer> termCount = new HashMap<>();

        String tweet;
        String docId;

        JSONParser parser = new JSONParser();

        try {
            Object obj = parser.parse(JSONTweet);

            JSONObject jsonObject = (JSONObject) obj;

            tweet = (String) jsonObject.get("text");
            docId = (String) jsonObject.get("id_str");

            for (String term : tweet.split("\\s+")) {
                if (termCount.containsKey(term.toLowerCase())) {
                    termCount.put(term,
termCount.get(term.toLowerCase()) + 1);
                } else {
                    termCount.put(term.toLowerCase(), 1);
                }
            }

            for (Entry<String, Integer> entry : termCount.entrySet())
{
                emitter.emit(Pair.of(entry.getKey(), new TF(entry.
getKey(), docId, entry.getValue()))));
            }
        } catch (ParseException e) {
            e.printStackTrace();
        }
    }
  }
}
```

Document frequency is straightforward. For each `Pair<String, TF>` generated in the term frequency step, we emit the term — the first element of the pair. We aggregate and count the resulting `PCollection` of terms to obtain document frequency, as follows:

```
class DocumentFrequencyString extends DoFn<Pair<String, TF>, String> {
@Override
    public void process(Pair<String, TF> tfAvro,
        Emitter<String> emitter) {
        emitter.emit(tfAvro.first());
    }
}
```

We finally join the `PTable` TF with the `PTable` DF on the shared key (term) and feed the resulting `Pair<String, Pair<TF, Long>>` object to `TermFrequencyInvertedDocumentFrequency`.

For each term and document, we calculate TF-IDF and return a `term`, `docIf`, and `tfIdf` triple:

```
class TermFrequencyInvertedDocumentFrequency extends
MapFn<Pair<String, Pair<TF, Long>>, Tuple3<String, String, Double> >
{
    @Override
    public Tuple3<String, String, Double> map(
        Pair<String, Pair<TF, Long>> input) {

    Pair<TF, Long> tfDf = input.second();
    Long df = tfDf.second();

    TF tf = tfDf.first();
    double idf = 1.0+Math.log(numDocs / df);
    double tfIdf = idf * tf.frequency;

    return  Tuple3.of(tf.term, tf.docId, tfIdf);
    }

}
```

We use `MapFn` because we are going to output one record for each input. The source code for this example can be found at `https://github.com/learninghadoop2/book-examples/blob/master/ch9/crunch/src/main/java/com/learninghadoop2/crunch/CrunchTermFrequencyInvertedDocumentFrequency.java`.

The example can be compiled and executed with the following commands:

```
$ ./gradlew jar
$ ./gradlew copyJars
```

If not already done, add the Crunch and Avro dependencies downloaded with `copyJars` to the `LIBJARS` environment variable, as follows:

```
$ export CRUNCH_DEPS=build/libjars/crunch-example/lib
$ export LIBJARS=${LIBJARS},${CRUNCH_DEPS}/crunch-core-0.9.0-
cdh5.0.3.jar,${CRUNCH_DEPS}/avro-1.7.5-cdh5.0.3.jar,${CRUNCH_DEPS}/avro-
mapred-1.7.5-cdh5.0.3-hadoop2.jar
```

Furthermore, add the `json-simple` JAR to `LIBJARS`:

```
$ export LIBJARS=${LIBJARS},${CRUNCH_DEPS}/json-simple-1.1.1.jar
```

Finally, run `CrunchTermFrequencyInvertedDocumentFrequency` as a MapReduce job, as follows:

```
$ hadoop jar build/libs/crunch-example.jar \
com.learninghadoop2.crunch.CrunchTermFrequencyInvertedDocumentFrequency
\
-libjars ${LIBJARS} \
tweets.json tweets.avro-out
```

Kite Morphlines

Kite Morphlines is a data transformation library, inspired by Unix pipes, originally developed as part of Cloudera Search. A morphline is an in-memory chain of transformation commands that relies on a plugin structure to tap heterogeneous data sources. It uses declarative commands to carry out ETL operations on records. Commands are defined in a configuration file, which is later fed to a driver class.

The goal is to make embedding ETL logic into any Java codebase a trivial task by providing a library that allows developers to replace programming with a series of configuration settings.

Concepts

Morphlines are built around two abstractions: `Command` and `Record`.

Records are implementations of the `org.kitesdk.morphline.api.Record` interface:

```
public final class Record {
  private ArrayListMultimap<String, Object> fields;
  ...

    private Record(ArrayListMultimap<String, Object> fields) {…}
  public ListMultimap<String, Object> getFields() {…}
  public List get(String key) {…}
  public void put(String key, Object value) {…}

    ...

}
```

A record is a set of named fields, where each field has a list of one or more values. A `Record` is implemented on top of Google Guava's `ListMultimap` and `ArrayListMultimap` classes. Note that a value can be any Java object, fields can be multivalued, and two records don't need to use common field names. A record can contain an _attachment_body field that can be a `java.io.InputStream` or a byte array.

Commands implement the `org.kitesdk.morphline.api.Command` interface:

```
public interface Command {
    void notify(Record notification);
    boolean process(Record record);
    Command getParent();
}
```

A command transforms a record into zero or more records. Commands can call the methods on the `Record` instance provided for read and write operations as well as for adding or removing fields.

Commands are chained together, and at each step of a morphline the parent command sends records to its child, which in turn processes them. Information between parents and children is exchanged using two communication channels (planes); notifications are sent via a control plane, and records are sent over a data plane. Records are processed by the `process()` method, which returns a Boolean value to indicate whether a morphline should proceed or not.

Commands are not instantiated directly, but via an implementation of the
`org.kitesdk.morphline.api.CommandBuilder` interface:

```
public interface CommandBuilder {
    Collection<String> getNames();
    Command build(Config config,
        Command parent,
        Command child,
        MorphlineContext context);
}
```

The `getNames` method returns the names with which the command can be invoked.
Multiple names are supported to allow backwards compatible name changes. The
`build()` method creates and returns a command rooted at the given morphline
configuration.

The `org.kitesdk.morphline.api.MorphlineContext` interface allows additional
parameters to be passed to all morphline commands.

The data model of morphlines is structured following a source-pipe-sink pattern,
where data is captured from a source, piped through a number of processing steps,
and its output is then delivered into a sink.

Morphline commands

Kite Morphlines comes with a number of default commands that implement data
transformations on common serialization formats (plaintext, Avro, JSON). Currently
available commands are organized as subprojects of morphlines and include:

- `kite-morphlines-core-stdio`: will read data from binary large objects
  (BLOBs) and text

- `kite-morphlines-core-stdlib`: wraps around Java data types for data
  manipulation and representation

- `kite-morphlines-avro`: is used for serialization into and deserialization
  from data in the Avro format

- `kite-morphlines-json`: will serialize and deserialize data in
  JSON format

- `kite-morphlines-hadoop-core`: is used to access HDFS

- `kite-morphlines-hadoop-parquet-avro`: is used to serialize and deserialize data in the Parquet format

- `kite-morphlines-hadoop-sequencefile`: is used to serialize and deserialize data in the Sequencefile format

- `kite-morphlines-hadoop-rcfile`: is used to serialize and deserialize data in RCfile format

A list of all available commands can be found at `http://kitesdk.org/docs/0.17.0/kite-morphlines/morphlinesReferenceGuide.html`.

Commands are defined by declaring a chain of transformations in a configuration file, `morphline.conf`, which is then compiled and executed by a driver program. For instance, we can specify a `read_tweets` morphline that will load tweets stored as JSON data, serialize and deserialize them using Jackson, and print the first 10, by combining the default `readJson` and `head` commands contained in the `org.kitesdk.morphline` package, as follows:

```
morphlines : [{
  id : read_tweets
  importCommands : ["org.kitesdk.morphline.**"]

  commands : [{
    readJson {
      outputClass : com.fasterxml.jackson.databind.JsonNode
    }}
    {
      head {
      limit : 10
    }}
  ]
}]
```

We will now show how this morphline can be executed both from a standalone Java program as well as from MapReduce.

`MorphlineDriver.java` shows how to use the library embedded into a host system. The first step that we carry out in the `main` method is to load morphline's JSON configuration, build a `MorphlineContext` object, and compile it into an instance of `Command` that acts as the starting node of the morphline. Note that `Compiler.compile()` takes a `finalChild` parameter; in this case, it is `RecordEmitter`. We use `RecordEmitter` to act as a sink for the morphline, by either printing a record to stdout or storing it into HDFS. In the `MorphlineDriver` example, we use `org.kitesdk.morphline.base.Notifications` to manage and monitor the morphline life cycle in a transactional fashion.

A call to `Notifications.notifyStartSession(morphline)` starts the transformation chain within a transaction defined by calling `Notifications.notifyBeginTransaction`. Upon success, we terminate the pipeline with `Notifications.notifyShutdown(morphline)`. In the event of failure, we roll back the transaction, `Notifications.notifyRollbackTransaction(morphline)`, and pass an exception handler from the morphline context to the calling Java code:

```java
public class MorphlineDriver {
    private static final class RecordEmitter implements Command {
        private final Text line = new Text();

        @Override
        public Command getParent() {
            return null;
        }

        @Override
        public void notify(Record record) {

        }

        @Override
        public boolean process(Record record) {
            line.set(record.get("_attachment_body").toString());

            System.out.println(line);

            return true;
        }
    }

    public static void main(String[] args) throws IOException {
        /* load a morphline conf and set it up */
        File morphlineFile = new File(args[0]);
        String morphlineId = args[1];
        MorphlineContext morphlineContext = new MorphlineContext.
Builder().build();
        Command morphline = new Compiler().compile(morphlineFile,
morphlineId, morphlineContext, new RecordEmitter());

        /* Prepare the morphline for execution
         *
```

```
    * Notifications are sent through the communication channel
    * */

   Notifications.notifyBeginTransaction(morphline);

   /* Note that we are using the local filesystem, not hdfs*/
   InputStream in = new BufferedInputStream(new
FileInputStream(args[2]));

   /* fill in a record and pass  it over */
   Record record = new Record();
   record.put(Fields.ATTACHMENT_BODY, in);

   try {

        Notifications.notifyStartSession(morphline);
        boolean success = morphline.process(record);
        if (!success) {
           System.out.println("Morphline failed to process record:
" + record);
        }
     /* Commit the morphline */
   } catch (RuntimeException e) {
        Notifications.notifyRollbackTransaction(morphline);
        morphlineContext.getExceptionHandler().handleException(e,
null);
     }
   finally {
        in.close();
   }

   /* shut it down */
   Notifications.notifyShutdown(morphline);
  }
}
```

In this example, we load data in JSON format from the local filesystem into
an InputStream object and use it to initialize a new Record instance. The
RecordEmitter class contains the last processed record instance of the chain,
on which we extract _attachment_body and print it to standard output. The
source code for MorphlineDriver can be found at https://github.com/
learninghadoop2/book-examples/blob/master/ch9/kite/src/main/java/com/
learninghadoop2/kite/morphlines/MorphlineDriver.java.

Using the same morphline from a MapReduce job is straightforward. During the setup phase of the Mapper, we build a context that contains the instantiation logic, while the map method sets the `Record` object up and fires off the processing logic, as follows:

```
public static class ReadTweets
        extends Mapper<Object, Text, Text, NullWritable> {
    private final Record record = new Record();
    private Command morphline;

    @Override
    protected void setup(Context context)
            throws IOException, InterruptedException {
        File morphlineConf = new File(context.getConfiguration()
                .get(MORPHLINE_CONF));
        String morphlineId = context.getConfiguration()
                .get(MORPHLINE_ID);
        MorphlineContext morphlineContext =
new MorphlineContext.Builder()
                .build();

        morphline = new org.kitesdk.morphline.base.Compiler()
                .compile(morphlineConf,
                    morphlineId,
                    morphlineContext,
                    new RecordEmitter(context));
    }

    public void map(Object key, Text value, Context context)
            throws IOException, InterruptedException {
        record.put(Fields.ATTACHMENT_BODY,
                new ByteArrayInputStream(
value.toString().getBytes("UTF8")));
        if (!morphline.process(record)) {
            System.out.println(
"Morphline failed to process record: " + record);
        }

        record.removeAll(Fields.ATTACHMENT_BODY);
    }
}
```

In the MapReduce code we modify `RecordEmitter` to extract the `Fields` payload from post-processed records and store it into context. This allows us to write data into HDFS by specifying a `FileOutputFormat` in the MapReduce configuration boilerplate:

```
private static final class RecordEmitter implements Command {
    private final Text line = new Text();
    private final Mapper.Context context;

    private RecordEmitter(Mapper.Context context) {
        this.context = context;
    }

    @Override
    public void notify(Record notification) {
    }

    @Override
    public Command getParent() {
        return null;
    }

    @Override
    public boolean process(Record record) {
        line.set(record.get(Fields.ATTACHMENT_BODY).toString());
        try {
            context.write(line, null);
        } catch (Exception e) {
            e.printStackTrace();
            return false;
        }
        return true;
    }
}
```

Notice that we can now change the processing pipeline behavior and add further data transformations by modifying `morphline.conf` without the explicit need to alter the instantiation and processing logic. The MapReduce driver source code can be found at https://github.com/learninghadoop2/book-examples/blob/master/ch9/kite/src/main/java/com/learninghadoop2/kite/morphlines/MorphlineDriverMapReduce.java.

Both examples can be compiled from `ch9/kite/` with the following commands:

```
$ ./gradlew jar
$ ./gradlew copyJar
```

We add the `runtime` dependencies to `LIBJARS`, as follows

```
$ export KITE_DEPS=/home/cloudera/review/hadoop2book-private-reviews-
gabriele-ch8/src/ch8/kite/build/libjars/kite-example/lib
export LIBJARS=${LIBJARS},${KITE_DEPS}/kite-morphlines-core-
0.17.0.jar,${KITE_DEPS}/kite-morphlines-json-0.17.0.jar,${KITE_
DEPS}/metrics-core-3.0.2.jar,${KITE_DEPS}/metrics-healthchecks-
3.0.2.jar,${KITE_DEPS}/config-1.0.2.jar,${KITE_DEPS}/jackson-databind-
2.3.1.jar,${KITE_DEPS}/jackson-core-2.3.1.jar,${KITE_DEPS}/jackson-
annotations-2.3.0.jar
```

We can run the MapReduce driver with the following:

```
$ hadoop jar build/libs/kite-example.jar \
com.learninghadoop2.kite.morphlines.MorphlineDriverMapReduce \
-libjars ${LIBJARS} \
morphline.conf \
read_tweets \
tweets.json \
morphlines-out
```

The Java standalone driver can be executed with the following command:

```
$ export CLASSPATH=${CLASSPATH}:${KITE_DEPS}/kite-morphlines-core-
0.17.0.jar:${KITE_DEPS}/kite-morphlines-json-0.17.0.jar:${KITE_
DEPS}/metrics-core-3.0.2.jar:${KITE_DEPS}/metrics-healthchecks-
3.0.2.jar:${KITE_DEPS}/config-1.0.2.jar:${KITE_DEPS}/jackson-databind-
2.3.1.jar:${KITE_DEPS}/jackson-core-2.3.1.jar:${KITE_DEPS}/jackson-
annotations-2.3.0.jar:${KITE_DEPS}/slf4j-api-1.7.5.jar:${KITE_DEPS}/
guava-11.0.2.jar:${KITE_DEPS}/hadoop-common-2.3.0-cdh5.0.3.jar
$ java -cp $CLASSPATH:./build/libs/kite-example.jar \
com.learninghadoop2.kite.morphlines.MorphlineDriver \
morphline.conf \
read_tweets tweets.json \
morphlines-out
```

Summary

In this chapter, we introduced four tools to ease development on Hadoop. In particular, we covered:

- How Hadoop streaming allows the writing of MapReduce jobs using dynamic languages
- How Kite Data simplifies interfacing with heterogeneous data sources
- How Apache Crunch provides a high-level abstraction to write pipelines of Spark and MapReduce jobs that implement common design patterns
- How Morphlines allows us to declare chains of commands and data transformations that can then be embedded in any Java codebase

In *Chapter 10, Running a Hadoop 2 Cluster*, we will shift our focus from the domain of software development to system administration. We will discuss how to set up, manage, and scale a Hadoop cluster, while taking aspects such as monitoring and security into consideration.

10
Running a Hadoop Cluster

In this chapter, we will change our focus a little and look at some of the considerations you will face when running an operational Hadoop cluster. In particular, we will cover the following topics:

- Why a developer should care about operations and why Hadoop operations are different
- More detail on Cloudera Manager and its capabilities and limitations
- Designing a cluster for use on both physical hardware and EMR
- Securing a Hadoop cluster
- Hadoop monitoring
- Troubleshooting problems with an application running on Hadoop

I'm a developer – I don't care about operations!

Before going any further, we need to explain why we are putting a chapter about systems operations in a book squarely aimed at developers. For anyone who has developed for more traditional platforms (for example, web apps, database programming, and so on) then the norm might well have been for a very clear delineation between development and operations. The first group builds the code and packages it up, and the second group controls and operates the environment in which it runs.

In recent years, the DevOps movement has gained momentum with a belief that it is best for everyone if these silos are removed and that the teams work more closely together. When it comes to running systems and services based on Hadoop, we believe this is absolutely essential.

Hadoop and DevOps practices

Even though a developer can conceptually build an application ready to be dropped into YARN and forgotten about, the reality is often more nuanced. How many resources are allocated to the application at runtime is most likely something the developer wishes to influence. Once the application is running, the operations staff likely want some insight into the application when they are trying to optimize the cluster. There really isn't the same clear-cut split of responsibilities seen in traditional enterprise IT. And that's likely a really good thing.

In other words, developers need to be more aware of the operations aspects, and the operations staff need to be more aware of what the developers are doing. So consider this chapter our contribution to help you have those discussions with your operations staff. We don't intend to make you an expert Hadoop administrator by the end of this chapter; that really is emerging as a dedicated role and skillset in itself. Instead, we will give a whistle-stop tour of issues you do need some awareness of and that will make your life easier once your applications are running on live clusters.

By the nature of this coverage, we will be touching on a lot of topics and going into them only lightly; if any are of deeper interest, then we provide links for further investigation. Just make sure you keep your operations staff involved!

Cloudera Manager

In this book, we used as the most common platform the **Cloudera Hadoop Distribution** (CDH) with its convenient QuickStart virtual machine and the powerful Cloudera Manager application. With a Cloudera-based cluster, Cloudera Manager will become (at least initially) your primary interface into the system to manage and monitor the cluster, so let's explore it a little.

Note that Cloudera Manager has extensive and high-quality online documentation. We won't duplicate this documentation here; instead we'll attempt to highlight where Cloudera Manager fits into your development and operational workflows and how it might or might not be something you want to embrace. Documentation for the latest and previous versions of Cloudera Manager can be accessed via the main Cloudera documentation page at `http://www.cloudera.com/content/support/en/documentation.html`.

To pay or not to pay

Before getting all excited about Cloudera Manager, it's important to consult the current documentation concerning what features are available in the free version and which ones require subscription to a paid-for Cloudera offering. If you absolutely want some of the features offered only in the paid-for version but either can't or don't wish to pay for subscription services, then Cloudera Manager, and possibly the entire Cloudera distribution, might not be a good fit for you. We'll return to this topic in *Chapter 11, Where to Go Next*.

Cluster management using Cloudera Manager

Using the QuickStart VM, it won't be obvious, but Cloudera Manager is the primary tool to be used for management of all services in the cluster. If you want to enable a new service, you'll use Cloudera Manager. To change a configuration, you will need Cloudera Manager. To upgrade to the latest release, you will again require Cloudera Manager.

Even if the primary management of the cluster is handled by operational staff, as a developer you'll likely still want to become familiar with the Cloudera Manager interface just to look to see exactly how the cluster is configured. If your jobs are running slowly, then looking into Cloudera Manager to see just how things are currently configured will likely be your first start. The default port for the Cloudera Manager web interface is `7180`, so the home page will usually be connected to via a URL such as `http://<hostname>:7180/cmf/home`, and can be seen in the following screenshot:

Cloudera Manager home page

It's worth poking around the interface; however, if you are connecting with a user account with admin privileges, be careful!

Click on the **Clusters** link, and this will expand to give a list of the clusters currently managed by this instance of Cloudera Manager. This should tell you that a single Cloudera Manager instance can manage multiple clusters. This is very useful, especially if you have many clusters spread across development and production.

For each expanded cluster, there will be a list of the services currently running on the cluster. Click on a service, and then you will see a list of additional choices. Select **Configuration**, and you can start browsing the detailed configuration of that particular service. Click on **Actions**, and you will get some service-specific options; this will usually include stopping, starting, restarting, and otherwise managing the service.

Click on the **Hosts** option instead of **Clusters**, and you can start drilling down into the servers managed by Cloudera Manager, and from there, see which service components are deployed on each.

Cloudera Manager and other management tools

That last comment might raise a question: how does Cloudera Manager integrate with other systems management tools? Given our earlier comments regarding the importance of DevOps philosophies, how well does it integrate with the tools favored in DevOps environments?

The honest answer: not always very well. Though the main Cloudera Manager server can itself be managed by automation tools, such as Puppet or Chef, there is an explicit assumption that Cloudera Manager will control the installation and configuration of all the software Cloudera Manager needs on all the hosts that will be included in its clusters. To some administrators, this makes the hardware behind Cloudera Manager look like a big, black box; they might control the installation of the base operating system, but the management of the configuration baseline going forward is entirely managed by Cloudera Manager. There's nothing much to be done here; it is what it is — to get the benefits of Cloudera Manager, it will add itself as a new management system in your infrastructure, and how well that fits in with your broader environment will be determined on a case-by-case basis.

Monitoring with Cloudera Manager

A similar point can be made regarding systems monitoring as Cloudera Manager is also conceptually a point of duplication here. But start clicking around the interface, and it will become apparent very quickly that Cloudera Manager provides an exceptionally rich set of tools to assess the health and performance of managed clusters.

From graphing the relative performance of Impala queries through showing the job status for YARN applications and giving low-level data on the blocks stored on HDFS, it is all there in a single interface. We'll discuss later in this chapter how troubleshooting on Hadoop can be challenging, but the single point of visibility provided by Cloudera Manager is a great tool when looking to assess cluster health or performance. We'll discuss monitoring in a little more detail later in this chapter.

Finding configuration files

One of the first confusions faced when running a cluster managed by Cloudera Manager is trying to find the configuration files used by the cluster. In the vanilla Apache releases of products, such as the core Hadoop, there would be files typically stored in /etc/hadoop, similarly /etc/hive for Hive, /etc/oozie for Oozie, and so on.

In a Cloudera Manager managed cluster, however, the config files are regenerated each time a service is restarted, and instead of sitting in the /etc locations on the filesystem, will be found at /var/run/cloudera-scm-agent-process/<pid>-<task name>/, where the last directory might have a name such as 7007-yarn-NODEMANAGER. This might seem odd to anyone used to working on earlier Hadoop clusters or other distributions that don't do such a thing. But in a Cloudera Manager-controlled cluster, it might often be easier to use the web interface to browse the configuration instead of looking for the underlying config files. Which approach is best? This is a little philosophical, and each team needs to decide which works best for them.

Cloudera Manager API

We've only given the highest level of overview of Cloudera Manager, and in doing so, have completely ignored one area that might be very useful for some organizations: Cloudera Manager offers an API that allows integration of its capabilities into other systems and tools. Consult the documentation if this might be of interest to you.

Cloudera Manager lock-in

This brings us to the point that is implicit in the whole discussion around Cloudera Manager: it does cause a degree of lock-in to Cloudera and their distribution. That lock-in might only exist in certain ways; code, for example, should be portable across clusters modulo the usual caveats about different underlying versions — but the cluster itself might not easily be reconfigured to use a different distribution. Assume that switching distributions would be a complete remove/reformat/reinstall activity.

We aren't saying don't use it, rather that you need to be aware of the lock-in that comes with the use of Cloudera Manager. For small teams with little dedicated operations support or existing infrastructure, the impact of such a lock-in is likely outweighed by the significant capabilities that Cloudera Manager gives you.

For larger teams or ones working in an environment where integration with existing tools and processes has more weight, the decision might be less clear. Look at Cloudera Manager, discuss with your operations people, and determine what is right for you.

Note that it is possible to manually download and install the various components of the Cloudera distribution without using Cloudera Manager to manage the cluster and its hosts. This might be an attractive middle ground for some users as the Cloudera software can be used, but deployment and management can be built into the existing deployment and management tools. This is also potentially a way of avoiding the additional expense of the paid-for levels of Cloudera support mentioned earlier.

Ambari – the open source alternative

Ambari is an Apache project (`http://ambari.apache.org`), which in theory, provides an open source alternative to Cloudera Manager. It is the administration console for the Hortonworks distribution. At the time of writing Hortonworks employees are also the vast majority of the project contributors.

Ambari, as one would expect given its open source nature, relies on other open source products, such as Puppet and Nagios, to provide the management and monitoring of its managed clusters. It also has high-level functionality similar to Cloudera Manager, that is, the installation, configuration, management, and monitoring of a Hadoop cluster, and the component services within it.

It is good to be aware of the Ambari project as the choice is not just between full lock-in to Cloudera and Cloudera Manager or a manually managed cluster. Ambari provides a graphical tool that might be worth consideration, or indeed involvement, as it matures. On an HDP cluster, the Ambari UI equivalent to the Cloudera Manager home page shown earlier can be reached at `http://<hostname>:8080/#/main/dashboard` and looks like the following screenshot:

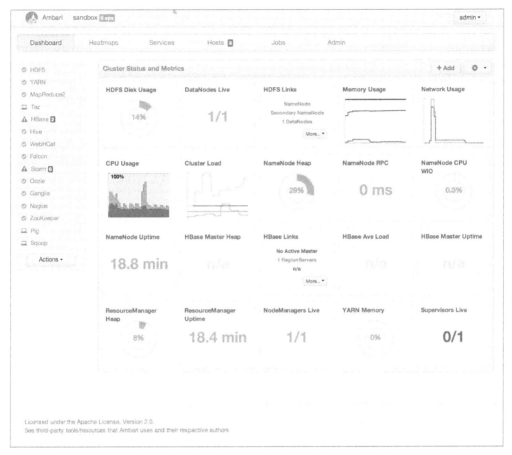

Ambari

Operations in the Hadoop 2 world

As mentioned in *Chapter 2, Storage*, some of the most significant changes made to HDFS in Hadoop 2 involve its fault tolerance and better integration with external systems. This is not just a curiosity, but the NameNode High Availability features, in particular, have made a massive difference in the management of clusters since Hadoop 1. In the bad old days of 2012 or so, a significant part of the operational preparedness of a Hadoop cluster was built around mitigations for, and restoration processes around failure of the NameNode. If the NameNode died in Hadoop 1, and you didn't have a backup of the HDFS `fsimage` metadata file, then you basically lost access to all your data. If the metadata was permanently lost, then so was the data.

Hadoop 2 has added the in-built NameNode HA and the machinery to make it work. In addition, there are components such as the NFS gateway into HDFS, which make it a much more flexible system. But this additional capability does come at the expense of more moving parts. To enable NameNode HA, there are additional components in the JournalManager and FailoverController, and the NFS gateway requires Hadoop-specific implementations of the portmap and nfsd services.

Hadoop 2 also now has extensive other integration points with external services as well as a much broader selection of applications and services that run atop it. Consequently, it might be useful to view Hadoop 2 in terms of operations as having traded the simplicity of Hadoop 1 for additional complexity, which delivers a substantially more capable platform.

Sharing resources

In Hadoop 1, the only time one had to consider resource sharing was in considering which scheduler to use for the MapReduce JobTracker. Since all jobs were eventually translated into MapReduce code having a policy for resource sharing at the MapReduce level was usually sufficient to manage cluster workloads in the large.

Hadoop 2 and YARN changed this picture. As well as running many MapReduce jobs, a cluster might also be running many other applications atop other YARN ApplicationMasters. Tez and Spark are frameworks in their own right that run additional applications atop their provided interfaces.

If everything runs on YARN, then it provides ways of configuring the maximum resource allocation (in terms of CPU, memory, and soon I/O) consumed by each container allocated to an application. The primary goal here is to ensure that enough resources are allocated to keep the hardware fully utilized without either having unused capacity or overloading it.

Things get somewhat more interesting when non-YARN applications, such as Impala, are running on the cluster and want to grab allocated slices of capacity (particularly memory in the case of Impala). This could also happen if, say, you were running Spark on the same hosts in its non-YARN mode or indeed any other distributed application that might benefit from co-location on the Hadoop machines.

Basically, in Hadoop 2, you need to think of the cluster as much more of a multi-tenancy environment that requires more attention given to the allocation of resources to the various tenants.

There really is no silver bullet recommendation here; the right configuration will be entirely dependent on the services co-located and the workloads they are running. This is another example where you want to work closely with your operations team to do a series of load tests with thresholds to determine just what the resource requirements of the various clients are and which approach will give the maximum utilization and performance. The following blog post from Cloudera engineers gives a good overview of how they approach this very issue in having Impala and MapReduce coexist effectively: `http://blog.cloudera.com/blog/2013/06/ configuring-impala-and-mapreduce-for-multi-tenant-performance/`.

Building a physical cluster

There is one minor requirement before thinking about allocation of hardware resources: defining and selecting the hardware used for your cluster. In this section, we'll discuss a physical cluster and move on to Amazon EMR in the next.

Any specific hardware advice will be out of date the moment it is written. We advise perusing the websites of the various Hadoop distribution vendors as they regularly write new articles on the currently recommended configurations.

Instead of telling you how many cores or GB of memory you need, we'll look at hardware selection at a slightly higher level. The first thing to realize is that the hosts running your Hadoop cluster will most likely look very different from the rest of your enterprise. Hadoop is optimized for low(er) cost hardware, so instead of seeing a small number of very large servers, expect to see a larger number of machines with fewer enterprise reliability features. But don't think that Hadoop will run great on any junk you have lying around. It might, but recently the profile of typical Hadoop servers has been moving away from the bottom-end of the market, and instead, the sweet spot would seem to be in mid-range servers where the maximum cores/disks/ memory can be achieved at a price point.

You should also expect to have different resource requirements for the hosts running services such as the HDFS NameNode or the YARN ResourceManager, as opposed to the worker nodes storing data and executing the application logic. For the former, there is usually much less requirement for lots of storage, but frequently, a need for more memory and possibly faster disks.

For Hadoop worker nodes, the ratio between the three main hardware categories of cores, memory, and I/O is often the most important thing to get right. And this will directly inform the decisions you make regarding workload and resource allocation.

For example, many workloads tend to become I/O bound and having many times as many containers allocated on a host than there are physical disks might actually cause an overall slowdown due to contention for the spinning disks. At the time of writing, current recommendations here are for the number of YARN containers to be no more than 1.8 times the number of disks. If you have workloads that are I/O bound, then you will most likely get much better performance by adding more hosts to the cluster instead of trying to get more containers running or indeed faster processors or more memory on the current hosts.

Conversely, if you expect to run lots of concurrent Impala, Spark, and other memory-hungry jobs, then memory might quickly become the resource most under pressure. This is why even though you can get current hardware recommendations for general-purpose clusters from the distribution vendors, you still need to validate against your expected workloads and tailor accordingly. There is really no substitute for benchmarking on a small test cluster or indeed on EMR, which can be a great platform to explore the resource requirements of multiple applications that can inform hardware acquisition decisions. Perhaps EMR might be your main environment; if so, we'll discuss that in a later section.

Physical layout

If you do use a physical cluster, there are a few things you will need to consider that are largely transparent on EMR.

Rack awareness

The first of these aspects for clusters large enough to consume more than one rack of data center space is building rack awareness. As mentioned in *Chapter 2*, *Storage*, when HDFS places replicas of new files, it attempts to place the second replica on a different host than the first, and the third in a different rack of equipment in a multi-rack system. This heuristic is aimed at maximizing resilience; there will be at least one replica available even if an entire rack of equipment fails. MapReduce uses similar logic to attempt to get a better-balanced task spread.

If you do nothing, then each host will be specified as being in the single default rack. But, if the cluster grows beyond this point, you will need to update the rack name.

Under the covers, Hadoop discovers a node's rack by executing a user-supplied script that maps node hostname to rack names. Cloudera Manager allows rack names to be set on a given host, and this is then retrieved when its rack awareness scripts are called by Hadoop. To set the rack for a host, click on **Hosts-><hostname>->Assign Rack**, and then assign the rack from the Cloudera Manager home page.

Service layout

As mentioned earlier, you are likely to have two types of hardware in your cluster: the machines running the workers and those running the servers. When deploying a physical cluster, you will need to decide which services and which subcomponents of the services run on which physical machines.

For the workers, this is usually pretty straightforward; most, though not all, services have a model of a worker agent on all worker hosts. But, for the master/server components, it requires a little thought. If you have three master nodes, then how do you spread your primary and backup NameNodes: the YARN ResourceManager, maybe Hue, a few Hive servers, and an Oozie manager? Some of these features are highly available, while others are not. As you add more and more services to your cluster, you'll also see this list of master services grow substantially.

In an ideal world, you might have a host per service master but that is only tractable for very large clusters; in smaller installations it is prohibitively expensive. Plus it might always be a little wasteful. There are no hard-and-fast rules here either, but do look at your available hardware, and try to spread the services across the nodes as much as possible. Don't, for example, have two nodes for the two NameNodes and then put everything else on a third. Think about the impact of a single host failure and manage the layout to minimize it. As the cluster grows across multiple racks of equipment, the considerations will also need to consider how to survive single-rack failures. Hadoop itself helps with this since HDFS will attempt to ensure each block of data has replicas across at least two racks. But, this type of resilience is undermined if, for example, all the master nodes reside in a single rack.

Upgrading a service

Upgrading Hadoop has historically been a time-consuming and somewhat risky task. This remains the case on a manually deployed cluster, that is, one not managed by a tool such as Cloudera Manager.

If you are using Cloudera Manager, then it takes the time-consuming part out of the activity, but not necessarily the risk. Any upgrade should always be viewed as an activity with a high chance of unexpected issues, and you should arrange enough cluster downtime to account for this surprise excitement. There's really no substitute for doing a test upgrade on a test cluster, which underlines the importance of thinking about Hadoop as a component of your environment that needs to be treated with a deployment life cycle like any other.

Sometimes an upgrade requires modification to the HDFS metadata or might otherwise affect the filesystem. This is, of course, where the real risks lie. In addition to running a test upgrade, be aware of the ability to set HDFS in upgrade mode, which effectively makes a snapshot of the filesystem state prior to the upgrade and which will be retained until the upgrade is finalized. This can be really helpful as even an upgrade that goes badly wrong and corrupts data can potentially be fully rolled back.

Building a cluster on EMR

Elastic MapReduce is a flexible solution that, depending on requirements and workloads, can sit next to, or replace, a physical Hadoop cluster. As we've seen so far, EMR provides clusters preloaded and configured with Hive, Streaming, and Pig as well as with custom JAR clusters that allow the execution of MapReduce applications.

A second distinction to make is between transient and long-running life cycles. A transient EMR cluster is generated on demand; data is loaded in S3 or HDFS, some processing workflow is executed, output results are stored, and the cluster is automatically shut down. A long-running cluster is kept alive once the workflow terminates, and the cluster remains available for new data to be copied over and new workflows to be executed. Long-running clusters are typically well-suited for data warehousing or working with datasets large enough that loading and processing data would be inefficient compared to a transient instance.

In a must-read white paper for prospective users (found at `https://media.amazonwebservices.com/AWS_Amazon_EMR_Best_Practices.pdf`), Amazon gives a heuristic to estimate which cluster type is a better fit as follows:

> *If number of jobs per day * (time to setup cluster including Amazon S3 data load time if using Amazon S3 + data processing time) < 24 hours, consider transient Amazon EMR clusters or physical instances. Long-running instances are instantiated by passing the –alive argument to the ElasticMapreduce command, which enables the Keep Alive option and disables auto termination.*

Note that transient and long-running clusters share the same properties and limitations; in particular, data on HDFS is not persisted once the cluster is shut down.

Considerations about filesystems

In our examples so far we assumed data to be available in S3. In this case, a bucket is mounted in EMR as an `s3n` filesystem, and it is used as input source as well as a temporary filesystem to store intermediate data in computations. With S3 we introduce potential I/O overhead, operations such as reads and writes fire off `GET` and `PUT` `HTTP` requests.

 Note that EMR does not support S3 block storage. The s3 URI maps to s3n.

Another option would be to load data into the cluster HDFS and run processing from there. In this case, we do have faster I/O and data locality, but we would lose persistence. When the cluster is shut down, our data disappears. As a rule of thumb, if you are running a transient cluster, it makes sense to use S3 as a backend. In practice, one should monitor and take decisions based on the workflow characteristics. Iterative, multi-pass MapReduce jobs would greatly benefit from HDFS; one could argue that for those types of workflows, an execution engine like Tez or Spark would be more appropriate.

Getting data into EMR

When copying data from HDFS to S3, it is recommended to use s3distcp (`http://docs.aws.amazon.com/ElasticMapReduce/latest/DeveloperGuide/UsingEMR_s3distcp.html`) instead of Apache distcp or Hadoop distcp. This approach is suitable also to transfer data within EMR and from S3 to HDFS. To move very large amounts of data from the local disk into S3, Amazon recommends parallelizing the workload using Jets3t or GNU Parallel. In general, it's important to be aware that PUT requests to S3 are capped at 5 GB per file. To upload larger files, one needs to rely on Multipart Upload (`https://aws.amazon.com/about-aws/whats-new/2010/11/10/Amazon-S3-Introducing-Multipart-Upload/`), an API that allows splitting large files into smaller parts and reassembles them when uploaded. Files can also be copied with tools such as the AWS CLI or the popular S3CMD utility, but these do not have the parallelism advantages of as s3distcp.

EC2 instances and tuning

The size of an EMR cluster depends on the dataset size, the number of files and blocks (determines the number of splits) and the type of workload (try to avoid spilling to disk when a task runs out of memory). As a rule of thumb, a good size is one that maximizes parallelism. The number of mappers and reducers per instance as well as heap size per JVM daemon is generally configured by EMR when the cluster is provisioned and tuned in the event of changes in the available resources.

Cluster tuning

In addition to the previous comments specific to a cluster run on EMR, there are some general thoughts to keep in mind when running workloads on any type of cluster. This will, of course, be more explicit when running outside of EMR as it often abstracts some of the details.

JVM considerations

You should be running the 64-bit version of a JVM and using the server mode. This can take longer to produce optimized code, but it also uses more aggressive strategies and will re-optimize code over time. This makes it a much better fit for long-running services, such as Hadoop processes.

Ensure that you allocate enough memory to the JVM to prevent overly-frequent **Garbage Collection** (**GC**) pauses. The concurrent mark-and-sweep collector is currently the most tested and recommended for Hadoop. The **Garbage First** (**G1**) collector has become the GC option of choice in numerous other workloads since its introduction with JDK7, so it's worth monitoring recommended best practice as it evolves. These options can be configured as custom Java arguments within each service's configuration section of Cloudera Manager.

The small files problem

Heap allocation to Java processes on worker nodes will be something you consider when thinking about service co-location. But there is a particular situation regarding the NameNode you should be aware of: the small files problem.

Hadoop is optimized for very large files with large block sizes. But sometimes particular workloads or data sources push many small files onto HDFS. This is most likely suboptimal as it suggests each task processing a block at a time will read only a small amount of data before completing, causing inefficiency.

Having many small files also consumes more NameNode memory; it holds in-memory the mapping from files to blocks and consequently holds metadata for each file and block. If the number of files and hence blocks increases quickly, then so will the NameNode memory usage. This is likely to only hit a subset of systems as, at the time of writing this, 1 GB of memory can support 2 million files or blocks, but with a default heap size of 2 or 4 GB, this limit can easily be reached. If the NameNode needs to start very aggressively running garbage collection or eventually runs out of memory, then your cluster will be very unhealthy. The mitigation is to assign more heap to the JVM; the longer-term approach is to combine many small files into a smaller number of larger ones. Ideally, compressed with a splittable compression codec.

Map and reduce optimizations

Mappers and reducers both provide areas for optimizing performance; here are a few pointers to consider:

- The number of mappers depends on the number of splits. When files are smaller than the default block size or compressed using a non splittable format, the number of mappers will equal the number of files. Otherwise, the number of mappers is given by the total size of each file divided by the block size.

- Compress mappers output to reduce writes to disk and increase I/O. LZO is a good format for this task.

- Avoid spill to disk: the mappers should have enough memory to retain as much data as possible.

- Number of Reducers: it is recommended that you use fewer reducers than the total reducer capacity (this avoids execution waits).

Security

Once you built a cluster, the first thing you thought about was how to secure it, right? Don't worry, most people don't. But, as Hadoop has moved on from being something running in-house analysis in the research department to directly driving critical systems, it's not something to ignore for too long.

Securing Hadoop is not something to be done on a whim or without significant testing. We cannot give detailed advice on this topic and cannot stress strongly enough the need to take this topic seriously and do it properly. It might consume time, it might cost money, but weigh this against the cost of having your cluster compromised.

Security is also a much bigger topic than just the Hadoop cluster. We'll explore some of the security features available in Hadoop, but you do need a coherent security strategy into which these discrete components fit.

Evolution of the Hadoop security model

In Hadoop 1, there was effectively no security protection as the provided security model had obvious attack vectors. The Unix user ID with which you connected to the cluster was assumed to be valid, and you had all the privileges of that user. Plainly, this meant that anyone with administrative access on a host that could access the cluster could effectively impersonate any other user.

This led to the development of the so-called "head node" access model, whereby the Hadoop cluster was firewalled off from every host except one, the head node, and all access to the cluster was mediated through this centrally-controlled node. This was an effective mitigation for the lack of a real security model and can still be useful in situations even when richer security schemes are utilized.

Beyond basic authorization

Core Hadoop has had additional security features added, which address the previous concerns. In particular, they address the following:

- A cluster can require a user to authenticate via Kerberos and prove they are who they say they are.

- In secure mode, the cluster can also use Kerberos for all node-node communications, ensuring that all communicating nodes are authenticated and preventing malicious nodes from attempting to join the cluster.

- To ease management, users can be collected into groups against which data-access privileges can be defined. This is called **Role Based Access Control (RBAC)** and is a prerequisite for a secure cluster with more than a handful of users. The user-group mappings can be retrieved from corporate systems, such as LDAP or active directory.

- HDFS can apply ACLs to replace the current Unix-inspired owner/group/ world model.

These capabilities give Hadoop a significantly stronger security posture than in the past, but the community is moving fast and additional dedicated Apache projects have emerged to address specific areas of security.

Apache Sentry `https://sentry.incubator.apache.org` is a system to provide much finer-grained authorization to Hadoop data and services. Other services build Sentry mappings, and this allows, for example, specific restrictions to be placed not only on particular HDFS directories, but also on entities such as Hive tables.

Whereas Sentry focuses on providing much richer tools for the internal, fine-grained aspects of Hadoop security, Apache Knox (`http://knox.apache.org`) provides a secure gateway to Hadoop that integrates with external identity management systems and provides access control mechanisms to allow or disallow access to specific Hadoop services and operations. It does this by presenting a REST-only interface to Hadoop and securing all calls to this API.

The future of Hadoop security

There are many other developments happening in the Hadoop world. Core Hadoop 2.5 added extended file attributes to HDFS, which can be used as the basis of additional access control mechanisms. Future versions will incorporate capabilities for better support of encryption for data in transit as well as at rest, and the Project Rhino initiative led by Intel (`https://github.com/intel-hadoop/project-rhino/`) is building out richer support for filesystem cryptographic modules, a secure filesystem, and, at some point, a fuller key-management infrastructure.

The Hadoop distribution vendors are moving fast to add these capabilities to their releases, so if you care about security (you do, don't you!), then consult the documentation for the latest release of your distribution. New security features are being added even in point updates and aren't being delayed until major upgrades.

Consequences of using a secured cluster

After teasing you with all the security goodness that is now available and that which is coming, it's only fair to give some words of warning. Security is often hard to do correctly, and often the feeling of security wrongly employed with a buggy deployment is worse than knowing you have no security.

However, even if you do it right, there are consequences to running a secure cluster. It makes things harder for the administrators certainly and often the users, so there is definitely an overhead. Specific Hadoop tools and services will also work differently depending on what security is employed on a cluster.

Oozie, which we discussed in *Chapter 8, Data Lifecycle Management*, uses its own delegation tokens behind the scenes. This allows the oozie user to submit jobs that are then executed on behalf of the originally submitting user. In a cluster using only the basic authorization mechanism, this is very easily configured, but using Oozie in a secure cluster will require additional logic to be added to the workflow definitions and the general Oozie configuration. This isn't a problem with Hadoop or Oozie; however, similarly as with the additional complexity resulting from the much better HA features of HDFS in Hadoop 2, better security mechanisms will simply have costs and consequences that you need take into consideration.

Monitoring

Earlier in this chapter, we discussed Cloudera Manager as a visual monitoring tool and hinted that it could also be programmatically integrated with other monitoring systems. But before plugging Hadoop into any monitoring framework, it's worth considering just what it means to operationally monitor a Hadoop cluster.

Hadoop – where failures don't matter

Traditional systems monitoring tends to be quite a binary tool; generally speaking, either something is working or it isn't. A host is alive or dead, and a web server is responding or it isn't. But in the Hadoop world, things are a little different; the important thing is service availability, and this can still be treated as live even if particular pieces of hardware or software have failed. No Hadoop cluster should be in trouble if a single worker node fails. As of Hadoop 2, even the failure of the server processes, such as the NameNode shouldn't really be a concern if HA is configured. So, any monitoring of Hadoop needs to take into account the service health and not that of specific host machines, which should be unimportant. Operations people on 24/7 pager are not going to be happy getting paged at 3 AM to discover that one worker node in a cluster of 10,000 has failed. Indeed, once the scale of the cluster increases beyond a certain point, the failure of individual pieces of hardware becomes an almost commonplace occurrence.

Monitoring integration

You won't be building your own monitoring tools; instead, you might likely want to integrate with existing tools and frameworks. For popular open source monitoring tools, such as Nagios and Zabbix, there are multiple sample templates to integrate Hadoop's service-wide and node-specific metrics.

This can give the sort of separation hinted previously; the failure of the YARN ResourceManager would be a high-criticality event that should most likely cause alerts to be sent to operations staff, but a high load on specific hosts should only be captured and not cause alerts to be fired. This then provides the duality of firing alerts when bad things happen in addition to capturing and providing the information needed to delve into system data over time to do trend analysis.

Cloudera Manager provides a REST interface, which is another point of integration against which tools such as Nagios can integrate and pull the Cloudera Manager-defined service-level metrics instead of having to define its own.

For heavier-weight enterprise-monitoring infrastructure built on frameworks, such as IBM Tivoli or HP OpenView, Cloudera Manager can also deliver events via SNMP traps that will be collected by these systems.

Application-level metrics

At times, you might also want your applications to gather metrics that can be centrally captured within the system. The mechanisms for this will differ from one computational model to another, but the most well-known are the application counters available within MapReduce.

When a MapReduce job completes, it outputs a number of counters, gathered by the system throughout the job execution, that deal with metrics such as the number of map tasks, bytes written, failed tasks, and so on. You can also write application-specific metrics that will be available alongside the system counters and which are automatically aggregated across the map/reduce execution. First define a Java enum, and name your desired metrics within it, as follows:

```
public enum AppMetrics{
   MAX_SEEN,
   MIN_SEEN,
   BAD_RECORDS
};
```

Then, within the map, reduce, setup, and cleanup methods of your Map or Reduce implementations, you can do something like the following to increment a counter by one:

```
Context.getCounter(AppMetrics.BAD_RECORDS).increment(1);
```

Refer to the JavaDoc of the `org.apache.hadoop.mapreduce.Counter` interface for more details of this mechanism.

Troubleshooting

Monitoring and logging counters or additional information is all well and good, but it can be intimidating to know how to actually find the information you need when troubleshooting a problem with an application. In this section, we will look at how Hadoop stores logs and system information. We can distinguish three typologies of logs, as follows:

- YARN applications, including MapReduce jobs
- Daemon logs (NameNode and ResourceManager)
- Services that log non-distributed workloads, for example, HiveServer2 logging to /var/log

Next to these log typologies, Hadoop exposes a number of metrics at filesystem (the storage availability, replication factor, and number of blocks) and system level. As mentioned, both Apache Ambari and Cloudera Manager, which centralize access to debug information, do a nice job as the frontend. However, under the hood, each service logs to either HDFS or the single-node filesystem. Furthermore, YARN, MapReduce, and HDFS expose their logfiles and metrics via web interfaces and programmatic APIs.

Logging levels

Hadoop logs messages to Log4j by default. Log4j is configured via log4j.properties in the classpath. This file defines what is logged and with which layout:

```
log4j.rootLogger=${root.logger}
root.logger=INFO,console
log4j.appender.console=org.apache.log4j.ConsoleAppender
log4j.appender.console.target=System.err
log4j.appender.console.layout=org.apache.log4j.PatternLayout
log4j.appender.console.layout.ConversionPattern=%d{yy/MM/dd HH:mm:ss}
%p %c{2}: %m%n
```

The default root logger is INFO,console, which logs all messages at the level INFO and above to the console's stderr. Single applications deployed on Hadoop can ship their own log4j.properties and set the level and other properties of their emitted logs as required.

Hadoop daemons have a web page to get and set the log level for any Log4j property. This interface is exposed by the /LogLevel endpoint in each service web UI. To enable debug logging for the ResourceManager class, we will visit http://resourcemanagerhost:8088/LogLevel, and the screenshot can be seen as follows:

Getting and setting the log level on ResourceManager

Alternatively, the YARN daemonlog <host:port> command interfaces with the service /LogLevel endpoint. We can inspect the level associated with mapreduce. map.log.level for the ResourceManager class using the -getlevel <property> parameter, as follows:

```
$ hadoop daemonlog -getlevel localhost.localdomain:8088  mapreduce.map.
log.level
```

Connecting to http://localhost.localdomain:8088/logLevel?log=mapreduce. map.log.level Submitted Log Name: mapreduce.map.log.level Log Class: org. apache.commons.logging.impl.Log4JLogger Effective level: INFO

The effective level can be modified using the -setlevel <property> <level> option:

```
$ hadoop daemonlog -setlevel localhost.localdomain:8088  mapreduce.map.
log.level   DEBUG
```

Connecting to http://localhost.localdomain:8088/logLevel?log=mapreduce. map.log.level&level=DEBUG

```
Submitted Log Name: mapreduce.map.log.level
Log Class: org.apache.commons.logging.impl.Log4JLogger
Submitted Level: DEBUG
Setting Level to DEBUG ...
Effective level: DEBUG
```

Note that this setting will affect all logs produced by the `ResourceManager` class. This includes system-generated entries as well as the ones generated by applications running on YARN.

Access to logfiles

Logfile locations and naming conventions are likely to differ based on the distribution. Apache Ambari and Cloudera Manager centralize access to logfiles, both for services and single applications. On Cloudera's QuickStart VM, an overview of the currently running processes and links to their logfiles, the `stderr` and `stdout` channels can be found at `http://localhost.localdomain:7180/cmf/hardware/hosts/1/processes`, and the screenshot can be seen as follows:

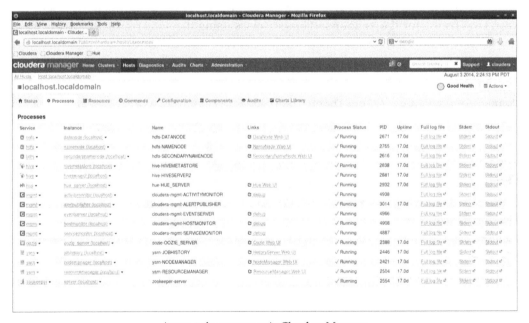

Access to log resources in Cloudera Manager

Ambari provides a similar overview via the **Services** dashboard found at `http://127.0.0.1:8080/#/main/services` on the HDP Sandbox, and the screenshot can be seen as follows:

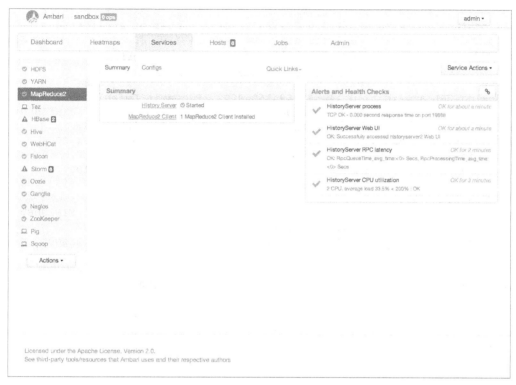

Access to log resources on Apache Ambari

Non-distributed logs are usually found under `/var/log/<service>` on each cluster node. YARN containers and MRv2 logs locations also depend on the distribution. On CDH5 these resources are available in HDFS under `/tmp/logs/<user>`.

The standard modality to access distributed logs is either via command-line tools or using services web UIs.

For instance, the command is as follows:

```
$ yarn application -list -appStates ALL
```

The preceding command will list all running and retried YARN applications. The URL in the task column points to a web interface that exposes the task log, as follows:

```
14/08/03 14:44:38 INFO client.RMProxy: Connecting to ResourceManager
at localhost.localdomain/127.0.0.1:8032 Total number of applications
(application-types: [] and states: [NEW, NEW_SAVING, SUBMITTED, ACCEPTED,
RUNNING, FINISHED, FAILED, KILLED]):4                    Application-
Id      Application-Name      Application-Type      User
Queue               State           Final-State         Progress
Tracking-URL application_1405630696162_0002  PigLatin:DefaultJobNa
me          MAPREDUCE      cloudera  root.cloudera           FINISHED
SUCCEEDED            100%  http://localhost.localdomain:19888/
jobhistory/job/job_1405630696162_0002 application_1405630696162_0004
PigLatin:DefaultJobName          MAPREDUCE      cloudera  root.
cloudera           FINISHED          SUCCEEDED            100%
http://localhost.localdomain:19888/jobhistory/job/job_1405630696162_0004
application_1405630696162_0003  PigLatin:DefaultJobNa
me          MAPREDUCE      cloudera  root.cloudera           FINISHED
SUCCEEDED            100%  http://localhost.localdomain:19888/
jobhistory/job/job_1405630696162_0003 application_1405630696162_0005  Pi
gLatin:DefaultJobName          MAPREDUCE      cloudera  root.cloudera
FINISHED          SUCCEEDED            100%  http://localhost.
localdomain:19888/jobhistory/job/job_1405630696162_0005
```

For instance, `http://localhost.localdomain:19888/jobhistory/job/` `job_1405630696162_0002`, a link to a task belonging to user cloudera, is a frontend to the content stored under `hdfs:///tmp/logs/cloudera/logs/` `application_1405630696162_0002/`.

In the following sections, we will give an overview of the available UIs for different services.

Provisioning an EMR cluster with the `-log-uri` `s3://<bucket>` option will ensure that Hadoop logs are copied into the `s3://<bucket>` location.

ResourceManager, NodeManager, and Application Manager

On YARN the ResourceManager web UI provides information and general job statistics of the Hadoop cluster, running/completed/failed jobs, and a job history logfile. By default, the UI is exposed at `http://<resourcemanagerhost>:8088/` and can be seen in the following screenshot:

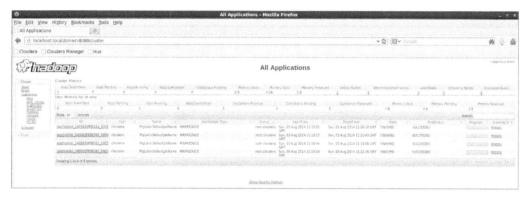

Resource Manager

Applications

On the left-hand sidebar, it is possible to review the application status of interest: NEW, SUBMITTED, ACCEPTED, RUNNING, FINISHING, FINISHED, FAILED, or KILLED. Depending on the application status, the following information is available:

- The application ID
- The submitting user
- The application name
- The scheduler queue in which the application is placed
- Start/finish times and state
- Link to the Tracking UI for application history

In addition, the `Cluster Metrics` view gives you information on the following:

- Overall application status
- Number of running containers
- Memory usage
- Node status

Nodes

The `Nodes` view is a frontend to the NodeManager service menu, which shows health and location information on the node's running applications, as follows:

Nodes status

Each individual node of the cluster exposes further information and statistics at host level via its own UI. These include which version of Hadoop is running on the node, how much memory is available on the node, the node status, and a list of running applications and containers, as shown in the following screenshot:

Single node info

Scheduler

The following screenshot shows the Scheduler window:

Scheduler

MapReduce

Though the same information and logging details are available in MapReduce v1 and MapReduce v2, the access modality is slightly different.

MapReduce v1

The following screenshot shows the MapReduce JobTracker UI:

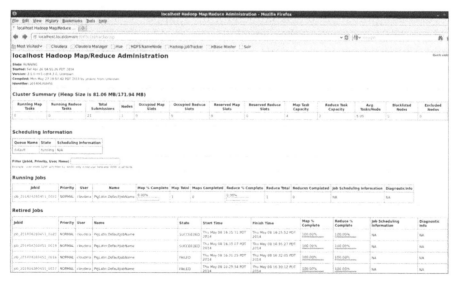

The Job Tracker UI

The Job Tracker UI, available by default at `http://<jobtracker>:50070`, exposes information on all currently running as well as retired MapReduce jobs, a summary of the cluster resources and health, as well as scheduling information and completion percentage, as shown in the following screenshot:

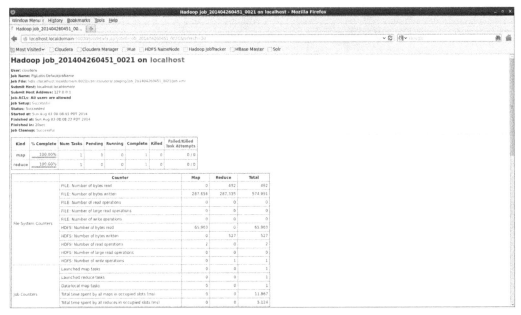

Job details

For each running and retired job, details are available, including its ID, owner, priority, task assignment, and task launch for the mapper. Clicking on a `jobid` link will lead to a job details page—the same URL exposed by the `mapred job -list` command. This resource gives details about both the map and reduce tasks as well as general counter statistics at the job, filesystem, and MapReduce levels; these include the memory used, number of read/write operations, and the number of bytes read and written.

For each Map and Reduce operation, the JobTracker exposes the total, pending, running, completed, and failed tasks, as shown in the following screenshot:

Job tasks overview

Clicking on the links in the Job table will lead to a further overview at the task and task-attempt levels, as shown in the following screenshot:

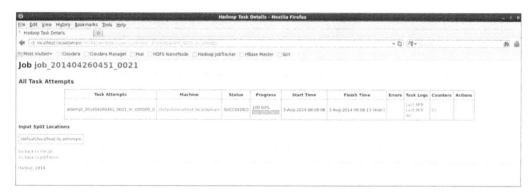

Task attempts

From this last page, we can access the logs of each task attempt, both for successful and failed/killed tasks on each individual TaskTracker host. This log contains the most granular information about the status of the MapReduce job, including the output of Log4j appenders as well as output piped to the stdout and stderr channels and syslog, as shown in the following screenshot:

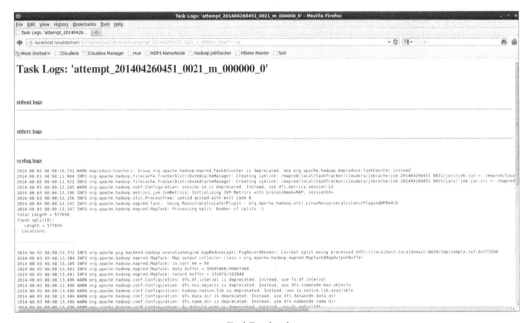

TaskTracker logs

MapReduce v2 (YARN)

As we have seen in *Chapter 3, Processing – MapReduce and Beyond*, with YARN, MapReduce is only one of many processing frameworks that can be deployed. Recall from previous chapters that the JobTracker and TaskTracker services have been replaced by the ResourceManager and NodeManager, respectively. As such, both the service UIs and the logfiles from YARN are more generic than MapReduce v1.

The `application_1405630696162_0002` name shown in Resource Manager corresponds to a MapReduce job with the `job_1405630696162_0002` ID. That application ID belongs to the task running inside the container, and clicking on it will reveal an overview of the MapReduce job and allow a drill-down to the individual tasks from either phase until the single-task log is reached, as shown in the following screenshot:

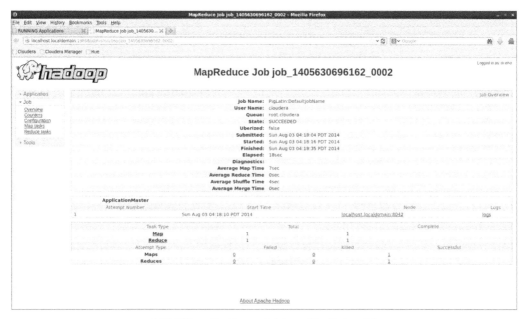

A YARN application containing a MapReduce job

JobHistory Server

YARN ships with a JobHistory REST service that exposes details on finished applications. Currently, it only supports MapReduce and provides information on finished jobs. This includes the job final status SUCCESSFUL or FAILED, who submitted the job, the total number of map and reduce tasks, and timing information.

A UI is available at `http://<jobhistoryhost>:19888/jobhistory`, as shown in the following screenshot:

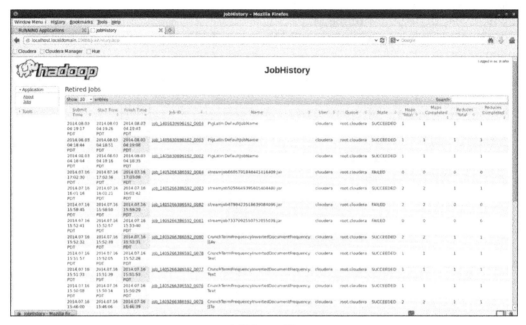

JobHistory UI

Clicking on each job ID will lead to the MapReduce job UI shown in the YARN application screenshot.

NameNode and DataNode

The web interface for the **Hadoop Distributed File System** (HDFS) shows information about the NameNode itself as well as the filesystem generally.

By default, it is located at `http://<namenodehost>:50070/`, as shown in the following screenshot:

NameNode UI

The **Overview** menu exposes NameNode information about DFS capacity and usage and the block pool status, and it gives a summary of the status of DataNode health and availability. The information contained in this page is for the most part equivalent to what is shown at the command-line prompt:

```
$ hdfs dfsadmin -report
```

The DataNodes menu gives more detailed information about the status of each node and offers a drill-down at the single-host level, both for available and decommissioned nodes, as shown in the following screenshot:

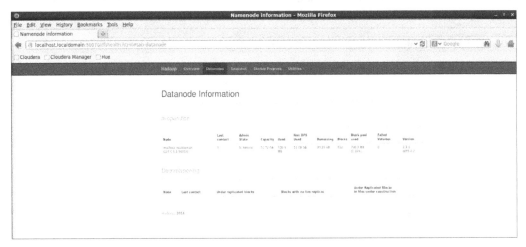

Datanode UI

Summary

This has been quite a whistle-stop tour around the considerations of running an operational Hadoop cluster. We didn't try to turn developers into administrators, but hopefully, the broader perspective will help you to help your operations staff. In particular, we covered the following topics:

- How Hadoop is a natural fit for DevOps approaches as its multilayered complexity means it's not possible or desirable to have substantial knowledge gaps between development and operations staff

- Cloudera Manager, and how it can be a great management and monitoring tool; it might cause integration problems though, if you have other enterprise tools, and it comes with a vendor lock-in risk

- Ambari, the Apache open source alternative to Cloudera Manager, and how it is used in the Hortonworks distribution

- How to think about selecting hardware for a physical Hadoop cluster, and how this naturally fits into the considerations of how the multiple workloads possible in the world of Hadoop 2 can peacefully coexist on shared resources

- The different considerations for firing up and using EMR clusters and how this can be both an adjunct to, as well as an alternative to, a physical cluster

- The Hadoop security ecosystem, how it is a very fast moving area, and how the features available today are vastly better than some years ago and there is still much around the corner

- Monitoring of a Hadoop cluster, considering what events are important in the Hadoop model of embracing failure, and how these alerts and metrics can be integrated into other enterprise-monitoring frameworks

- How to troubleshoot issues with a Hadoop cluster, both in terms of what might have happened and how to find the information to inform your analysis

- A quick tour of the various web UIs provided by Hadoop, which can give very good overviews of happenings within various components in the system

This concludes our treatment of Hadoop in depth. In the final chapter, we will express some thoughts on the broader Hadoop ecosystem, give some pointers for useful and interesting tools and products that we didn't have a chance to cover in the book, and suggest how to get involved with the community.

11
Where to Go Next

In the previous chapters we have examined many parts of Hadoop 2 and the ecosystem around it. However, we have necessarily been limited by page count; some areas we didn't get into as much depth as was possible, other areas we referred to only in passing or did not mention at all.

The Hadoop ecosystem, with distributions, Apache and non-Apache projects, is an incredibly vibrant and healthy place to be right now. In this chapter, we hope to complement the previously discussed more detailed material with a travel guide, if you will, for other interesting destinations. In this chapter, we will discuss the following topics:

- Hadoop distributions
- Other significant Apache and non-Apache projects
- Sources of information and help

Of course, note that any overview of the ecosystem is both skewed by our interests and preferences, and is outdated the moment it is written. In other words, don't for a moment think this is all that's available, consider it instead a whetting of the appetite.

Alternative distributions

We've generally used the Cloudera distribution for Hadoop in this book, but have attempted to keep the coverage distribution independent as much as possible. We've also mentioned the **Hortonworks Data Platform (HDP)** throughout this book but these are certainly not the only distribution choices available to you.

Before taking a look around, let's consider whether you need a distribution at all. It is completely possible to go to the Apache website, download the source tarballs of the projects in which you are interested, then work to build them all together. However, given version dependencies, this is likely to consume more time than you would expect. Potentially, vastly more so. In addition, the end product will likely lack some polish in terms of tools or scripts for operational deployment and management. For most users, these areas are why employing an existing Hadoop distribution is the natural choice.

A note on free and commercial extensions — being an open source project with a quite liberal license, distribution creators are also free to enhance Hadoop with proprietary extensions that are made available either as free open source or commercial products.

This can be a controversial issue as some open source advocates dislike any commercialization of successful open source projects; to them, it appears that the commercial entity is freeloading by taking the fruits of the open source community without having to build it for themselves. Others see this as a healthy aspect of the flexible Apache license; the base product will always be free, and individuals and companies can choose whether to go with commercial extensions or not. We don't give judgment either way, but be aware that this is another of the controversies you will almost certainly encounter.

So you need to decide if you need a distribution and if so for what reasons, which specific aspects will benefit you most above rolling your own? Do you wish for a fully open source product or are you willing to pay for commercial extensions? With these questions in mind, let's look at a few of the main distributions.

Cloudera Distribution for Hadoop

You will be familiar with the Cloudera distribution (http://www.cloudera.com) as it has been used throughout this book. CDH was the first widely available alternative distribution and its breadth of available software, proven level of quality, and its free cost has made it a very popular choice.

Recently, Cloudera has been actively extending the products it adds to its distribution beyond the core Hadoop projects. In addition to Cloudera Manager and Impala (both Cloudera-developed products), it has also added other tools such as Cloudera Search (based on Apache Solr) and Cloudera Navigator (a data governance solution). While CDH versions prior to 5 were focused more on the integration benefits of a distribution, version 5 (and presumably beyond) is adding more and more capability atop the base Apache Hadoop projects.

Cloudera also offers commercial support for its products in addition to training and consultancy services. Details can be found on the company web page.

Hortonworks Data Platform

In 2011, the Yahoo! division responsible for so much of the development of Hadoop was spun off into a new company called Hortonworks. They have also produced their own pre-integrated Hadoop distribution called the **Hortonworks Data Platform (HDP)**, available at `http://hortonworks.com/products/hortonworksdataplatform/`.

HDP is conceptually similar to CDH but both products have differences in their focus. Hortonworks makes much of the fact HDP is fully open source, including the management tool Ambari, which we discussed briefly in *Chapter 10, Running a Hadoop Cluster*. They have also positioned HDP as a key integration platform through its support for tools such as Talend Open Studio. Hortonworks does not offer proprietary software; its business model focuses instead on offering professional services and support for the platform.

Both Cloudera and Hortonworks are venture-backed companies with significant engineering expertise; both companies employ many of the most prolific contributors to Hadoop. The underlying technology is, however, comprised of the same Apache projects; the distinguishing factors are how they are packaged, the versions employed, and the additional value-added offerings provided by the companies.

MapR

A different type of distribution is offered by MapR Technologies, although the company and distribution are usually referred to simply as MapR. The distribution available from `http://www.mapr.com` is based on Hadoop, but has added a number of changes and enhancements.

The focus of the MapR distribution is on performance and availability. For example, it was the first distribution to offer a high-availability solution for the Hadoop NameNode and JobTracker, which you will remember from *Chapter 2, Storage*, was a significant weakness in core Hadoop 1. It also offered native integration with NFS filesystems long before Hadoop 2, which makes processing of existing data much easier. To achieve these features, MapR replaced HDFS with a full POSIX compliant filesystem that also features no NameNode, resulting in a true distributed system with no master, and a claim of much better hardware utilization than Apache HDFS.

MapR provides both a community and enterprise edition of its distribution; not all the extensions are available in the free product. The company also offers support services as part of the enterprise product subscription in addition to training and consultancy.

And the rest…

Hadoop distributions are not just the territory of young start-ups, nor are they a static marketplace. Intel had its own distribution until early 2014 when it decided to fold its changes into CDH instead. IBM has its own distribution called IBM Infosphere Big Insights available in both free and commercial editions. There are also various stories of numerous large enterprises rolling their own distributions, some of which are made openly available while others are not. You will have no shortage of options with so many high-quality distributions available.

Choosing a distribution

This raises the question: how to choose a distribution? As can be seen, the available distributions (and we didn't cover them all) range from convenient packaging and integration of fully open source products through to entire bespoke integration and analysis layers atop them. There is no overall best distribution; think carefully about your requirements and consider the alternatives. Since all these offer a free download of at least a basic version, it's good to simply play and experience the options for yourself.

Other computational frameworks

We've frequently discussed the myriad possibilities brought to the Hadoop platform by YARN. We went into details of two new models, Samza and Spark. Additionally, other more established frameworks such as Pig are also being ported to the framework.

To give a view of the much bigger picture in this section, we will illustrate the breadth of processing possible using YARN by presenting a set of computational models that are currently being ported to Hadoop on top of YARN.

Apache Storm

Storm (`http://storm.apache.org`) is a distributed computation framework written (mainly) in the Clojure programming language. It uses custom-created spouts and bolts to define information sources and manipulations to allow distributed processing of streaming data. A Storm application is designed as a topology of interfaces that creates a stream of transformations. It provides similar functionality to a MapReduce job with the exception that the topology will theoretically run indefinitely until it is manually terminated.

Though initially built distinct from Hadoop, a YARN port is being developed by Yahoo! and can be found at `https://github.com/yahoo/storm-yarn`.

Apache Giraph

Giraph originated as the open source implementation of Google's Pregel paper (which can be found at `http://kowshik.github.io/JPregel/pregel_paper.pdf`). Both Giraph and Pregel are inspired by the **Bulk Synchronous Parallel (BSP)** model of distributed computation introduced by Valiant in 1990. Giraph adds several features including master computation, sharded aggregators, edge-oriented input, and out-of-core computation. The YARN port can be found at `https://issues.apache.org/jira/browse/GIRAPH-13`.

Apache HAMA

Hama is a top-level Apache project that aims, like other methods we've encountered so far, to address the weakness of MapReduce with regard to iterative programming. Similar to the aforementioned Giraph, Hama implements the BSP techniques and has been heavily inspired by the Pregel paper. The YARN port can be found at `https://issues.apache.org/jira/browse/HAMA-431`.

Other interesting projects

Whether you use a bundled distribution or stick with the base Apache Hadoop download, you will encounter many references to other related projects. We've covered several of these such as Hive, Samza, and Crunch in this book; we'll now highlight some of the others.

Note that this coverage seeks to point out the highlights (from the authors' perspective) as well as give a taste of the breadth of types of projects available. As mentioned earlier, keep looking out, as there will be new ones launching all the time.

HBase

Perhaps the most popular Apache Hadoop-related project that we didn't cover in this book is HBase (`http://hbase.apache.org`). Based on the BigTable model of data storage publicized by Google in an academic paper (sound familiar?), HBase is a nonrelational data store sitting atop HDFS.

While both MapReduce and Hive focus on batch-like data access patterns, HBase instead seeks to provide very low-latency access to data. Consequently HBase can, unlike the aforementioned technologies, directly support user-facing services.

The HBase data model is not the relational approach that was used in Hive and all other RDBMSs, nor does it offer the full ACID guarantees that are taken for granted with relational stores. Instead, it is a key-value schema-less solution that takes a column-oriented view of data; columns can be added at runtime and depend on the values inserted into HBase. Each lookup operation is then very fast, as it is effectively a key-value mapping from the row key to the desired column. HBase also treats timestamps as another dimension on the data so one can directly retrieve data from a point in time.

The data model is very powerful but does not suit all use cases just as the relational model isn't universally applicable. But if you have a requirement for structured low-latency views on large-scale data stored in Hadoop, then HBase is absolutely something you should look at.

Sqoop

In *Chapter 7, Hadoop and SQL*, we looked at tools for presenting a relational-like interface to data stored on HDFS. Often, such data either needs to be retrieved from an existing relational database or the output of its processing needs to be stored back.

Apache Sqoop (`http://sqoop.apache.org`) provides a mechanism for declaratively specifying data movement between relational databases and Hadoop. It takes a task definition and from this generates MapReduce jobs to execute the required data retrieval or storage. It will also generate code to help manipulate relational records with custom Java classes. In addition, it can integrate with HBase and Hcatalog/Hive and it provides a very rich set of integration possibilities.

At the time of writing, Sqoop is slightly in flux. Its original version, Sqoop 1, was a pure client-side application. Much like the original Hive command-line tool, Sqoop 1 has no server and generates all code on the client. This unfortunately means that each client needs to know a lot of details about physical data sources, including exact host names as well as authentication credentials.

Sqoop 2 provides a centralized Sqoop server that encapsulates all these details and offers the various configured data sources to the connecting clients. It is a superior model but at the time of writing, the general community recommendation is to stick with Sqoop 1 until the new version evolves further. Check on the current status if you are interested in this type of tool.

Whir

When looking to use cloud services such as Amazon AWS for Hadoop deployments, it is usually a lot easier to use a higher level service such as Elastic MapReduce as opposed to setting up your own cluster on EC2. Though there are scripts to help, the fact is that the overhead of Hadoop-based deployments on cloud infrastructures can be involved. That's where Apache Whir (`http://whir.apache.org`) comes in.

Whir isn't focused on Hadoop; it's about supplier-independent instantiation of cloud services of which Hadoop is a single example. Whir aims to provide a programmatic way of specifying and creating Hadoop-based deployments on cloud infrastructures in a way that handles all the underlying service aspects for you. It does this in a provider-independent fashion so that once you've launched on say EC2 then you can use the same code to create the identical setup on another provider such as Rightscale or Eucalyptus. This makes vendor lock-in, often a concern with cloud deployments, less of an issue.

Whir isn't quite there yet. Today, it is limited in services it can create and providers it supports, however, if you are interested in cloud deployment with less pain then it's worth watching its progress.

 If you are building out your full infrastructure on Amazon Web Services then you might find cloud formation gives much of the same ability to define application requirements, though obviously in an AWS-specific fashion.

Mahout

Apache Mahout (`http://mahout.apache.org/`) is a collection of distributed algorithms, Java classes, and tools for performing advanced analytics on top of Hadoop. Similar to Spark's MLLib briefly mentioned in *Chapter 5, Iterative Computation with Spark*, Mahout ships with a number of algorithms for common use cases: recommendation, clustering, regression, and feature engineering. Although the system is focused on natural language processing and text-mining tasks, its building blocks (linear algebra operations) are suitable to be applied to a number of domains. As of Version 0.9, the project is being decoupled from the MapReduce framework in favor of richer programming models such as Spark. The community end goal is to obtain a platform-independent library based on a Scala DSL.

Hue

Initially developed by Cloudera and marketed as the "User Interface for Hadoop", Hue (`http://gethue.com/`) is a collection of applications, bundled together under a common web interface, that act as clients for core services and a number of components of the Hadoop ecosystem:

The Hue Query Editor for Hive

Hue leverages many of the tools we discussed in previous chapters and provides an integrated interface for analyzing and visualizing data. There are two components that are remarkably interesting. On one hand, there is a query editor that allows the user to create and save Hive (or Impala) queries, export the result set in CSV or Microsoft Office Excel format as well as plot it in the browser. The editor features the capability of sharing both HiveQL and result sets, thus facilitating collaboration within an organization. On the other hand, there is an Oozie workflow and coordinator editor that allows a user to create and deploy Oozie jobs manually, automating the generation of XML configurations and boilerplate.

Both Cloudera and Hortonworks distributions ship with Hue and typically include the following:

- A file manager for HDFS
- A Job Browser for YARN (MapReduce)
- An Apache HBase browser
- A Hive metastore explorer
- Query editors for Hive and Impala
- A script editor for Pig
- A job editor for MapReduce and Spark
- An editor for Sqoop 2 jobs
- An Oozie workflow editor and dashboard
- An Apache ZooKeeper browser

On top of this, Hue is a framework with an SDK that contains a number of web assets, APIs, and patterns for developing third-party applications that interact with Hadoop.

Other programming abstractions

Hadoop isn't just extended by additional functionality, there are tools to provide entirely different paradigms for writing the code used to process your data within Hadoop.

Cascading

Developed by Concurrent, and open sourced under an Apache license, Cascading (`http://www.cascading.org/`) is a popular framework that abstracts the complexity of MapReduce away and allows us to create complex workflows on top of Hadoop. Cascading jobs can compile to, and be executed on, MapReduce, Tez, and Spark. Conceptually, the framework is similar to Apache Crunch, covered in *Chapter 9, Making Development Easier*, though practically there are differences in terms of data abstractions and end goals. Cascading adopts a tuple data model (similar to Pig) rather than arbitrary objects, and encourages the user to rely on a higher level DSL, powerful built-in types, and tools to manipulate data.

Put in simple terms, Cascading is to PigLatin and HiveQL what Crunch is to a user-defined function.

Like Morphlines, which we also saw in *Chapter 9, Making Development Easier*, the Cascading data model follows a source-pipe-sink approach, where data is captured from a source, piped through a number of processing steps, and its output is then delivered into a sink, ready to be picked up by another application.

Cascading encourages developers to write code in a number of JVM languages. Ports of the framework exist for Python (PyCascading), JRuby (Cascading.jruby), Clojure (Cascalog), and Scala (Scalding). Cascalog and Scalding in particular have gained a lot of traction and spawned off their very own ecosystems.

An area where Cascading excels is documentation. The project provides comprehensive javadocs of the API, extensive tutorials (`http://www.cascading.org/documentation/tutorials/`) and an interactive exercise-based learning environment (`https://github.com/Cascading/Impatient`).

Another strong selling point of Cascading is its integration with third-party environments. Amazon EMR supports Cascading as a first-class processing framework and allows us to launch Cascading clusters both with the command line and web interfaces (`http://docs.aws.amazon.com/ElasticMapReduce/latest/DeveloperGuide/CreateCascading.html`). Plugins for the SDK exist for both the IntelliJ IDEA and Eclipse integrated development environments. One of the framework's top projects, Cascading Patterns, a collection of machine-learning algorithms, features a utility for translating **Predictive Model Markup Language (PMML)** documents into applications on Apache Hadoop, thus facilitating interoperability with popular statistical environments and scientific tools such as R (`http://cran.r-project.org/web/packages/pmml/index.html`).

AWS resources

Many Hadoop technologies can be deployed on AWS as part of a self-managed cluster. However, just as Amazon offers support for Elastic MapReduce, which handles Hadoop as a managed service, there are a few other services that are worth mentioning.

SimpleDB and DynamoDB

For some time, AWS has offered SimpleDB as a hosted service providing an HBase-like data model.

It has, however, largely been superseded by a more recent service from AWS, DynamoDB, located at `http://aws.amazon.com/dynamodb`. Though its data model is very similar to that of SimpleDB and HBase, it is aimed at a very different type of application. Where SimpleDB has quite a rich search API but is very limited in terms of size, DynamoDB provides a more constrained though constantly evolving API, but with a service guarantee of near-unlimited scalability.

The DynamoDB pricing model is particularly interesting; instead of paying for a certain number of servers hosting the service, you allocate a certain capacity for read-and-write operations, and DynamoDB manages the resources required to meet this provisioned capacity. This is an interesting development as it is a more pure service model, where the mechanism of delivering the desired performance is kept completely opaque to the service user. Have a look at DynamoDB but if you need a much larger scale of data store than SimpleDB can offer; however, do consider the pricing model carefully as provisioning too much capacity can become very expensive very quickly. Amazon provides some good best practices for DynamoDB at the following URL that illustrate that minimizing the service costs can result in additional application-layer complexity: `http://docs.aws.amazon.com/amazondynamodb/latest/developerguide/BestPractices.html`.

 Of course the discussion of DynamoDB and SimpleDB assumes a non-relational data model; there is the **Amazon Relational Database Service** (**Amazon RDS**) for a relational database in the cloud service.

Kinesis

Just as EMR is hosted Hadoop and DynamoDB has similarities to a hosted HBase, it wasn't surprising to see AWS announce Kinesis, a hosted streaming data service in 2013. This can be found at `http://aws.amazon.com/kinesis` and it has very similar conceptual building blocks to the stack of Samza atop Kafka. Kinesis provides a partitioned view of messages as a stream of data and an API to have callbacks that execute when messages arrive. As with most AWS services, there is tight integration with other services making it easy to get data into and out of locations such as S3.

Data Pipeline

The final AWS service that we'll mention is Data Pipeline, which can be found at `http://aws.amazon.com/datapipeline`. As the name suggests, it is a framework for building up data-processing jobs that involve multiple steps, data movements, and transformations. It has quite a conceptual overlap with Oozie, but with a few twists. Firstly, Data Pipeline has the expected deep integration with many other AWS services, enabling easy definition of data workflows that incorporate diverse repositories such as RDS, S3, and DynamoDB. In addition however, Data Pipeline does have the ability to integrate agents installed on local infrastructure, providing an interesting avenue for building workflows that span across the AWS and on-premises environments.

Sources of information

You don't just need new technologies and tools—even if they are cool. Sometimes, a little help from a more experienced source can pull you out of a hole. In this regard, you are well covered, as the Hadoop community is extremely strong in many areas.

Source code

It's sometimes easy to overlook, but Hadoop and all the other Apache projects are after all fully open source. The actual source code is the ultimate source (pardon the pun) of information about how the system works. Becoming familiar with the source and tracing through some of the functionality can be hugely informative. Not to mention helpful when you are hitting unexpected behavior.

Mailing lists and forums

Almost all the projects and services listed in this chapter have their own mailing lists and/or forums; check out the home pages for the specific links. Most distributions also have their own forums and other mechanisms to share knowledge and get (non-commercial) help from the community. Additionally, if using AWS, make sure to check out the AWS developer forums at `https://forums.aws.amazon.com`.

Always remember to read posting guidelines carefully and understand the expected etiquette. These are tremendous sources of information; the lists and forums are often frequently visited by the developers of the particular project. Expect to see the core Hadoop developers on the Hadoop lists, Hive developers on the Hive list, EMR developers on the EMR forums, and so on.

LinkedIn groups

There are a number of Hadoop and related groups on the professional social network LinkedIn. Do a search for your particular areas of interest, but a good starting point might be the general Hadoop users' group at `http://www.linkedin.com/groups/Hadoop-Users-988957`.

HUGs

If you want more face-to-face interaction then look for a **Hadoop User Group (HUG)** in your area, most of which will be listed at `http://wiki.apache.org/hadoop/HadoopUserGroups`. These tend to arrange semi-regular get-togethers that combine things such as quality presentations, the ability to discuss technology with like-minded individuals, and often pizza and drinks.

No HUG near where you live? Consider starting one.

Conferences

Though some industries take decades to build up a conference circuit, Hadoop already has some significant conference action involving the open source, academic, and commercial worlds. Events such as the Hadoop Summit and Strata are pretty big; these and some other are linked from `http://wiki.apache.org/hadoop/Conferences`.

Summary

In this chapter, we took a quick gallop around the broader Hadoop ecosystem, looking at the following topics:

- Why alternative Hadoop distributions exist and some of the more popular ones
- Other projects that provide capabilities, extensions, or Hadoop supporting tools
- Alternative ways of writing or creating Hadoop jobs
- Sources of information and how to connect with other enthusiasts

Now, go have fun and build something amazing!

Index

B

block replication 35
Bulk Synchronous Parallel (BSP) model 337

C

Cascading
  about 341, 342
  reference links 342
  URL 341
Cloudera
  URL 16
  URL, for blog post 305
  URL, for documentation 298
Cloudera distribution, for Hadoop
  about 334
  URL 334
Cloudera Kitten
  URL 98
Cloudera Manager
  about 298
  cluster management, performing 299, 300
  configuration, finding 301
  integrating, with management tools 300
  monitoring with 300
  payment, for subscription services 299
Cloudera Manager API 301
Cloudera Manager lock-in 301, 302
Cloudera QuickStart VM
  about 19
  advantages 19
cluster, Apache Spark
  computing, with working sets 132, 133
cluster, on EMR
  building 308
  data, obtaining into EMR 309
  EC2 instances 310
  EC2 tuning 310
  filesystem, considerations 309
cluster startup, HDFS
  about 34
  DataNode startup 35
  NameNode startup 34
cluster tuning
  about 310
  JVM considerations 310

map optimization 311
  reduce optimization 311
columnar stores 196
column-oriented data formats
  about 53
  Avro 54
  Java API, using 55-58
  ORC 54
  Parquet 54
  RCFile 54
combiner class, Java API to MapReduce 65
combineValues operation 276
command-line access, HDFS filesystem
  about 36
  dfsadmin command 36
  dfs command 36
  hdfs command 36
Comparable interface 51
complex data types
  bag 160
  map 160
  tuple 160
complex event processing (CEP) 106
components, Hadoop
  about 10
  common building blocks 10
  computation 11
  storage 11
components, YARN
  about 95
  NodeManager (NM) 95
  ResourceManager (RM) 95
computation 11
computational frameworks
  about 336
  Apache Giraph 337
  Apache Storm 336
computation, Hadoop 2 14-16
conferences
  about 345
  reference link 345
configuration file, Samza 112, 113
containers 51
contributed UDFs
  about 167
  Apache DataFu 168

macros 163
map 162
math 162
reference link, for built-in functions 160
string 162
tuple 162

G

Garbage Collection (GC) 310
Garbage First (G1) collector 310
general availability (GA) 8
general-purpose file formats
  about 52
  SequenceFile 53
  Text files 52
Giraph. *See* **Apache Giraph**
Google Chubby system
  reference link 41
Google File System (GFS)
  reference link 9
Gradle
  URL 23
GraphX
  about 140
  URL 140
groupByKey(GroupingOptions options)
    method 278
groupByKey(int numPartitions) method 278
groupByKey() method 278
GROUP operator 164
Grunt
  about 156
  exec command 156
  fs command 156
  help command 156
  kill command 156
  sh command 156
Guava library
  URL 79

H

Hadoop
  about 18
  alternative distributions 333
  AWS credentials 21

  AWS resources 342
  background 8, 9
  components 10
  computational frameworks 336
  data processing 24
  dual approach 17
  EMR, using 20
  interesting projects 337
  operations 297
  practices 298
  programming abstractions 341
  sources of information 344
  using 20
  versioning 7
Hadoop 2
  about 12
  computation 14-16
  diagrammatic representation,
    architecture 15
  operations 303, 304
  reference link 18
  storage 13
Hadoop 2 NameNode HA
  about 38
  enabling 39
  keeping, in sync 39
Hadoop Distributed File System. *See* **HDFS**
Hadoop distributions
  about 16
  Cloudera 16
  Hortonworks 16
  MapR 16
  reference link 17
Hadoop filesystems
  about 48
  Hadoop interfaces 48
  reference link 48
Hadoop interfaces
  about 48
  Apache Thrift 49
  Java FileSystem API 48
  Libhdfs 49
Hadoop-provided InputFormat,
    MapReduce job
  about 92
  FileInputFormat 92

Hortonworks Data Platform (HDP)
about 333, 335
URL 335
Hue
about 340, 341
URL 340
HUGs
about 345
reference link 345

I

IAM console
URL 208
IBM Infosphere Big Insights 336
Identity and Access Management (IAM) 21
Impala
about 216
architecture 217
co-existing, with Hive 217, 218
references 216, 217
indices attribute, entity 170
InputFormat, MapReduce job 91, 92
input/output, MapReduce job 91
in-sync replicas (ISR) 114

J

Java
WordCount 138, 139
Java API
about 138
versus Scala API 138
Java API to MapReduce
about 61
combiner class 65
Driver class 63-65
Hadoop-provided Mapper and
Reducer implementations 67
Mapper class 61, 62
partitioning 66
Reducer class 62, 63
reference data, sharing 67, 68
Java FileSystem API 48
JDBC 212

JobTracker monitoring, MapReduce job 89
join node 242
JOIN operator 165, 166, 198
JSON 193, 194
JSON Simple
URL 111
JVM considerations, cluster tuning
about 310
small files problem 310, 311

K

Kite Data
about 270
Data Core 271, 272
Data Crunch 274
Data HCatalog 272, 273
Data Hive 273
Data MapReduce 273
Data Spark 274
Kite examples
reference link 270
Kite JARs
reference link 271
Kite Morphlines
about 286
commands 288-294
concepts 287
Record abstractions 287
kite-morphlines-avro command 288
kite-morphlines-core-stdio command 288
kite-morphlines-core-stdlib command 288
kite-morphlines-hadoop-core command 288
kite-morphlines-hadoop-parquet-avro
command 289
kite-morphlines-hadoop-rcfile
command 289
kite-morphlines-hadoop-sequencefile
command 289
kite-morphlines-json command 288
Kite SDK
URL 270
KVM
reference link 19

V

versioning, Hadoop 7
VirtualBox
  reference link 19
VMware
  reference link 19

W

Whir
  about 339
  URL 339
Who to Follow service
  reference link 178
window function
  adding 117, 118
WordCount
  in Java 138, 139
WordCount example, MapReduce programs
  about 70-72
  reference link, for source code 74
workflow-app 224
workflows
  building, Oozie used 256
workflow.xml file
  reference link 233
workloads
  Hive tables, structuring from 199
wrapper classes 50
WritableComparable interface 51
Writable interface 49, 50

Y

YARN
  about 14, 15, 94, 99
  Apache Samza 102
  Apache Spark 102
  architecture 95
  components 95
  examples, running on 142
  future 103
  issues, with MapReduce 99, 100
  present situation 103
  processing frameworks 98
  processing models 98

  Samza, integrating 109
  Tez 100
  URL 142
YARN API 97
YARN application
  anatomy 95, 96
  ApplicationMaster (AM) 95
  execution models 98
  fault tolerance 97
  life cycle 96
  monitoring 97
Yet Another Resource Negotiator. *See*
    YARN

Z

ZooKeeper. *See* Apache ZooKeeper
ZooKeeper Failover Controller (ZKFC) 45
ZooKeeper quorum 45

Thank you for buying
Learning Hadoop 2

About Packt Publishing

Packt, pronounced 'packed', published its first book, *Mastering phpMyAdmin for Effective MySQL Management*, in April 2004, and subsequently continued to specialize in publishing highly focused books on specific technologies and solutions.

Our books and publications share the experiences of your fellow IT professionals in adapting and customizing today's systems, applications, and frameworks. Our solution-based books give you the knowledge and power to customize the software and technologies you're using to get the job done. Packt books are more specific and less general than the IT books you have seen in the past. Our unique business model allows us to bring you more focused information, giving you more of what you need to know, and less of what you don't.

Packt is a modern yet unique publishing company that focuses on producing quality, cutting-edge books for communities of developers, administrators, and newbies alike. For more information, please visit our website at www.packtpub.com.

About Packt Open Source

In 2010, Packt launched two new brands, Packt Open Source and Packt Enterprise, in order to continue its focus on specialization. This book is part of the Packt Open Source brand, home to books published on software built around open source licenses, and offering information to anybody from advanced developers to budding web designers. The Open Source brand also runs Packt's Open Source Royalty Scheme, by which Packt gives a royalty to each open source project about whose software a book is sold.

Writing for Packt

We welcome all inquiries from people who are interested in authoring. Book proposals should be sent to author@packtpub.com. If your book idea is still at an early stage and you would like to discuss it first before writing a formal book proposal, then please contact us; one of our commissioning editors will get in touch with you.

We're not just looking for published authors; if you have strong technical skills but no writing experience, our experienced editors can help you develop a writing career, or simply get some additional reward for your expertise.

Big Data Analytics with R and Hadoop

ISBN: 978-1-78216-328-2   Paperback: 238 pages

Set up an integrated infrastructure of R and Hadoop to turn your data analytics into Big Data analytics

1. Write Hadoop MapReduce within R.

2. Learn data analytics with R and the Hadoop platform.

3. Handle HDFS data within R.

4. Understand Hadoop streaming with R.

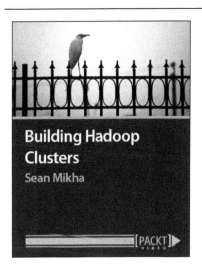

Building Hadoop Clusters [Video]

ISBN: 978-1-78328-403-0   Duration: 02:34 hrs

Deploy multi-node Hadoop clusters to harness the Cloud for storage and large-scale data processing

1. Familiarize yourself with Hadoop and its services, and how to configure them.

2. Deploy compute instances and set up a three-node Hadoop cluster on Amazon.

3. Set up a Linux installation optimized for Hadoop.

Please check **www.PacktPub.com** for information on our titles

Microsoft SQL Server 2012 with Hadoop

ISBN: 978-1-78217-798-2   Paperback: 96 pages

Integrate data between Apache Hadoop and SQL Server 2012 and provide business intelligence on the heterogeneous data

1. Integrate data from unstructured (Hadoop) and structured (SQL Server 2012) sources.

2. Configure and install connectors for a bi-directional transfer of data.

3. Full of illustrations, diagrams, and tips with clear, step-by-step instructions and practical examples.

Hadoop Beginner's Guide

ISBN: 978-1-84951-730-0   Paperback: 398 pages

Learn how to crunch big data to extract meaning from the data avalanche

1. Learn tools and techniques that let you approach big data with relish and not fear.

2. Shows how to build a complete infrastructure to handle your needs as your data grows.

3. Hands-on examples in each chapter give the big picture while also giving direct experience.

Please check **www.PacktPub.com** for information on our titles